THE LIKENESS *of* THINGS UNLIKE

Sharon Cameron

THE LIKENESS *of* THINGS UNLIKE

A Poetics of Incommensurability

The University of Chicago Press
CHICAGO AND LONDON

The University of Chicago Press, Chicago 60637
The University of Chicago Press, Ltd., London

Published 2025
Printed in the United States of America

34 33 32 31 30 29 28 27 26 25   1 2 3 4 5

ISBN-13: 978-0-226-83704-8 (cloth)
ISBN-13: 978-0-226-83705-5 (paper)
ISBN-13: 978-0-226-83706-2 (e-book)
DOI: https://doi.org/10.7208/chicago/9780226837062.001.0001

Library of Congress Cataloging-in-Publication Data

Names: Cameron, Sharon, author.
Title: The likeness of things unlike : a poetics of incommensurability / Sharon Cameron.
Description: Chicago : The University of Chicago Press, 2025. | Includes bibliographical references and index.
Identifiers: LCCN 2024024445 | ISBN 9780226837048 (cloth) | ISBN 9780226837055 (paperback) | ISBN 9780226837062 (ebook)
Subjects: LCSH: American literature—History and criticism—Theory, etc. | Literature—Philosophy. | Literature—Aesthetics.
Classification: LCC PS31 .C36 2025 | DDC 811.009/41—dc23/eng/20240626
LC record available at https://lccn.loc.gov/2024024445

♾ This paper meets the requirements of ANSI/NISO Z39.48-1992 (Permanence of Paper).

IN MEMORY *of* JANET MALCOLM
***and* JONATHAN GOLDBERG**

Contents

Introduction

Entities, qualities, manifestations of being, discordant expressive modes, and all manner of other phenomena that are alien to, but inseparable from, each other possess a nearly inscrutable affinity—a state of affairs for which understanding can't facilely be prescribed. Wallace Stevens termed this kinship "the likeness of things unlike."[1] We see such compacts in the radical claim of astrophysicists that "every atom of your body was once inside a star that exploded. . . . Our bodies are made of stardust,"[2] and also in the entangled particles of quantum theory, whereby measuring one particle instantly affects the measurement of another particle even if the two are millions of miles apart. We see this in Alfred North Whitehead's paradoxical claim that "the ultimate metaphysical truth is atomism. . . . But atomism does not exclude complexity and universal relativity [since] each atom is a system of all things."[3] In Gottfried Leibniz's philosophy, too, "each thing involves the others in such a way that, supposing it did not exist or were otherwise, all things in the universe would be different from what they now are."[4] Many of the elements of the paradoxical doublets that William James anatomizes in *Essays in Radical Empiricism* must be understood not in terms of separate entities ("thoughts and things," consciousness and its contents) but as an affair of relations, in which two processes or contexts converge. In "one context," a room is an object occupying that "environment for thirty years." In another, it figures as a mental state; "as your field of consciousness it may never have existed until now." Thus "one identical room can be in two places" just as "one identical point can be on two lines . . . if it be situated at their intersection."[5] For James, experience unfolds in incongruous contiguous elements that inhabit the same space. In an example from Exodus 15:11, the rhetorical question in part of the song that Miriam sings after the crossing of the sea is *mi kamocha baelim Adonai?*—literally "who among the gods is like you, God?"—and is meant to be answered: *no one is like you.* At the same time everyone is like God because everyone is made in His image.[6]

These examples embody different kinds of incommensurability. The explanation that tempers the incongruity between "living organisms and fallen stars" corrects "the myth that God falls into human form so that we may be born again."[7] Here the incongruences are conflicting understandings offered by "scientific theory" and "religious fable," even as both convictions coincide in positing a convergence of the human and the nonhuman.[8] For Leibniz, all generalizing categories—everything that would allow one to subsume different objects in a shared class and thus to render them commensurable—are purely mental constructs. "Real entities, i.e., monads, are particularized entities with no relations, either causal or conceptual, to one another. Leibniz's principle of the identity of indiscernibles means that every entity must differ from any other in at least one respect, or else they would simply be the same thing. So the universe is, in a sense, composed entirely of incommensurable particularities. At the same time monads are internally accommodated to one another by the principle of compossibility so as to optimize the universe as a whole."[9] William James's spider-webby explanations that draw together entity and function suggest "there is no possible point of view from which the world can appear an absolutely single fact."[10] At the core of these very different incommensurables, we find improbable composites of things that can't be integrated but also can't be separated. Writing of a very different coincidence in William Wordsworth's poetry of "line-endings" as an "emblem of what the poet values," Christopher Ricks concludes: "the might of poetry is, like that of mind and world, 'a blended might,' something which overrides 'our puny boundaries.'"[11] The transcendence of boundary also applies to the incommensurables described above and to its kindred presence in the literary works I examine in the following essays, which consider incomparables that converge in the poetry and prose of Ralph Waldo Emerson, Walt Whitman, Emily Dickinson, Willa Cather, and Wallace Stevens. I have introduced nonliterary manifestations of incommensurables straight off because such adjacencies are not purely literary, or even exclusively American. At the same time, I mean my assessments of these literary texts to reveal the novel ways in which an analysis of style and form—within a phenomenological practice of reading—might awaken a reader to the uncanny strangeness of things that are tethered or enmeshed beyond rational congruence. By a phenomenological practice, I mean reading that responds at various levels and in disproportionate ways to the textual experience of repetitions, reversals, rhythms, pauses, chiasmic phrases, literary tropes, undertones, overtones, and even bursts of sensory detail that strain against the logic of explication and, sometimes, against deciphering.

My essays are not linked by a single argument and may be read in any order. In each work the interconnections across disjunctive phenomena emerge in sui generis terms and to singular ends. In Ralph Waldo Emerson's essays, nonnarrative paratactic tropes bind the personal and impersonal outside the polemic whose narrative conflict structures the advance of Emerson's ideas. Beyond a common basis, measure, or logical standard of comparison, Walt Whitman's "I" is submerged in a "you" and in everything else imaginable in an intermingling he termed "translation." Abstraction and sensation entwine in Emily Dickinson's off-the-map scenes—sites that can't be placed but that pulse with an immediacy requiring no key. Their coupling becomes the precondition of access to uninhabitable spaces—the journey upward toward God's "Residence -"; forward to "Eternity -"; through mute psychic states that are "inner than the Bone."[12] Abstraction provides entry to such far-flung zones, while sensation enfleshes these regions, thus tearing down the wall between what can be recognized and the vast space that supplants identification. Polyphonic rhythms govern episodic passages and provide breathers of sorts from the rush of plot across Willa Cather's novels. In Wallace Stevens's poems, phenomena that are not isomorphic open to each other beyond form or kind and propose a metaphysics with no organizing matrix. Such shape-shifting, unevenly matched incommensurables, not convertible one to the other, each constellation numinous in distinctive ways—in the prose and poetry of Emerson, Whitman, Dickinson, Cather, and Stevens—are the subject of my essays. I argue that such challenges to literary systems are essentially philosophical in their rethinking of categories and thus go beyond the aesthetic particulars that exemplify them, and even beyond aesthetics tout court into philosophy. From another vantage, one might say that it is precisely the workings of literature that reveal these sometimes stunning constellations to be philosophical through and through. My essays show how literary texts philosophize. In a different book, the confluence of such incomparables in literary texts might be discussed in relation to the philosophers themselves.

As is well known, Wallace Stevens was familiar with the writings of Gottfried Wilhelm Leibniz and Alfred North Whitehead, and Willa Cather with Henri Bergson's *Creative Evolution*. While I touch on Cather's and Stevens's fascination with their theories, I am not arguing that the latter were influences, but rather touchstones within a philosophic register that, albeit methodically, anticipate the ways in which asymmetric entities in these texts—in Whitehead's word—"prehend" each other (*PR* 52),[13] even when they are remote. Whitehead's most extensive example is "God and the World," about which he claimed: "Opposed elements stand to each other in mutual requirement" (*PR* 348). For Whitehead, there are divergent ways to formulate the reach of that imperative. For instance, the "standpoint" of "every actual entity in its relationship to other actual entities is . . . somewhere in the continuum" of the whole. "But in another sense [each entity] is everywhere throughout the continuum. . . . Thus the continuum is present in each actual entity, and each actual entity pervades the continuum" (*PR* 67). Similarly, for Leibniz: "This *interconnection*, . . . of all created things to each other and of each to all the rest, means that each simple substance has relations which express all the others, and that consequently it is a perpetual living mirror of the universe."[14] The concord of the one and the many ("God and the World" [*PR* 349]), the one *in* all the others, and all the others in the one, constitute a *system*. In distinction, the quirky enmeshments of diverse entities, qualities, phenomena in general, in the texts I consider, pull toward each other, mingle, are pushed apart, almost it seems at whim. Throughout, my essays suggest a triangulation between literary figuration and ontological questions that are not contingent on the transmission of analytic ideas. Yes, Emerson read Spinoza, and a recent article (cited in the Emerson essay) posits a genealogy from Spinoza to Charles Sanders Peirce that is mediated through Emerson's knowledge of Spinoza. But, to repeat, influence is not how my analysis links them. Spinoza is important to my argument about Emerson because both chart progressions across types of consciousness—from a kind of knowledge based on sensation or reason to a kind of knowledge based on an "adequate knowledge of the essence of things."[15] The question for Emerson, as for Spinoza, is how the human mind can move from a confused knowledge of things to the conception of "its body's essence under a species of eternity" (*Et* 258; V P31) when Emerson's essays, like Spinoza's *Ethics*, refuse sequence, development, and teleology, even as, paradoxically, each espouses a hierarchy among the stages, while claiming there is no evolutionary means to graduate from one to the other. In this paradox, and, importantly, in the fact that, for both, the "intuitive . . . knowledge of the third kind" (*Et* 261; V P36) can only be registered in the body as a fully corporeal phenomenon, I note a *structural congruity*—thus something substantive—shared, however inadvertently, by the *Ethics* and Emerson's essays. The affiliations between Cather and Bergson and between Stevens and Leibniz and Whitehead, though only indicated rather than developed, are also substantive.

To pause for a moment on Stevens's relation to Leibniz, which also bears on the cognate methods of my other authors. In "A Collect of Philosophy," Stevens wrote that Leibniz "was a poet without flash. . . . Leibniz . . . was a man who thought like a poet but did not write like one."[16] He concluded that Leibniz "stands for a class: the philosopher afraid of ornament. Men engaged in the elucidation of obscurity might well feel a horror of the metaphor,"[17] whereas "the class I have in mind is the class to which metaphor is native and inescapable" (*CPP* 853). Stevens had the highest regard for what in "Effects of Analogy" he called "the appositeness of the image" (*CPP* 711)—for "the discipline that comes from appositeness in the highest degree" (*CPP* 712), since "it is often the case that the concepts of philosophy are poetic"

(*CPP* 856). Thus philosophical "obscurity" is uncharacteristically "elucidat[ed]" (*CPP* 853) in a poetic register. Even minor effects of figuration can express existential percepts—but nondiscursively. Cather has her own characterization of the nondiscursive: "It is the inexplicable presence of the thing not named, of the undertone divined by the ear but not heard by it, the verbal mood, the emotional aura of the fact or the thing or the deed, that gives high quality to the novel or drama, as well as to poetry itself."[18] Whitman enacts, but does not explain, and certainly cannot systematize the throng of incommensurable particulars he draws into an aggregate. Emerson's essays break out of expository discourse into adversarial figures—asymmetrical tropes or impacted genitives like "the life of life,"[19] an apposition that is also an opposition eluding concept.

With these examples in mind, then, let me clarify: I call literary works philosophical when *thematically* they raise questions about the nature of reality—as when a writer's project is to designate what Stevens called "things as they are"[20] or "being without description," where (in the "Latest Freed Man") "to be without description of to be" is to come upon "everything bulging and blazing and big in itself" (*CP* 205); as in Dickinson's poems, where speakers contemplate posthumous experience from "that odd Fork in Being's Road -" (F 453), from a beyond devoid of orientation in time and space; and as in Emerson's essays, where the being that differently constitutes personality and impersonality is not binary, since impersonality is not the negation of the human particular but a penetration to a region that disrupts the elementary categories we suppose are basic to human distinctiveness. Such issues brought to the surface and phrased as above are prima facie philosophical.

More crucial to my sense of the philosophical than the *thematic* subject-domains indicated above, the literary works discussed are *structurally* philosophical because the elements of the couplings formed by diverse phenomena lie beyond the ideational strictures that dictate the single context they could share. We see this in Whitman's poetry where "the old knot of contrariety"[21] is somehow contributive to the law of affiliation that "fuses me into you" (CBF 8:97) and both "I" and "you" into "any on[e]" (CBF 9:117). We see it in a poem like Stevens's "Pieces" (*CP* 351–52), where things said to be "like" each other are alien to each other, but also inextricable. We see it in Dickinson's poems, where sensation and abstraction constitute a complex of differences that frictively unfold in a single register, even though these expressive modes would seem to be antithetical ways of representing experience. We see it in the mesh of images held up to view as counterparts in *The Professor's House* when Tom Outland can't extricate the Latin of Virgil's *Aeneid* from the cliff dwellings on the mesa. ("I can always see two pictures: the one on the page, and another behind that: blue and purple rocks . . . little clustered houses."[22]) Their confluence reveals some third, near-nameless, thing—a thing that has no single name but, rather, is first identified as "happiness," then as a bare particular, "summer, high and blue," then as a distillation (or is it a surplus?): "a life in itself" composed of elements whose boundaries are implicitly traced and then erased (*PH* 253). For although the phrase "in itself" denotes what "life" intrinsically is, it also harks back to these inequivalent aspects of experience that compose the "in itself." In distinction, Whitman's conjunctions of incommensurables are serial, nonadditive, and often inconsequential—no sooner proposed than passed over. This is true of the "hieroglyph" in section 6 of "Song of Myself," whose translation enfolds incomparable entities in a union that has no stable form or logic, a transient "knit of identity"[23] like that which comprises Whitman's massified self. In distinctly different terms, in Cather's prose the changes that wash over all experience also deprive it of calcification. While for Bergson, in *Creative Evolution*, discontinuous novelty is an intuitive *principle* ("reality appears as a ceaseless upspringing of something new"[24]), for Cather it is a style entangling every aspect of her writing so that no manifestation of experience—whether a quality, a color, a movement—can be secured, but all are rather subject to the transmutations that link one feature of experience with another. As in the couplings of Whitman's catalogues, Emerson's tropes, Stevens's appositions, and Dickinson's syntactical yoking of "things unlike" (*OP* 109), any gloss of the proximal things juxtaposed in Cather's fiction leaves some aspect of them unaccommodated—within a drift of literary experience that cannot be tacked down to any of its parts. These conjunctions, these cognitive adjacencies, these condensations of aspects of reality that logically dispute each other but are affixed to each other, are a challenge to category and paradigm. They present phenomena that cannot be identified as this or as that, being rather something that emerges in excess of either. In this way, things that are *like* replace things that *are* as well as things that *become*. The passages I consider amass, subvert, and reshape what could never be a given, since in them resemblance and difference are matters of immediate, unscripted perception.[25]

While I leave the particulars of the argument to the reader's discovery in the essays themselves, I briefly outline the trajectory of each. "Beginning to Be: Emerson's Paratactic Images" charts the conflicts between personal and impersonal manifestations of experience, as these are registered in the narrative agons whose crisis is inscribed in the representative essays "Circles," "Fate," "Montaigne," and "Illusions" written across the range of Emerson's work. My essay then turns to certain tropes that condense manifestations of unlike experience that do not eliminate the person, but also do not consign him to the enclosures of personality. These asymmetrical tropes are almost permeable to each other. The truth of one cannot be exiled from the truth of the other, but overlap. I argue that Emerson's nondiscursive images are coupled by a technique that Walter Benjamin would call "literary montage"[26] and that the mysterious transit from one to the other, outside of narrative sequence, can be analogized to the anomalous movement across the discordant types of consciousness proposed in Spinoza's *Ethics*.

"Translation" is a word that Whitman culls to describe the transformation of something unlike to something like, writing: "The great translator and joiner of the whole is the poet."[27] In "Whitman's Translations," I argue that it is not just "hell" that he will "translate into a new tongue" (SM 21:423–24) but also the dead into the living (SM 6:126), and the "I" into the you and all. The essay considers the various ways in which these transmutations of unlike into like assault a classical view of identity where there is an equivalence relation that everything has to itself and to nothing else, and asks whether these transmutations can be theorized. With special attention to "Song of Myself," I suggest that Whitman's practice of conjoining things that are incommensurable does not read as contradictory because Whitman's visions of likeness at each moment begin anew. Thus each moment that draws serial manifestations of unlikeness together is original. That which is experienced as occurring for the first time cannot be seen to dispute anything that came before it.

In "Done with the Compass, Done with the Chart: Off-the-Map Scenes in Dickinson's Poems," I consider the incongruent counterparts of abstraction and sensation in Dickinson's journey poems that posit scenes where it is prohibitive to do so—in the spaces her speakers inhabit between death and eternity, and between death and immortality. Such placeholders dissolve in these thought experiments that foil the impotence of thought much as they do in another speaker's journey to locate God's "Face" and "his Residence" (F 525). In other poems, states of mind represented scenically cannot be isolated from scenes suffused with states of mind. Throughout, Dickinson's poems provide tropes for "reportless places" (F 1404), whether the locus glossed is a mental state or an improbable site, while some poems—for instance, "I started early took my dog" (F 656)—render perceptible what could not be attributed to mind or place. In Dickinson's poems, abstraction and sensation are in motion around each other along with the shifting mental states they register. Therefore I suggest that Dickinson's renditions of abstraction and sensation cannot squeeze into the narrow model offered by a deconstructionist critic and that their unique interactions would get lost within the exhaustive model of a cultural theorist.

"Something like Nebraska and Something like Virginia: Cather's Incommensurables,"[28] the title of my essay on Cather, exemplifies the way that, in an anecdote from *My Ántonia*, two states situated in discrepant regions of the country and states that conjoin discordant manifestations of being (crisis and serenity) and of condition (marrying and dying) abut each other or meet in junctures of unlikeness whose incongruences have no logical corollary. The transmutations in which a phenomenon becomes obliquely combinatory with something alien is at the heart of Cather's writing and affects the construction of the image; the sentence; the depiction of character; and even life experienced as that sensation which intermeshes the natural and the human; as well as the micro-vibrations of Cather's phrases and rhythms. Such composites are not an anomaly in Cather's writing. The flux and transpositions that couple incommensurate states sweep through Cather's writing. They do not drive the story forward but disrupt continuities of narrative that divide things into units in a compulsively linear way. One premise of the essay is that Cather's plots, her gripping portraits of character, of the Nebraska settlers, of the prairie's pictorial splendor, for which she is justly celebrated, momentarily fade from attention before certain astonishing moments that dilate on a vision in which something is seen to be inequivalent to itself—as when in *The Professor's House* a lake undergoes a metamorphosis in consciousness that renders it alienated from the characteristics that define it and also from the properties of an alternative body of water to which it is compared: "it is a sea, and yet it is not salt. It is blue, but quite another blue" (*PH* 30–31)—"quite another blue" being absolutely if elusively separable from its look-alike, even if the distinction has no graspable name.

While in Emerson's essays, tropes that arise to quash the agon of argument are crucial but intermittent presences, in Stevens's poems such relations evolve continuously by juxtaposition. In "Wallace Stevens's Entangled Objects," I argue that for Stevens in the tumble of conditions, moods, and thoughts, there could be no "in itself" (*PH* 253) or "things as they are"—only things on the move that repel a solid nature. Thus in "The Blue Guitar," there is no "Dichtung und Wahrheit, all / Confusion solved, as in a refrain." Rather, "one keeps on playing year by year, / Concerning the nature of things as they are" (*CP* 177), which could never be systematized, since they emerge from what you "say of what you see in the dark" (*CP* 183), of "things as they are" (*CP* 178) . . . "That it is this or that it is that" (*CP* 183). But since "the swarm of thoughts, the swarm of dreams" (*CP* 179) reshape the "this" and the "that," "things as they were" diverge from "things as they are" or "will be" (*CP* 178): "The world had worlds . . . / The grass turned green and the grass turned gray" (*CP* 178). From a more capacious vantage, in Stevens's "Description Without Place," things unambiguously *seem* rather than *are*: each thing is "alive with its own seemings, seeming to be / Like rubies reddened by rubies reddening" (*CP* 346). "Seeming" inflects what has been and what comes to be—but not necessarily in that order. For the past ("rubies reddened") is colored by the present progressive ("rubies reddening"), that continuous tense which casts its shadow backward—"seeming" (like the infinitive form in which it is here expressed) retains a fluency that overturns chronology, rebuking its divisions and direction—since all manifestations of time, however conceptually sundered, are tinged by the same hue.

As the diverse characterizations above suggest, the unevenly matched set of incommensurables investigated in the following essays—all articulated within a unique idiom, not in the same way, not to the same effect, and not with regard to the same incongruences—are outliers, each a bearer of "a life in itself" (*PH* 253), one not assimilable to another. They thus repel a genealogy and an overarching theory. As for a paradigm or theory that would clinch such analysis, I have not sought such closure. Perhaps this resistance to the closure of theory is itself philosophical. My readings are site-specific and differential. Anything syncretic seems to me antithetical to the subtlety on which these works insist. My essays investigate the particulars that validate such a claim.

I should add that of course Stevens read Emerson and Whitman, and he also read Cather's 1940 *Sapphira and the Slave Girl.*[29] There is no record that he read Dickinson: Thomas Johnson's edition of her poems was published in 1955, the year Stevens died. Yet in Stevens's poetry, the conjunction of abstraction and sensation seems uncannily to echo the admixture of the two forms of expression in his predecessor. For Dickinson, sensation is a retort to things that can't be experienced and which therefore requires the presence of things that *can* be to ameliorate the lived emptiness of abstraction. For Stevens, sensation arises from what in "The Creations of Sound" he called "spontaneous particulars" (*CP* 311) that sear through the philosophical meandering weighing down a poem like "An Ordinary Evening in New Haven" (*CP* 465–89). I thus see the two poets who did not read each other as kin in their shared "intuition"—for Whitehead it was a "Category" explaining "concrescence" (*PR* 21, 22)—that "opposed elements stand to each other in mutual requirement. In their unity [their "novel togetherness" (*PR* 21)] they inhibit or contrast" (*PR* 348). One "is the instrument of novelty for the other" (*PR* 349). Even so, the essays that follow are not patterned overall by the structuring principle of opposition that sets the person against an overarching impersonality as explored in my 2007 *Impersonality*. Nor do these essays focus on the opposition in general that organizes my 2017 *The Bond of the Furthest Apart*. For example, the current essay on Emerson's paratactic images is a peripheral and partly remedial corrective to the claims of my two earlier assessments, in which I argued that Emerson uniformly dismisses the person for a bloodless abstraction. In this essay, I consider paratactic tropes that demonstrate how the human mind can leap from a person's bounded understanding to an intuitive grasp of the essence of things. Such tropes conjoin antitheses that can't be extricated from each other and introduce the mystery of paradox without contradiction.

The authors I consider are not the only American writers whose originality is rooted in incommensurables. In Edgar Allan Poe's *Eureka*, "an absolute *reciprocity of adaptation*" governs cause and effect[30] and also a related pairing of atoms in which "two Principles . . . *Attraction* and *Repulsion*" (consolidation and diffusion), personified as "the Material and the Spiritual" factors that "accompany each other, in the strictest fellowship, forever" (EAP 256), are truths discovered by "illimitable intuition" (EAP 219) that in Poe's treatise far exceeds any axiom (EAP 216–20). Incommensurables are hardly an American phenomenon, as illustrated by an extravagant example of that mode in Jorge Luis Borges's "The Aleph": "the place where, without admixture or confusion, all the places of the world, seen from every angle, coexist."[31] Incommensurables considered in my essays do not arrive at such a synchronicity, though the reckoning of Whitman's native catalogues moves toward a visionary apex. But there are other manifestations of extremity where, in Borges's words, incongruent phenomena come together, not temporally, but existentially, to "occup[y] the same point, without superposition and without transparency" (A 129).

An American version of this mode of conjunction begins with the logic of Emerson's essays that harks back to Michel de Montaigne's "metaphysics" and "physics" elaborated in "Of Experience," where "resemblance does not make things so much alike as difference makes them unlike."[32] Emerson's understanding of that co-optation is to run it backward to a moment in which a "ravishment of the intellect" breaks out by "coming nearer to the fact."[33] In that proximity, "intellect," a faculty of mind associated with knowledge or objective understanding, is carried away by transport—bliss and "intellect" each emerging from discordant zones that here cannot be kept apart. Incommensurables lean into each other in Dickinson's fascicle experiments, in which word choices on the poetic line and their variants in the margin cannot both be accommodated by metrical rule, but also can't be detached from each other. Two of Thoreau's representations of nature are written at the same time but instigated by forms of attention that could not be corralled into the same project: *Walden* is polemical and instructive, the *Journal* enthralled by heterogeneous particulars that spill over the bounds of argument and exhortation. In *Moby-Dick* Melville contemplates a fate arrived at by the answer to the formulation posed by Ahab's alternative understandings—"be the white whale agent, or be the white whale principle"[34]—a determination that, however settled, would be dimmed by the novel's corollary focus on a primitive corporeality, for bodies are not susceptible to hermeneutic dissection.[35] At the end of F. Scott Fitzgerald's *The Great Gatsby*, where a romantic dream is everywhere complicated by an imaginative mismatch between phenomena and their apprehension, any true wonder will be thrown back not just on romantic illusion or colonial ambition but on the incommensurability of response and what incites it—notwithstanding the disclaimer that protests otherwise:

> . . . for a transitory enchanted moment man must have held his breath in the presence of this continent, compelled into an aesthetic contemplation he neither understood nor desired, face to face for the last time in history with something commensurate to his capacity for wonder.[36]

"Wonder," as described above, might satisfy a meager "capacity," but is incompatible with the immensity of the continent—whose vastness opens beyond the beauty of "aesthetic contemplation"—and thus falls short of the sublimity evoked by, and "commensurate" with, a spectacle exceeding human scale. At the same time, the passage records a climactic moment, perhaps the utmost that can be experienced within the insufficiencies of the American Dream represented in Fitzgerald's novel.

Something of the disparity that defines these American incommensurables is not just italicized but also worried in the last stanza of Dickinson's "The brain is wider than the sky":

> The Brain is just the weight of God -
> For - Heft them - Pound for Pound -
> And they will differ - if they do -
> As Syllable from Sound -
> (F 598)

The stanza bears a relation to Whitehead's claim that "God and the World"—those monumental synecdoches of the inner and the outer—"stand in mutual requirement" (*PR* 348), except that the posterior, non-God trope has migrated inward. Dickinson wants to specify the difference between these entities, while at the same time insisting on the possibility that the entities do not differ. The stanza above separates the claim that "God" and "the Brain" are the same ("The Brain is just the weight of God") from the claim that they are different ("And they will differ . . . / As Syllable from Sound") by an interpolated question about whether they are really different ("And they will differ - if they do"). A cognate hesitation arises for a reader in the junctures of Stevens's "The Motive for Metaphor" (*CP* 288), a poem whose tropes are incomparably and, in one instance, inexplicably affixed to each other by contiguity and thus might have been called "The Motive for Metonymy." A magnetic constellation gathers the instances touched on above—each manifesting in its own terms "the likeness of things unlike" (*OP* 108–9) to form a loose commonality in a strain of American writing, and these examples form a backdrop against which to consider the incommensurables examined in the essays that follow. For this reader they also offer more than an intrinsic interest across a differential spectrum. Crammed full of cognitive and affective experience speaking for itself—that *is* an "in itself" (*PH* 253) outside of any name or category that could be attributed to it—these instances of incommensurability bestow an unstabilized pleasure, a wobbly thrill, at aspects of things that can't be extracted from each other and can't be integrated, at an intertwining whose fascination lies beyond what we can make of it.

Beginning to Be

EMERSON'S PARATACTIC IMAGES

A novice reader of Emerson soon comes to the startling conclusion that while persons provide entrances to "the power and order that lie at the heart of things,"[1] they quickly become stepping-stones to the recognition that "the human mind cannot be enshrined in a person."[2] The person—including the famous person in *Representative Men*—is serviceable beyond "conveniency in household matters"[3] only when he introduces us to universals. Moreover, even up close, persons cannot be recognized as sui generis: "they melt so fast into each other, that they are like grass and trees," "a rack of clouds, or a fleet of ripples which the wind drives over the water" (NR 580). And though "we are associated . . . with some friends, who, like skies and waters, are coextensive with our idea; who, answe[r] to a certain affection of the soul" so that "we cannot choose but love them," as is the case with the "ideal" friend at the end of the "Discipline" section of *Nature*—any "standard of excellence" (*N* 31) such a friend might provide is fleeting. We must uproot our affections for him when he is chillingly replaced by a bloodless abstraction: "solid and sweet wisdom" (*N* 31) that demands no personal engagement.

Whether the abjured person is a friend, the influential man in *Representative Men* who is "greater when he can abolish himself"[4] (thus enabling an "irresistible upward force, into our thought . . . [that] destroy[s] individualism" with a "power so great, that the potentate is nothing" [U 625]), or even one's own person as when we are "throw[n] . . . on the party and interest of the Universe, against all and sundry; against ourselves, as much as others,"[5] these passages suggest value is only secure in tropes of vastness like the "Over-soul,"[6] the "superpersonal Heart,"[7] the "immeasurable mind"[8] that "resist the usurpation of particulars"[9] and the "encumb[rance]" of "personality" (NR 579) to affirm a "catholic sense" (M 709), even a "catholic" existence.

One consequence of this coolness toward the person affects Emerson's dissociation from his own person and its losses. "I cannot get it nearer to me,"[10] he remarks at the death of his child about an evanescence that can only be examined once it is posited as a property of all experience. Though the "lubricity of all objects, which lets them slip through our fingers then when we clutch hardest" (E 473) is discoverable everywhere Emerson turns his attention, and thus gives the lie to his claim that "this calamity . . . does not touch me" (E 473), he himself never acknowledges the feeling he insists escapes him. I have argued that this expunging of the person from empathetic representation (and this muffling of feeling) creates a fissure in the life picture Emerson constructs from which we see something crucial has been omitted.[11]

In the following pages, I mean to revise a characterization to which I have contributed by considering certain crisis moments that offer a corrective to Emerson's routine slighting of the person. In part i, I examine passages that render substantial and even highlight the conflict experienced by the "individual" (along with "man," Emerson's synonym for "person") who is torn between the imperative to embrace an "alien energy" (OS 385) exemplified by tropes of vastness that give access to infinite regions ("the common heart" [OS 396]; the "universal soul" [OS 393]; "an influx of the Divine mind into our mind" [OS 392]) and, conversely, to repel that buoyant consent to a sacrifice of "the will I call mine" (OS 385) on which such an embrace is premised because of the suffering it exacts—a friction to which I was blind in my earlier essays when I claimed that Emerson exerted no resistance to the demands of impersonality. Here I look with fresh eyes at manifestations of that anguish: As when "a man" sees he must vow allegiance to a "power transcending all limit and privacy,"[12] a commitment that in "Fate" compels his "ruin" (F 967). As when in "Circles," a "man" forgoes this compliance because its assault on everything that "hem[s] in the life"[13] savages the boundaries that define and preserve *him*. As when in "Montaigne," surrender to a "world saturated with deity" (M 708) is compromised by a corollary: to embrace such magnitude is to consent to its "parsimony" for oneself personally (M 708). As when in "Illusions," the mythological Thor is swept into the profusion of impersonal energies rendered conceptually, at a remove, outside the representation of his direct experience. Notwithstanding the diversity of such crisis moments, as I will elaborate, they uniformly distill the agon of aversion and surrender, often played out at an essay's penultimate moments in a conceptual rift: on the one side, the person who incarnates a perspective and who recoils from a "better and universal self . . . new and unsearchable" when it "sweeps away all cherished hopes . . . and projects . . . in its flood" (OS 398); on the other side, an "unbounded substance" (E 485) indifferent to the suffering inflicted by that metamorphosis.

In opposition to such a schism that characterizes Emerson's prose (either in explicit logic or in its undertone), in part ii I argue that disjunctive paratactic images—dissonant images placed side by side, without subordination or hierarchy, and located outside of narrative expositions from which they break free—reveal an ontology not founded on the splitting anatomized above. These tropes provide a corrective to Emerson's segregation of the person from totalities like "the immeasurable mind" (DSA 89). They evoke a plenitude of being that is not outside the person, but is an embodied experience. Yet even if one is a discerning and practiced reader of Emerson, these paratactic conjunctive images, the smallest units of an Emerson essay that both preserve and transform the person, are easy to miss. They flash by without duration or consequence. Moreover, though riveting when noticed, the disjunctive images (like the terminological association of the chiastic phrases "Beautiful Necessity" and the "necessity of beauty" [F 967] entangled with each other at the conclusion of "Fate" that have something of the same contrastive effect) are nonidentical in logic but affixed to each other. They can't be visualized or even adequately penetrated. Even so, the paratactic images that elliptically conjoin incommensurables of the person and a magnitude that surpasses his limits are a solution to the inadequacy of exposition for Emerson—exposition being inclined to drive a wedge between differences and then to build toward conclusions that stabilize and thus terminate thought.

In part iii, I examine the kinship of Emerson's paratactic emblems with other anti-expository and nonlinear systems of thought that similarly juxtapose understandings of being that can't be assimilated to each other, but also can't be separated. One such metaphysics is Spinoza's *Ethics*, in which a "mode" (a finite mind and body) can't be separated from infinite "substance" ("God or Nature"), and in which, in one "kind" of knowledge, consciousness of the body can't be segregated from a consciousness that sees "intuitive[ly]" from the point of view of eternity,[14] for between the two there is a "lived transition."[15] In that transition, as I shall explain, Emerson, like Spinoza, corrects the notions that a perception of the "Unity" (F 967) of things must be notional, lying outside of direct experience. For both, such knowledge could only be validated as an embodied phenomenon, something grasped from within.

Emerson has a well-documented relation to Spinoza,[16] even though the former's designation of "person" is not the same as Spinoza's unique understandings of the "individual," whose boundaries are heterogeneously defined, since for Emerson the limits of the person do not fluctuate across categories.[17] Nonetheless, the denominations are comparable, because both "individual" and "person" are equivalently counterpointed to Emerson's "infinite enlargement . . . with a power of growth to a new infinity on every side" (OS 398) and to Spinoza's "substance which is . . . infinite" and "indivisible" (*Et* 93; I P13). Both reconceive singularity, though not on the same ground. In the following pages, what draws Spinoza and Emerson into a kindred universe is not influence of the former on the latter, but a like fascination for each with how the human mind can move from a bounded, "mutilated, confused . . . knowledge" that is "represented to us through the senses" or from "common notions" and "reason" (*Et* 141; II P40S2) to an "adequate" understanding that opens to "the knowledge of singular things . . . called intuitive" (*Et* 261; V P36), when both theories refuse sequence as well as teleology. Part iii asks how it comes about that a lived experience of an infinite—no longer soaring above him—could traverse a person with a vitality that changes but does not efface him.

i

While "Circles," "Fate," and "Montaigne" have argumentative threads clearly drawn from one end of an essay to another, these are intertwined with dramatized hesitations that challenge each essay's unshakable polemic. To borrow Charles Altieri's word from a discussion of style in another context, both the polemic and a reactive relation to its logic are "displayed,"[18] producing a cacophony of voice positions that obliquely contend with each other. Such contested points of view remake perception from one moment to the next, each perspective being saturated in the particulars of its own validity. There is no fixity to an orientation, since a perspective is uprooted from one moment to the next and from one frame of reference to another, superseded by a vision that incarnates a dissimilar perspective, equally persuasive but not persuasive in relation to the same conditions, the same vantage, or the same ground. These disparately voiced perspectives exhibit the incongruity of moods and convictions; they are energies or patterns of intensity whose vehemence appears, passes across the page, then passes away. They can no more be simplified, codified, or immobilized than can the numerous incommensurabilities that constitute any insolid self. An essay like "Circles" both conceives and models the deviation of perspective such that the essay's central proposition—"The universe is fluid and volatile. Permanence is but a word of degrees" (C 403)—applies to everything, including point of view, the context that authenticates it, and what kind of person can endure the knowledge that "there is no outside, no enclosing wall, no circumference to us" (C 405) when this lack of fixture assaults the enclosure he calls himself.

In "Circles," impermanence pertains to our perception of a person (once we see past the edges of a man, the "sea to swim in" that he initially represents to us becomes "a pond" with "shores" [C 406]); to degrees of idealism ("the idealism of Berkeley is only a crude statement of the idealism of Jesus, and that again is a crude statement of the fact, that all nature is the rapid efflux of goodness" [C 407]); to preferences that cede to other preferences ("Good as is discourse, silence is better" [C 408]); and even to states that would seem to resist the "deep remedial force that underlies all facts,"[19] as when in the grip of Emerson's doctrine, selfishness becomes porous to what overcomes its recalcitrance (in "that unrestrained inundation of the principle of good into every chink and hole that selfishness has left open, yea, into selfishness and sin itself" [C 412]). Emerson's axiom of flux tenaciously demonstrates the impartial movement of everything without exception toward the "impersonal and illimitable" (C 409). No "building up our being" (C 413), or our conception of being, could prevent change. If all is "fugitive" (C 410), this *all* renders a person the repository of loss and pain, unrecognizable to himself while, in contrast, negligible for the universe: "All loss, all pain, is particular; the universe remains to the heart unhurt."[20] Moreover, the pronouncement "all that we reckoned settled shakes and rattles" (C 408) that can be celebrated in one set of circumstances must be lamented in another. In the context of inventions that facilitate travel ("see the investment of capital in aqueducts made useless by hydraulics; . . . roads and canals, by railways; sails, by steam; steam by electricity" [C 404]), mobility is synonymous with progress. The mercurial nature of everything inauspiciously also applies to the uncertain fortunes of the "merchant" when his materials gain and then lose value; to the variable weather that for a farmer erratically determines if there will be the "good tillage" propitious for a "crop" (C 404); and, of course, to the "ebb" and "flow" of moods, as when the feeling "I am God in nature" mutates to "I am a weed by the wall" (C 406). Such examples not only suggest that nothing is spared; they also inflict on the reader the role of passively attending to a current of change that resists pattern and conclusion. In "Circles" each instance of ephemerality momentarily brushes past the reader before it, too, is outflanked by another instance of the "partial," "the approximate," and the transient (C 410). This omnipresence—nothing exempt from passing away—provokes a hope that one could get behind the phenomenon with which there is an enforced intimacy by fathoming it, but the incessant flow of change never permits analysis.

Emerson's encomium on an intrepid embrace of change ("people wish to be settled; only as far as they are unsettled is there any hope for them" [C 413]) is repeatedly struck through by diction that accentuates hazard. Fearlessness is what the essay enjoins us to summon before the peril of incessant change, but in the charged language of the essay, we are also repeatedly reminded that we are "at the mercy of a new generalization," and this both constitutes and ameliorates the "thrill" of it (C 407). If there is danger when "God lets loose a thinker on this planet" (C 407), what happens when *you* become that thinker and realize "there is no virtue which is final; all are initial" (C 411)? These examples assail the edges that hold the person in place, edges that would preserve him as a person rather than as a force moved by "alien energy" (OS 385). "Circles" not only lingers on the precariousness of such instability, but the essay also ponders a specious prudence that would avert it: "Geoffrey draws on his boots to go through the woods, that his feet may be safer from the bite of snakes; Aaron never thinks of such a peril. In many years neither is harmed. . . . Yet it seems to me, that, with every precaution you take against such an evil, you put yourself into the power of the evil" (C 410). Emerson's stark preference for a "prudence" of risk rather than for a stranglehold of "pitiful calculations" (C 410) to ensure a welfare that in truth is always in doubt—as what counts as welfare will always be in doubt—is the moral of Aaron's vantage over Geoffrey's, and of the essay as a whole.

Yet at the essay's end, Aaron's come-what-may relation to experience is unexpectedly displaced by the essay's focus on a "semblance" of self-abandon which subverts the genuine self-yielding that would realize the "insatiable desire . . . to be surprised out of our propriety, to lose our sempiternal memory, and to do something without knowing how or why" extolled in the essay as a whole (C 414). The conclusion's pivot to a paralyzing caution casts a pall that reaches beyond Geoffrey's limitation, because it insists that others are as compromised as Geoffrey is when they mistake disinhibition for self-abandonment. The essay's last sentences compel attention less for what is revealed about Emerson's appeal to see that "the coming only is sacred" (C 413), an insistence that imbues the essay and is never in doubt, than for a question it raises about whether the impulse to preserve the self can be overcome—the one surprise for which the essay did not prepare us. While "the great man is not convulsible or tormentable; events pass over him without much impression" (C 413), the essay holds up the difficulty of becoming such a man or woman:

> Dreams and drunkenness, the use of opium and alcohol are the semblance and counterfeit of this oracular genius, and hence their dangerous attraction for men. For the like reason, they ask the aid of wild passions, as in gaming and war, to ape in some manner these flames and generosities of the heart. (C 414)

The travesties of self-abandonment—"opium," "alcohol," "gaming," "war"—mimic the deliverance from self the essay has espoused, thus turning the potentially great man (Aaron) whose equanimity is not "convulsible" (C 413) into another sort of man (Geoffrey), or into the same man at another moment (Aaron, when his courage falters, sliding into Geoffrey), one whose agitated self-preservation repels the greatness the essay has prescribed, made unattainable by a false liberation from self that enslaves him to intoxicating addictions. Though the final phrase rests its case on the magnanimity required by the essay's imperative and revealed in its examples, the intermittent hesitations that culminate in simulations of self-abandonment—amplified and ticked off in the essay's concluding sentence—expose a person's shuttered view, a self-imposed bondage that can only "ape . . . these flames and generosities of the heart" (C 414).

Emerson's essay "Fate" begins by enumerating inevitabilities that are darker than the manifestations of self-imprisonment glimpsed at the end of "Circles." "Fate" is physiological: "When each comes forth from his mother's womb . . . he has but one future . . . predetermined in his lobes . . . in that little fatty face, pig-eye, and squat form" (F 947). It is "temperament," a "prison of glass" (E 474). It is political determinacy: "with high magnifiers, Mr. Frauenhofer or Dr. Carpenter might come to distinguish in the embryo at the fourth day, this is a Whig, and that a Free-soiler" (F 948). Fate tears the mask off originality, since innovations "have all been invented over and over" (F 950) and so have inventors: "Copernicus, Newton, Laplace, are not new men or a new kind of men" (F 951). There could be only one conclusion: "the book of Nature is the book of Fate" (F 949). Only in the essay's middle section does logic transform fate into a mere segment of the whole: "if you . . . say, Fate is all; then we say, a part of Fate is the freedom of man" (F 953). Resisting the omnipresence of things that "hem in the life" (C 404), Emerson insists that freedom is "thought" (F 953); is "expansion" (F 954); is "the moral sentiment" (F 956); is "will" (F 957); is mobility ("The whole world is the flux of matter over the wires of thought" [F 965]). Thus the grim observation "The cold, inconsiderate of persons, . . . freezes a man like an apple" (F 945) is reformulated thirteen pages later, where ice bears a man up rather than freezing him solid and, in the flair of the skater who learns how to glide across it, shows him off to advantage: "the ice will give you a graceful, sweet, and poetic motion" (F 958). Advantage is more extravagantly demonstrated in a paragraph that illustrates the boast that "the cold will brace your limbs and brain to genius" (F 958): the one galvanized by cold and ice can "absorb and domineer . . . the secrets of water and steam, the spasms of electricity, the ductility of metals" (F 958). More: "cold and sea will train an imperial Saxon race, which nature cannot bear to lose" (F 958). Such gymnastic demonstrations indicate the plastic powers of thought, discipline, and language to transform impediments into instruments of power. Emerson marshals these resources into evidence that fate can even be made soluble: "see how fate slides into freedom, and freedom into fate" (F 961).

But the essay's resolution revokes the promise of "Fate" as "unpenetrated" "causes" (F 958), which could be penetrated: if "organization" "closes" "behind every individual," in compensation "before him, opens liberty" (F 960). It thus derides the "freedom" that the middle pages have wrested from "fate" with such virtuosity, compelling a surrender to fate that the essay has not prepared us to countenance, especially when in the essay's middle section an obligation to cultivate "pure sympathy with universal ends" (F 956) includes neither suffering nor sacrifice. This abdication is legitimated in compositional terms—"the omnipresence of law" "is not in us so much as we are in it" (F 955)—and even glamorized as mastery: "he who sees through the design, presides over it" (F 956). Yet the submission to fate extolled at the essay's end—man "is to rally on his relation to the Universe" "to take sides with the Deity who secures universal benefit by his pain" (F 967)—can only be clinched by the conspicuous substitution of caprice for freedom whose calamitous terms no one could accept:

> Let us build altars to the Beautiful Necessity. If we thought men were free in the sense, that, in a single exception one fantastical will could prevail over the law of things, it were all one as if a child's hand could pull down the sun. (F 967)

The essay's drift from "fate" to "freedom" and then to the *relinquishment* of freedom illegitimately made cognate with whim (the caricature of freedom), transgression (the exercise of liberty to derange a natural order), and an improvident will depends on a torque in the argument that jettisons one term for a non-synonym in a process of sublation (we "must will that which must be" [F 956]) and a display of sophistical equivalence ("why should we fear to be crushed by savage elements, we who are made up of the same elements?" [F 967]) that rhetorically—but only rhetorically—cancels distinctions initially upheld as essential. The person, once urged to cultivate a "stupendous antagonism" (F 953) to what thwarts him (he "ought to compare advantageously with a river, an oak, or a mountain" [F 954]), at the essay's end is enjoined to capitulate, to "build altars to the Beautiful Necessity" in response to a hypothetical apocalypse: the "child's hand" that "could pull down the sun" (F 967), a dictate which displaces the injunction to cultivate defiance by invoking a logic as capricious as the image that precipitates the essay's about-face.

The crisis of the person—the one who in "Fate" sacrifices himself to "Beautiful Necessity" (F 967) and the one who cannot do so in "Circles"—is accentuated at the end of "Montaigne," where all-consuming desire is rendered virtually synonymous with suffering, with "the universal grief" of *being* a person (as experienced by "young and ardent minds" [M 708]) crushed by the weight of an ethical imperative that trivializes this desire:

> Charles Fourier announced that "the attractions of man are proportioned to his destinies"; in other words, that every desire predicts its own satisfaction. Yet, all experience exhibits the reverse of this; the incompetency of power is the universal grief of young and ardent

> minds. They accuse the divine providence of a certain parsimony. It has shown the heaven and earth to every child, and filled him with a desire for the whole; a desire raging, infinite; a hunger, as of space to be filled with planets; a cry of famine, as of devils for souls. Then for the satisfaction,—to each man is administered a single drop, a bead of dew of vital power, *per day*,—a cup as large as space, and one drop of the water of life in it. Each man woke in the morning, with an appetite that could eat the solar system like a cake; a spirit for action and passion without bounds; he could lay his hand on the morning star: he could try conclusions with gravitation or chemistry; but, on the first motion to prove his strength,—hands, feet, senses, gave way, and would not serve him. . . . In every house, in the heart of each maiden, and of each boy, in the soul of the soaring saint, this chasm is found,—between the largest promise of ideal power, and the shabby experience. (M 708–9)

The passage's extravagant similes surpass each other in evoking unquenchable craving, as in the amplification "an appetite that could eat the solar system like a cake" (M 708), which resists being understood as a hyperbole because hunger intensified by the absence of objects to satisfy it could not be overstated. Ravenousness is experienced as so substantial—therefore so sensational—that anything it could identify, even the sun and all the planets, is insufficient to sate it; hence the depiction of the solar system as a sweet, something that ends a meal rather than constituting it. There could be no compensation for this omnivorousness—since its objects include "action and passion without bounds" and, in the designation of "space to be filled with planets," the infinite itself—notwithstanding these mitigative sentences:

> The expansive nature of truth comes to our succor. . . . Man helps himself by larger generalizations. The lesson of life is practically to generalize; to believe what the years and the centuries say against the hours; to resist the usurpation of particulars; to penetrate to their catholic sense. (M 709)

In the same vein, "the moral sentiment" is said to "outweig[h]" all "objections" and appease all "parsimony": it "is the drop which balances the sea" (M 708). But the "sea" equilibrated by the drop that is an ethical solvent more provocatively calls to mind the immensity identified in the paragraph I've examined—not of water, but of desire. Desire could not be glutted, just as "a single drop . . . of vital power, *per day*" could not fill "a cup as large as space" (M 708). In Emerson's passage, two incommensurate quantities ("sea" and "drop" / "space" and "drop") are inequivalently juxtaposed. "Sea" and "drop," as sketched above, could metaphorically be balanced, thanks to the heft attributed to the ethical globule, "the moral sentiment," while a "drop" that is an insufficiency ("a bead of dew of vital power, *per day*" [M 708]) could never balance "desire" figured as "a cup as large as space" (M 708), a near oxymoron for a void that could not be filled by anything. Rather, the "yawning gulf" between "drop" and "space" is reiterated as a "chasm" (M 709) in the revectored divide between the "sky of law and the pismire of performance" (M 706), "between the largest promise of ideal power, and the shabby experience" (M 709). Notwithstanding the ballast attributed to the compensatory lone "drop of the water of life" (M 708), the real weight at the essay's end subversively shifts to the scarcity of the person's satisfaction registered everywhere in its penultimate paragraphs and rendered unforgettable.

"Illusions" provides one last example of the friction between the person's fettered conception of experience and an aerial view that divulges its universal contours. In "Illusions" Emerson appropriates a Norse myth to exemplify how everyday "seeming trifles"[21] that illusorily seem paltry—the heroic feats narrated in the following passage are the god Thor's everyday—divulge their impersonal significance beyond the subjective and the apparently inconsequential so that he can taste the real quality of existence:

> That story of Thor, who was set to drain the drinking-horn in Asgard, and to wrestle with the old woman, and to run with the runner Lok, and presently found that he had been drinking up the sea, and wrestling with Time, and racing with Thought, describes us who are contending, amid these seeming trifles, with the supreme energies of Nature. (I 1121)

The refusal to explain the precise relation among the illimitable energies that Thor discovers pulsing through the undertakings dismissed as banal is the point of the formulation, not its mistake, suggesting that it is impossible to solve the enigma of how minute particulars that seemed to have no value could become a medium for the recognition of sovereign powers. Yet the very smoothness with which the sentence moves from Thor's incomprehension to his illumination—the discovery that his failed contests exemplify something unfathomable, rather than something meaningless—omits the deepening that would mark his experience as revelatory, that would show the process (or just the perceptible steps) through which we "who are contending, amid these seeming trifles" (I 1121), could also achieve wisdom, or through which he does. Rather all is described in an impassive past tense: he "found" (I 1121).[22] As there is no way to decipher the transition from Thor's blindness to his awakening, there is also nothing that exhibits Thor's registration of the import of the vision Emerson assigns him. His enlightenment changes everything without demonstrating how it changes anything. Of course Emerson is writing a parable that emphasizes a didactic point, not an empirical one. Nevertheless, the neutrality of the passage inadvertently raises the question whether the enlargement that occurs to Thor can only do so abstractly from a distance by omitting a felt sense of the realization imparted to him. "All our days are so unprofitable while they pass, that 'tis wonderful where or when we ever got anything of this which we call wisdom, poetry, virtue. We never got it on any dated calendar day" (E 471), Emerson laments. From Thor's perspective, however, it is life itself, "the real quality of existence" (I 1122), that escapes. Thor, a dumb spectator, believes he is "contending" with "seeming trifles" (I 1121) while life in its sublimity floats by and above him.

Glossed thus, the parable raises the question whether a person in Emerson's essays can experience the enlargement that surpasses him without resisting it ("Circles"); without being sacrificed to it ("Fate"); without suffering it as a tragedy ("Montaigne"); and without forgoing affect ("Illusions"). Although the passages I've touched on exemplify a range of ways in which the person is enjoined to embrace the sovereign powers that dictate an impersonal vision like Thor's, they all predictably demand a rupture (of the person from himself, as prescribed by "Fate" when he is urged to split himself into a "double consciousness" [F 966] so that he can approve his own "ruin" when it "secures universal benefit" [F 967]; of the person from his accumulated experience, as advocated by "Circles" on behalf of empty "[be]coming" [C 413]; of the person from his friend in the "Discipline" section of *Nature* when the larger-than-life succor, "solid and sweet wisdom," renders his presence gratuitous [*N* 31]; and of "circumstance," whether arduous or easy, from "the real quality of existence," which "in our thoughts . . . wear[s] no silks, and taste[s] no ice-creams" [I 1122–23]). The essays reveal a fissure in the self that pushes away the impersonal enlargement that is advocated at a distance, but cannot be tolerated close up for different reasons and different terms. In "Circles," to assent to the "impersonal and illimitable" (C 409) is to instigate a backlash of "pitiful calculations" (C 410), thereby "build[ing] up our being" (C 413) rather than diffusing it. In "Montaigne," the value term "the moral sentiment, . . . the drop which balances the sea," is no balance or succor for a person's "hunger, as of space to be filled with planets" (M 708). And in the caustic language of "Fate," the "freedom" that vanquishes necessity (F 953) is itself jettisoned for a sacrifice suddenly described as necessary (F 967). Expressed philosophically, these essays narrate "the absence of any appearance of reconciliation between the theory and practice of life" (M 705). Yet though the frequency of such ruptures in Emerson's essays suggests that they are all but inevitable, certain juxtaposed and intertwined images (associated with the person and with what surpasses his limits), to which I now turn, reveal an ontology not riven by splitting, not simplified by unity, and not purged of affect.

ii

These paratactic images, though embedded in exposition, in their condensation, announce a near independence from the partitions and subordinations described above. The emblems juxtapose a person's view—as exemplified by the Greek word *hupokritês*, which can mean "he who interprets"[23] according to his perspective—to an ontology, an embodied sense of what is real with regard to being and essence outside of subjectivity. Such a constellation does not eliminate the person but also does not consign him to the enclosure of personality, a feat that is realized by a fall out of exposition into emblems that reveal "cross-connections between elements" whose "relationships of tension have been brought, as it were, to a standstill"—hence that have an "affinity with the image" (to borrow Theodor Adorno's characterization of essayistic formulations that "pry open the aspect of... objects that cannot be accommodated by concepts, the aspect that reveals, through the contradictions in which concepts become entangled, that the net of their objectivity is a merely subjective arrangement"[24]). Adorno's characterization has an unintended application to those Emersonian images that permeate conceptual boundaries. These "intervoluted"[25] contrastive, paratactic images—one seeming to arise at an infinite distance from, the other in absolute proximity to, the person—veer into each other, notwithstanding their spatial and temporal disparity, and enigmatically cross, registering in the body as sensation and insight. Two examples follow.

Toward the end of "Fate," frictive images are bluntly linked to each other by an enigmatic "on," which emerges as a focus:

> How idle to choose a random sparkle here or there, when the indwelling necessity plants the rose of beauty on the brow of chaos, and discloses the central intention of Nature to be harmony and joy. (F 967)

"Rose of beauty" is an equative genitive, the rose that constitutes beauty—and maybe, more, a metonymy, the rose that epitomizes beauty. "Brow of chaos" is a synecdochic personification, signifying the disordered mind of the person, while a second metonymy, implied by the unsaid suggestion of *furrowed* "brow"—playing off of "*plants*" in the whole phrase—underscores the strange verb that, even as a figure of speech, raises questions about how a "rose of beauty" could be fixed on a "brow," or implanted in a mind so that, on the same plane as "chaos," "beauty" (F 967) might soothe its turbulence or smooth the creases on the brow. The preposition "on" draws these tropes into a configuration outside the classificatory distinctions that would segregate them, even as it renders their relation mysterious. "Beauty" implies the cosmos, a word it does not quite displace.[26] But how could a "rose" be lodged on a "brow"? How could the infinite disorder of "chaos," a word that retains its commonsense *and* cosmogonic associations, be crammed behind a finite brow? "Beauty" and "chaos" hang in a balance, while an intervening transition that would span the "chaos" of the human particular to reach "beauty," its slant counterweight, seems to have been excluded.[27] What is bypassed in Emerson's predicated phrase, however, is also missing from experience, since the sequel to "chaos" is primal order and form—the cosmos engendered at creation—which lies beyond what can be remembered, imagined, or reasoned. In the space between "chaos" and "beauty," a new relation to being is figured—not grounded in the subordination of hypotaxis or sequence, but in what is instantly realized, here named "the rose of beauty" that bestows "harmony and joy" (F 967)—even as how this comes about is occluded. What instigates the transformation from "chaos" to "beauty" happens behind our backs, without our agency, and beyond our ability to construe it.

Or, rather, it happens through an "indwelling Necessity" (F 967). The cluster of phrases—"*the necessity of beauty*"; "*Beautiful Necessity*"; "*indwelling necessity*" (F 967)—are permeable and reversible: "Beautiful Necessity" cannot be separated from "the necessity of beauty." Their kinship is not simply perceptible in the universe at large (a truth negotiated in the propositions, descriptions, and imperatives throughout the last paragraphs of "Fate"), but in the person's immersive sense of it.[28] Beauty resides in the potential to feel it, which cannot be separated from the potential to feel "chaos" in its stead.[29] Thus unlike the essay as a whole in which "Fate" and "freedom" are kept at a structural remove, or are represented in the "slid[e]" from one to the other (F 961), here "beauty" cannot be exiled from "chaos." Chaos, which has an ontological priority, is what precedes creation, and also what follows it. Chaos is what *is* without beauty's ministrations. That is why beauty is introduced as a "necessity." One could also contextualize the paratactic images thus: there is a "rose" to be seen everywhere. Beauty is not just in a "random sparkle" (F 967) that is someplace rather than everyplace. It is universally present, which means it also dwells in the person who is included in that universality. Thus it is "not personal nor impersonal" (F 968). Beauty has no coordinates that constrain it. While "indwelling necessity" (F 967) draws person and universe together, it never renders them interchangeable or equivalent, as in another register, *Sein* and *Dasein* are not equivalent.

Analogously in "Experience," a transport from discord ("inharmonious and trivial particulars") to "beauty and repose" is also empirically available only in images that break out of expository discourse, which charts a sequence from "distractions" that scatter the mind—to a concord intimated in Plato's "Idea"; in pastoral idyll; in "flashes of light"; and in "signs" that emanate from reading and thought (E 484). Yet while these archetypes and omens plot an access "to a new and excellent region" (E 484), they more conspicuously point to what, in the following passage, cannot be anticipated, to what eludes conception and presage:

> Bear with these distractions, with this coetaneous growth of the parts: they will one day be *members*, and obey one will. On that one will, on that secret cause, they nail our attention and hope. Life is hereby melted into an expectation or a religion. Underneath the inharmonious and trivial particulars, is a musical perfection, the Ideal journeying always with us, the heaven without rent or seam. Do but observe the mode of our illumination. . . . I do not at once arrive at satisfactions, as when, being thirsty, I drink water, or go to the fire, being cold: no! but I am first apprised of my vicinity to a new and excellent region of life. By persisting to read or to think, this region gives further sign of itself, as it were in flashes of light, in sudden discoveries of its profound beauty and repose, as if the clouds that covered it parted at intervals, and showed the approaching traveller the inland mountains, with the tranquil eternal meadows, whereon flocks graze, and shepherds pipe and dance. But every insight from this realm of thought is felt as initial, and promises a sequel. I do not make it; I arrive there, and behold what was there already. I make! O no! I clap my hands in infantine joy and amazement, before the first opening to me of this august magnificence, old with the love and homage of innumerable ages, young with the life of life, the sunbright Mecca of the desert. And what a future it opens! I feel a new heart beating with the love

> of the new beauty. I am ready to die out of nature, and be born again into this new yet unapproachable America I have found in the West. (E 484–85)

Only at the moment marked by "I do not make it" does a beyond time (no more "sequel" [E 485]), a beyond "hope . . . expectation or a religion" (E 484) emerge without counterpart. Occasioned by something that thought can't own and does not precipitate, agency disappears before that impacted genitive "the life of life" and its corollary "the sunbright Mecca of the desert" (E 485) that diversely gesture toward the *substance* to which those phrases refer—in an apposition that is also an opposition.

"The life of life" is bereft of metaphor and even sense, beyond the accent conferred by repetition—since the "life" that precedes the "of" (its essence or substance) cannot be figured apart from the life exemplified by what follows the preposition—assuming that the genitive is not a quintessentializing idiom or cognate intensifier to designate the innermost vitality or essence of life, which could not be so segregated. For life—could its essence be severed from its entirety—would have no existence. Conversely, "the sunbright Mecca of the desert" is nothing *but* metaphor. Though "the life of life" and "the sunbright Mecca of the desert" purport differently to name—through figure and what eludes figure—the *I*'s ecstatic discovery, neither appositional phrase can touch the substance each oppositely aims to denominate. The tag that associates the speaker's epiphany with a desert valley in western Saudi Arabia (then made synonymous with a "new yet unapproachable America I have found in the West"—but *not* in western Arabia), when severed from the semblance of a physical site, points to a reality that has no reference.[30] Although the chronicled Mecca—a pilgrim's goal—is made to contact the myth of the frontier in the American West, Emerson's image insists there is something more far-out than either trope, a beyond that could not be imagined or classified. Thus Mecca-America, though discoverable in a secluded, uncultivated region, is neither historical nor Messianic.[31]

In adjacent terms, then, both nodes of the expression (the genitive and the trope) are a cipher for what cannot be identified: it has no place, no time, no extractable core, no designation, and no antecedent, even as the expressions "born again" and "dy[ing] out of nature" (E 485) are viscerally experienced. Just as the trope of "beauty" arising out of "chaos" (F 967) in one formulation palpably registers "on the brow," in the other, "life of life" is sounded by the hands ("I clap") and pulses through the body as sensation ("a new heart beating") (E 485) so that the person is transformed by a realization that does not cut off insight from the materiality that gives it life.[32] At the same time, this integrity yields spatially irreconcilable coordinates: "the life of life, the sunbright Mecca of the desert," "this new . . . America" (E 485) is experienced as "unapproachable" (one could not advance toward it in time or space) by one who also stands in its midst (where but from a sensed midst, could this rapturous language issue?). In these conjunctions—and in distinction to "the absence of any . . . reconciliation between the theory and practice of life" (M 705)—Emerson's paratactic phrases manifest a vantage from which distance and proximity cannot be extracted from each other—in excess of any stylistic interest they might also exhibit.

Emerson's nondiscursive images are coupled by a technique that Walter Benjamin would call "literary montage," which "assemble[s] large-scale constructions of the smallest and most precisely cut components."[33] "Dialectical image" describes the method by which Benjamin will transmit a "primal history of the present" (*AP* 462), in which the relation between present and past will be expressed as "figural in nature," not as "temporal" (*AP* 463), arising in "an image" that is "suddenly emergent," rather than shown to evolve gradually through progression or continuity: "It's not that what is past casts its light on what is present, or what is present its light on what is past; rather, image is that wherein what has been comes together in a flash with the now to form a constellation. . . . Awakening" (*AP* 462). Any expectation of a recognizable whole is immediately overturned when Benjamin concludes that such a confluence opens to a heteromorphic vision that cannot be categorized: "Is awakening perhaps the synthesis of dream consciousness (as thesis) and waking consciousness (as antithesis)? Then the moment of awakening would be identical with the 'now of recognizability,' in which things put on their true—surrealist—face" (*AP* 463–64). "Surrealist" because the immediacy of any now cannot be mistaken for—or dissevered from—aboriginal time: "in the dialectical image, what has been within a particular epoch is always, simultaneously, 'what has been from time immemorial'" (*AP* 464). Hence Benjamin's fascination with Proust's "staking an entire life on life's supremely dialectical point of rupture: awakening. Proust begins with an evocation of the space of someone waking up" to this simultaneity (*AP* 464).[34] In spite of the tension between "chaos" and "beauty," "brow" and "rose" coincide in the phantasmagoric contact of that "on" (F 967), while in the juxtaposition "life of life . . . Mecca . . . America," figure and anti-figure (E 485) for what can be expressed by neither provoke and negate image for what cannot be visualized but is tangibly experienced. As with Benjamin's "dialectical images," whose "contrasts often seem indistinguishable from nuances" (*AP* 459), Emerson's antipodal images are momentary and nonteleological. Unlike the "clouds . . . parted at intervals" whose "mode of . . . illumination" (E 484) is temporal succession, the mode of insight delivered by the paratactic images is one of instantaneity and entirety.

Exposition can't, or Emerson's exposition doesn't, convey such immediacy. Discursive writing constructs hierarchies of value in which oppositions like *greater* and *lesser* are constantly refigured (as in the restless calculations performed in "Fate" and "Nominalist and Realist") to prove the nonconvergence of the person and what dwarfs him: that would be the point of an essay like "The Over-soul," which insists on what "Montaigne" calls "this parallelism of great and little, which never react on each other, nor discover the smallest tendency to converge" (M 705), so that "great" and "little" cannot encounter each other. Such nonconvergence marks the crisis moments of resistance, of sacrifice, of suffering, in the passages considered in part i where the person falls short of the comprehensive vision exacted of him, when it does not exclude him outright. In "Experience" and "Fate," Emerson's paratactic formulations resolve these schisms. They occupy a register in which divided things cohere. In such images, what is bounded and what could never be bounded lie on the same plane, as in Spinoza's third kind of knowledge, where the essence of the finite and infinite cleave to each other in a unity whose elements both preserve and dissolve distinctions. Hence an "awakening"—not Benjamin's to the truth of historical materialism; not Proust's to lost and found time; but Emerson's representation of the awakening to an ontology in which "life" is "born again" (E 485). The development proposed in Spinoza's geometric method to chart a progression across types of consciousness—from a kind of knowledge based on duration to one based on instantaneity in which "the mind conceives its body's essence under a species of eternity" (*Et* 258; V P31)—is inassimilable to Emerson's heuristic explorations.[35] Yet the idea of advance and what surpasses it are also, though not methodologically, Emerson's: "the consciousness in each man is a sliding scale, which identifies him now with the First Cause, and now with the flesh of his body; life above life, in infinite degrees" (E 485). Thus Emerson's spectrum of emphasis—now here, now there—also implies emanation and not only evolution. In conclusion, I turn to Spinoza's third kind of knowledge to underscore how the geometric method of the *Ethics* converges with Emerson's free-form prose to arrive inexplicably at the spontaneous discovery of "the essence of things" (*Et* 257; V P25) beyond calculation, method, and subjectivity.

iii

In Spinoza's first kind of knowledge, perception is dominated by the imagination: "we form universal notions . . . from singular things which have been represented to us through the senses" and from erroneous ideas gleaned from "opinion or imagination" (*Et* 141; II P40S2). Thus when we look at the sun, we might conceive it "at two hundred paces" away, since "what is specific to the imagination is exactly to relate everything to the 'self.'"[36] In the second kind of knowledge, "reason" dictates a practical comprehension of phenomena like that of the distance of the sun, based on "common notions and adequate ideas of the properties of things" (*Et* 141; II P40S2). The third kind of knowledge is no longer determined by sensory impressions or by reason, but rather by "an adequate knowledge of the essence of things" (*Et* 257; V P25). Specifically, "the essence of the body" is perceived "under a species of eternity" so that "we feel and know by experience that we are eternal" (*Et* 256; V P23S). Spinoza wrote: "Instantaneity is the modality of the affection of essence. . . . Eternity is the modality of essence."[37]

But how does one move from a sensory experience of the rays of the sun to an intuitive sense of "the essence of things" (*Et* 257; V P25) when the two are incompossible? Spinoza writes: "*The striving, or desire, to know things by the third kind of knowledge* [of essence] *cannot arise from the first kind of knowledge* [of sensory impression and imagination], *but can indeed arise from the second*" (*Et* 257; V P28). Thus the space between the first and third kind of knowledge cannot be traversed directly. Crucially, according to Étienne Balibar, there is also a "gap or break" of a different kind between the second and third kinds of knowledge: "in Spinoza's doctrine . . . consciousness in whatever sense has nothing to do" in the second stage, since "in Spinoza's doctrine it is never associated with . . . 'common notions' or 'scientific demonstrations' that constitute 'Reason.'"[38] In other words, no dynamic inner sense or psychic faculty performs the transition from the second to the third stage. Thus although the "*conatus* is nothing else than a transition from one form [of knowledge] to the other, there is no continuity between them" (NCC 49). Balibar continues: "This discontinuity in the history of modes of thought which, each for itself, are 'continuous' we might name *a process of consciousness without a subject*" since "there is nothing like a process of self-transformation within consciousness though reflexion" (NCC 49–50). Although one could consider the third kind of knowledge as "mystic" (as Deleuze does) rather than "intellectual and practical"[39] (as Balibar does), the implication of Balibar's conclusion is that it is not primarily the intuitive third form of essence-consciousness that troubles explanation but, more, the enigma of how one ever passes from the second to the third form when the subjectivity of the person momentarily vanishes in the transit. The "gap" in subjectivity that Balibar attributes to the stage of reason in Spinoza's doctrine finds a corollary in "Experience," where no agency precipitates the transit to "life" that is "born again": "I do not make it; I arrive there, and behold what was there already" (E 485). For Emerson, "every insight from this realm of thought is felt as initial, and promises a sequel" (E 485). That "sequel" is a "vast-flowing vigor" (E 485), the perception that "we have arrived as far as we can go," and "we give to this generalization the name of Being" (E 486). Spinoza touches on a cognate moment: it is "as if [the mind] were now beginning to be, and were now beginning to understand things under a species of eternity" (*Et* 259; V P31S). That "as if" edges onto the experience (E 485–86) from an outermost point—looking through and across it—to view how it comes about that the infinitive "to be" becomes singular "Being." In both texts, language is employed not to disclose, but rather "to cover this unbounded substance . . . which refuses to be named." In the same way, the "ineffable cause" (E 485), a manifestation of "substance," reveals a "mode of . . . illumination" that "will not be expounded" (E 484).

For Spinoza, the idea of stages suggests development—as when he glosses the relation between reason-consciousness en route to essence-consciousness by positing a chronology that signals attainment: "the more each of us is able to achieve in this kind of knowledge . . . the more perfect and blessed he is" (*Et* 259; V P31S). But such an advance is challenged by a second proposition in the *Ethics*, since if at every moment there is a transition from one stage to another—if, that is, in Spinoza's characterization, "the mind can undergo great changes, and pass now to a greater, now to a lesser perfection" (*Et* 160–61; III P11) between which there is more or less power, more or less joy, thus more or less "reality" (*Et* 263; V P40)—the process is not a linear movement but a fluctuation. Thus for Spinoza, changes in kinds of knowledge involve an advance (from one point of view) and (from another) a back-and-forth without beginning or end. Moreover, in both philosophies the flux from one mind state to another—in Emerson's formulation, "savage and serene in one hour" (M 704); in Spinoza's, propelled by the "great changes" of continuous variation (*Et* 160; III P11)—cannot be governed. Thus while Spinoza and Emerson engage similar questions in distinct terms, neither can systematize the way to arrive at the final point and abide there.

A rift in subjectivity between a perspective that relates everything to itself and an ontology, "a power transcending all limit and privacy" (P 467), haunts Emerson's essays. How astonishing that "Experience," the essay in which all is riven (child from father, loss from affect, subject from object, outside from inside), should open to an ecstatic immersion in "the life of life" (E 485), a state of affairs that incapacitates language, in which the instantaneous and the eternal could never be riven, even as this concord again gives way to the despair for which in that essay there is so much language: "I know better than to claim any completeness for my picture. I am a fragment, and this is a fragment of me" (E 491). Emerson's images move back and forth between a sense-based "infinite" ("a hunger, as of space to be filled with planets" [M 708]) that could not be mitigated, to an infinite beyond calculation but not beyond embodied experience. For "essence" gleaned "from the point of view of eternity"—for which "perfection" and "reality" are synonyms[40]—far from intangible, is only discoverable for the Emerson of "Experience," as for Spinoza, as a fully corporeal phenomenon. Thus Spinoza: "The mind conceives nothing under a species of eternity except insofar as it conceives its body's essence under a species of eternity" (*Et* 258; V P31). Again: "it is not *a* body . . . that is conceived from the point of view of eternity, it is 'my Body,' or better said, *a Body inasmuch as it is 'its own Body' for some Mind*" with "its singular essence and powers deriving causally from God (or Nature) as a proximate cause" (NCC 48). For Emerson, too, "essence" (*Et* 258; V P31) pulses through the body: "I clap my hands in infantine joy . . . before the first opening to me of this august magnificence. . . . I feel a new heart beating. . . . I am ready to die out of nature, and to be born again" (E 485). From distinct loci, essence emanates from "hands," "heart," and inclining mind—from a somatic basis. Such concurrence shows up, by contrast, the state of affairs that roil Emerson's narrative hierarchies, where "infinite enlargements" (OS 398), like the "immeasurable mind" (DSA 89), dwarf the lowly body and its frivolous needs. Such polarities can never be reconciled and require endless management. In distinction, Emerson's images place incompatibles as radical as "chaos" and "beauty" (F 967); instantaneity and eternity; and that wild pleonasm, "the life of life, the sunbright Mecca of the desert" (E 485), on a single plane, stripped of contingency, insoluble elements, that do not brook further reduction but for a moment, provisionally, are embodied as one, as things that seem fissured can ephemerally be one.

In conclusion, I must acknowledge that—to stress the conflictual strain of the basic units of an Emerson essay—in my analysis I have arranged to segregate exposition from image, and to isolate passages governed by abstractions like the "Over-soul" (E 385) that minimize the person from passages that depict his suffering in response to that diminution, and these from the dialectical images which conjoin perspective and ontology while never blending the states. The essays themselves, however, do not quarantine these diverse representations, nor do they demarcate a development from one to the other. Emerson's passages—those that abstract and decorporealize being in terms like the "Over-soul" (E 385) and the "superpersonal Heart" (E 1076) and, conversely, those that depict suffering as a response to such disembodiments—have no calculable order, like Spinoza's three kinds of knowledge and Emerson's "flux of moods" (E 485), seeming episodic, interludes disrupted by other interludes that have a contrary vantage and feel. The latter are themselves ruptured by the expression of inimical understandings, and on and on, thus shattering the hope that there could be a trajectory leading from a perspective to an ontology, or to put this in phenomenological terms: a path from the experience of our bodies as compromised and even damaged—which, to be endured, are devoured by sensation or smothered in abstraction—to the experience of the bodies we have yet to realize, which, in their full materiality, will be sensed as essence.

Because Emerson's breakthrough images occur intermedially, they more radically thwart the expectation not only of process but of arrival. If the joy of phrases like "the rose of beauty" (F 967) and "the sunbright Mecca of the desert" (E 485) suggest otherwise—that, in Spinoza's words, "it is as if [the mind] were now beginning to be, and were now beginning to understand things under a species of eternity" (*Et* 259; V P31), and thus that it is as if *we* "were now beginning to be"—ingress is repeatedly disrupted in Emerson's essays. "Beginning to be" could never be furthered, could only be experienced, if it is experienced at all, as a now that is a *not* now, not an end—"new, yet unapproachable," "yet" but not "yet," a "vast-flowing vigor" (E 486) that cannot be identified as personal or impersonal, a "metamorphosis of things into higher organic forms" (P 458) that then devolve into the conclusions of Emerson's expositions, which shifting mind states assemble, crystallize, undo, and recompose.

Whitman's Translations

> The truths I tell to you or any other may not be plain to you, because I do not translate them fully from my idiom into yours. If I could do so . . . they would be as apparent to you as they are to me; for they are truths—No two have exactly the same language, and the great translator and joiner of the whole is the poet.
>
> WALT WHITMAN[1]

In "Out of the Cradle Endlessly Rocking," Whitman "sings" "a reminiscence"[2] of himself as a boy listening to a bird's lament, the boy supposes, for the death of a mate. "Peering, absorbing" (OC 31), "I . . . [l]isten'd to keep, to sing, now translating the notes" (OC 67–69), as "he pour'd forth the meanings which I of all men know" (OC 60). Though translation usually refers to linguistic creations in which the meaning of a communication in one language is transmitted in a foreign tongue, in "Cradle" it involves converting the grief the prepoetic child discerns in birdsong into another medium, Whitman's own "solitary . . . singing" (OC 150), that is, into the semiotic and semantic structure of a poem. Whitman's reconstruction of these vocalizations into a linguistic expression of the relation between death and song could be identified as pathetic fallacy. But Whitman insistently calls the adaptation "translation." And translation is, also for Whitman, a word that indicates a metamorphosis in which the complete substance of a thing is even biologically altered,[3] as in the following transmutation: "The pleasures of heaven are with me and the pains of hell are with me, / The first, I graft and increase upon myself, the latter I translate into a new tongue."[4] The last example demonstrates a hybrid operation at once quasi-organic (in that the augmented pleasures of heaven are vitally implanted in Whitman's person) and linguistic—a sublimation of hell into a foreign "tongue" that purges hell of torment. "Tongue," of course, is an anatomical metonymy for language, thus straddling the metaphorical and linguistic senses of translation. Whitman's translations aren't always revealed in transfers of meaning from one language to another, but they always involve radical alterations of form, condition, or essence via linguistic, conceptual, and ontological recasting. Part i of my essay considers Whitman's translations of type or kind in which the essential quality or characteristics of an entity or phenomenon are restructured into a new compound or whole. My examples begin with incongruously paired nouns in a sustained passage on "prudence" in the 1855 Preface to *Leaves of Grass*; they then turn to Whitman's refigurings of the relation of "I" and "you" that transform the composition of intimacy and even individuality so that the latter becomes nonidentical with itself. Part ii considers the semantic and metaphysical translations performed on being when in section 6 of "Song of Myself"—in his cascading responses to the "is" in the question "*What is the grass?*" (SM 6:99)—Whitman proposes that a sign could have an equative relation to the multiform objects signified. The "uniform hieroglyphic" of "grass" (SM 6:106) is not said to *mean* but rather to *be* a series of incommensurable objects: "hair" (SM 6:110); "handkerchief of the Lord" (SM 6:102); "uttering tongues" (SM 6:119); "mothers' laps" (SM 6:115); "flag of my disposition" (SM 6:101); and more—a gloss that poses these as all but impossible ontological equivalents. The sequence of Whitman's decryptions presents such permutable objects as manifestations of being only gradually revealed to him before he even poetizes them: "To me the converging objects of the universe perpetually flow, / All are written to me, and I must get what the writing means" (SM 20:404–5). To "get what the writing means" is to see that objects also have a language that can be translated. In Walter Benjamin's characterization, "translation" applies not only to the transfer of meaning from one language to another, but also to the translation of "the language of things into that of man"[5]: "The language of things can pass into the language of knowledge and name only through translation" (LS 70–71). Whitman's translation of objects implicitly accords with such a theory.

Translation—the transformation of phenomena that we can't read, or that we misread, into forms that make them legible or that alter our perception of the nature of these phenomena—occurs in all the instances I consider, even when the tag "translation" is not used by Whitman, and even when other terms (metaphor, metonymy, syllepsis) indicating transference or displacement are also technically valid. Translation provides a rubric for diverse examples of transmutation that realize an unclouded perception of actuality. Such is Whitman's articulated objective as he departs from the poem: "Now I wash the gum from your eyes, / You must habit yourself to the dazzle of the light and of every moment of your life" (SM 46:1229–30). Part iii turns to the assaults on thinking that underlie such translations, and part iv posits a connection between Whitman and Benjamin that, strange and inexact, is nonetheless purposive. Benjamin's fascination with the translation of languages is founded on a near obsession with the devolution from "the creative word of God" to Adamic language, which does not create but is a "*mere* sign" communicating sense and meaning (LS 71); and then to the multiplicity of post-Babelian languages (LS 71–72). For Benjamin, translation not only illustrates that each language is only a fragment of a lost whole that can never be recovered (or can only be recovered in Messianic time), but it also gestures toward the lost integrity of an "undivided whole" (LS 73) in the way that piecing together fragments or shards evokes the fractured whole from which they have been shattered. In contrast to Benjamin's mystical theory, Whitman's transparent practice of translation reveals the whole to be perceptible now. In conclusion, I reflect on the counterintuitive metaphysics that Whitman's translations make tangible.

i

In the 1855 Preface to *Leaves of Grass*, there is a three-page exposition on two kinds of "prudence," one driven by "the toss and pallor of years of moneymaking"[6] parsimoniously calculated to assure "solid gains" (P 630) within an economy of splitting ("stuffing while others starve" [P 631]) and "higher notions of prudence" (P 630) "suitable for immortality" (P 631), impelled by the principle that true profit is only discoverable in the recognition of a totality. To see the "whole scope" (P 632) of anything, one part can't be excised from another, no matter how apparently incompatible its constitutive elements. Thus Whitman conceptually transforms time understood as a sequence of moments—each of which has a unique relation to a beginning—into a construct in which all moments are consolidated and uniform, because no instant of time has contact with that first moment which marks the genesis of time: "no result exists now without being from its long antecedent result, and that from its antecedent, and so backward without the farthest mentionable spot coming a bit nearer the beginning than any other spot" (P 633), since origin emerges from the nothing that precedes it and is related to nothing that could follow.

In a coupling that demonstrates the right understanding of prudence from another vantage, an odd conjuncture is ascribed to the "oneness of nature" and of "human affairs" structured by different kinds of genitives, each governed by "the propriety of the same spirit" (P 630). The doublets—singular "nature," diverse "human affairs"—not syntactically parallel, are also not logically comparable and raise the question of how "the same spirit" could regulate an absolute like the "sense of the oneness of nature," to which perfection is also ascribed and a relative as shallow as "propriety," especially since the phrasing of the sentence calls attention to the fault lines separating the yoked entities. The same passage also reveals other blocks of text simultaneously pulled together and driven apart:

> Extreme caution or prudence, the soundest organic health, large *hope and comparison* and fondness for women and children, large *alimentiveness and destructiveness* and causality, with a perfect sense of the oneness of nature and the propriety of the same spirit applied to human affairs . . . these are called up of the float of the brain of the world to be parts of the greatest poet from his birth out of his mother's womb and from her birth out of her mother's. (P 630; italics mine)

"Hope" and "comparison" are matched by a coordinate "and," but they are separated by semantic distinction, because the words belong to different classes of phenomena: "hope" is a state of mind, while "comparison" assesses differences. Such linkages are sometimes hendiadys, discrepant pairings of non-twins that should be subordinate, rather than compound ("toss and pallor" [P 631] is another example). But it would be impossible to find a single rhetorical term for the kind of disjunctive structures whose fault lines of distinction both threaten and constitute the integrity of Whitman's consolidations.[7] Their affiliations derail any facile understanding of relation and are not intelligible with reference to thin conceptions of "prudence," whose criteria for managing resources demand splitting one thing from another.[8] Whitman is translating a "melancholy prudence" (P 631) into another system of understanding in which nothing can be divided—"into a new tongue" (SM 21:424). In Whitman's "asyntactic sentence[s],"[9] antagonistic strains are perceptible in the category crossings that mark both limited phrasal units and the most expansive compounds of Whitman's writing, as in the constellation of the Whitmanian "I" initially proclaimed to be "well entretied, braced in the beams, / Stout as a horse, affectionate, haughty, electrical" whose preening breaks free of calculated self-depiction at the charge of the word "electrical" to yield a compound subject, "I and this mystery," a "we" (SM 3:49–51) composed of person and enigma, which could never be calculated.

We see the coincidence of incomparables most profoundly in the breach of the wall—or the wall torn down—between the "I" and "you" (these placeholders of identity that are not even names) of Whitman's multiform pairings. "Song of Myself" famously begins with Whitman's attribution of the irreducible elements of an "I" to a "you," declaring: "every atom belonging to me as good belongs to you" (SM 1:3), a supposition that perhaps conceives atoms as something like communal property, jointly possessed, that could nonetheless also be divided. But if Whitman means that each possess the same *kind* of atoms, rather than the *same* atoms, "good" might imply approbation for the similarity—in which case, atoms possessed by the "I" and the "you" would not literally be shared at all. A like question is raised toward the end of "Song of Myself" where

Whitman submits: "It is you talking, just as much as myself" (SM 47:1248), a claim suggesting that an equality imbues the exchanges between the "I" and the "you." Does Whitman mean that the "I" voices what the "you" wants to say and therefore *indirectly is* saying? "Just as much" cannot be taken to suggest that each is talking about the same things, in the same way, or even at the same time. Unless "just as much" is meant to be a pressure point for the reader's immediate translation of a written "I" into his own performative enunciation of it, a demonstration of Georges Poulet's theory in "Phenomenology of Reading" that when "the book is no longer a material reality," it has a "new existence: my innermost self"; "a book I am reading" contains "cogitations of another," "yet it is I who am their subject." In other words, for Poulet, "reading" becomes "the act by which a thought managed to bestow itself within me with a subject not myself."[10]

Yet in "Song of Myself," Poulet's paradigm is immediately undercut by questions evoked by Whitman's graphic attempts to literalize the effacement of identic boundaries in which the "*I* who thinks in me when I read a book" is indistinguishable from "the *I* of the one who writes the book."[11] For when Whitman continues, "I act as the tongue of you / Tied in your mouth, in mine it begins to be loosen'd" (SM 47: 1248–49), something more like an identity claim both emerges and is challenged, since the question of whose tongue (whose muscular organ permitting articulation) lingers past the clarification provided by the simile "as," which should put this interrogation to rest. Even though we can establish who speaks and who is silent, the line's intersections prevent us from deciphering whose speech is actually uttered. Does the "I" ventriloquize the "you"? Does the "I" compensate for the inability of the "you" to speak by giving tongue to an utterance all his own? In what sense is this an exchange? Whitman's I/you junctures are inconclusive about whether irreducible particles (like "atoms" in section 1) and essential faculties (like speech in section 47) are shared by persons, in the sense of each having the same atoms and speech, or are shared in the sense of each having separate but homologous atoms and speech. Even when decisive evidence tips the balance to the side of commensurability (atoms and speech are common factors of persons, rather than evidence of qualitative identity), vacillation still looms over Whitman's construction, because it is not clear whose intention and inclination to communicate are expressed.

Alternatively, Whitman's mobile I/you alliances seem to demonstrate Émile Benveniste's theory that these pronouns are shifters, "linguistic categories" that are positional: "the reality to which *I* or *you* refers" is a "'reality of discourse,'" because in Whitman's "Song," as in Benveniste's theory, "the form of *I* has no linguistic existence except in the act of speaking."[12] But when Benveniste adds that "neither of the terms can be conceived without the other; they are complementary, although according to an 'interior/exterior' opposition, and at the same time they are reversible,"[13] Whitman's I/you constellations no longer adhere to Benveniste's model, since in "Song" the "I" does not remain exterior to the "you," but systematically engulfs it: "I do not ask who you are . . . You can do nothing and be nothing but what I will infold you" (SM 40:1001–2). Thus these mercurial constellations of the I/you assimilation are not reversible. No reciprocal assimilation is imaginable. Rather, Whitman's incorporation of the "you" satisfies the criteria for "almost identity" or "relative identity" or "identity over time" (as in the notion of *becoming*)—understandable in terms of "mereological composition" (the relation of parts to wholes or parts to parts within a whole).[14]

One rubric for Whitman's signature "you" is "apostrophe" (in Barbara Johnson's definition, "a form of ventriloquism through which a speaker throws voice, life, and human form into the addressee, turning its silence into mute responsiveness"[15]). Yet these calls to a "you" (that also implicitly voice the power of the "I" to summon and animate an absent object or person) can be ostentatiously incongruent, even in the same poem. In "As I Ebb'd with the Ocean of Life," there is a "maze"—twenty-nine iterations of "you," and "your" that refer to assorted nouns, including a "reverse apostrophe" in which the speaker becomes a "you" to the "real Me"[16] that "stands yet untouch'd, untold"[17] (2:28), a state of affairs in which reference is not secured by apostrophic invocation, but rather drifts. And when Whitman declares he *is* the slave, the "wounded person," the "long-threaded moss," the "quadruped," the "fruit," the "rock" ("not a person or object missing / Absorbing all to myself and for this song" [SM 13:233–34]), as with the apostrophic "you," he is not each in the same way, and he is not each at the same time. Because Benveniste's *I* "is the individual who utters the present instance of discourse containing the linguistic instance *I*"[18] and Whitman's "I" can be defined in relation to a "being-with" each "you" or object that is successively hailed,[19] such conditionality might be construed as comparable. But for Benveniste contingency proves the "I" is an empty sign, whereas for Whitman such signs are full to the extent that they assail a "classical view of identity," which depends on "the equivalence relation which everything has with itself and to nothing else."[20]

In Whitman's writing, differentia are not only effaced between the "I" and the "you," they are also blotted out between discrete manifestations of the "you." The second-person singular, like the first-person singular (whose atoms are shared by affinity or identity, and whose tongue or language may not be his own), could not be conceived as individual. For instance, in "Song of Prudence," the linearity of reading first singles out a specific "you," who is then immediately deprived of particularity: "you whoever you are, or . . . any one."[21] In the syntactic equivalence occupied by the placeholders on either side of that "or," specificity could not survive when the individuated "you" is shown to be the same as an indiscriminate alternative—an impression substantiated by the context of the line: "All that is henceforth to be thought or done by you whoever you are, or by anyone, / These inure, have inured, shall inure, to the identities from which they sprang, or shall spring" (SP 34–35), a claim that disseminates benefit everywhere, even as it unsettles *whose* thought, *whose* action, *whose* identity will confer benefit and *whose* will reap it, as well as in *which* temporality the accrued advantage might lodge.

"Inure to the identities" is a common phrase in legal terminology to specify which individual will profit (often from inheritance of property). The twist in Whitman's use of the legalism is the disjuncture between the formula for specification and the subversion of the formula, since plural identities leave vague how many and which ones are designated as recipients. Thus the person identified as a "you" is numerically indistinct and temporally composite. A more abstract, but equally elastic, temporal scope conjoins the singular and plural in the juxtaposed first two words of a line that begins the stanza I've touched on: "Singly, wholly, to affect now, affected their time, will forever affect all of the past and all of the present and all of the future" (SP 21–22), where the infinitive "to affect" names an action without a subject, an omission that evades—except as an aggregate—specification of who or what affects. In these sundry ways, however we parse Whitman's diverse constellations of the "you" in "Song of Prudence," as in "Song of Myself," the person initially identified turns into the person who cannot be identified.

When a person is marked for recognition, by being selected, along with others who are also set apart from the totality designated as "everybody" ("This hour I tell things in confidence, / I might not tell everybody, but I will tell you" [SM 19:387–88]), the privilege is retracted by our memory of a counterclaim that precedes it in which visitations may be expected by "everybody" ("I make appointments with all" [SM 19:373]). In Whitman's writing, to be a person who is one of a kind, or who is the kind of person who enjoys acknowledgment, does not mean that only he or those like him receive special advantage, but rather, counterintuitively, that his unique characteristics—while not shared by each person—do not prohibit the latter from being identified by Whitman in the same way he is, as part of the "all" (SM 19:373), with whom Whitman arranges visitations. Thus what is individual and what effaces individuality as a criterion for receiving a particular advantage morph into each other, a merge that Whitman posits didactically in the image of a "knit of identity, always distinction, always a breed of life" (SM 3:47).

How should we theorize these variant couplings of the "I" and "you"? As glossed by Wai Chee Dimock, where Whitman combines Chomsky's belief in "innate structures of mind" perceptible in syntax and a Rawlsian "theory of justice" to produce "a grammatical entity (the 'myself')" who is "democratically defensible only as a formal universal"? According to Allen Grossman's theory of Whitman's inclusiveness founded on parataxis, on "a universal 'conjunctive principle'" that "rewrit[es] hierarchies"—"soul/body, collective/individual, nation/state—as equalities"? In relation to Charles Altieri's claim that Whitman's "mode of subjectivity [that] remains available to all" depends on understanding "what makes one identical to those pursuing quite different ends"? With reference to Ryan Cull's idea that Whitman practices an "improvisatory . . . sociality" in which intimacy is constructed outside of "normative categories"? Framed by Deleuze's insight that "the law [of Whitman's poetry] is that of fragmentation," which includes "samples . . . specimens . . . grains, 'granulations' . . . singular cases and minor scenes"? Such accounts, among the best of the transindividual Whitmanian self, are formalist, often grammatical, though it is a philosophical lens through which grammar is parsed. And they are political, as in Jane Bennett's claim that Whitman draws on a key term in nineteenth-century debates—on "a Smithian tradition of sympathy" and also on a "vitalist one"—from which Whitman contrives a transpersonal notion of self. Or should we structure our thinking along the lines of a historical/biographical account of Whitman's associations? One of the subtlest is Michael Moon's in which "the solitary" self can't be separated from the massified self involved in "the communal-utopian movement that swept the U.S. in the 1840s, from Brook Farm to Sodus Bay, and the free-love movement that became associated with it in the 1850s." These were discovered not in the closet but in social spaces like that of Pfaff's Tavern, where "Fourier's theories of social and sexual seriality" could be explored.[22]

No single theory of Whitman's pairings could account for the distracting prevalence of the permutations which assault any theory that does not add the tag: *and its variations*. "Crossing Brooklyn Ferry"'s sublime couplings ("what thought you have of me now, I had as much of you . . . I consider'd long and seriously of you before you were born" [7:88–89]) defy any single paradigm unless the prototype is seriality—Deleuze's or Moon's. The shifting terms of Whitman's vacillating I/you bonds—for instance, "I will be more to you than to any of the rest";[23] "If you do not say any thing how can I say any thing?" (SM 49:1301); "Do you suppose yourself advancing on real ground toward a real heroic man?"[24]—in which passionate declaration—the very capacity to speak; to draw closer to another; even to realize the *existence* of that other stripped of idealization—the mutable emotions that course through these utterances (in the above examples: adoration, coercion, scorn) resist any comprehensive principle. Each utterance erupts out of, and bears the residue of, a specific affinity, and is voiced out of a network of particulars, though not a vernacular, that confounds induction or conclusion. In "Song of the Answerer," where the "he" referred to is also the poet, Whitman proposes a linguistic explanation for such heterogeneity:

> Every existence has its idiom, every thing has an idiom and tongue,
> He resolves all tongues into his own and bestows it upon men, and
> any man translates, and any man translates himself also,
> One part does not counteract another part, he is the joiner, he sees
> how they join.
> (1:31–34)

The lines trouble the most rudimentary paraphrase: each "existence" has a particular language (an "idiom" and a "tongue") that Whitman assimilates, consolidates ("he is the joiner"), and singularizes in a conversion he names a translation. But just as it is unclear whether others require such a transformation to be performed for them or whether Whitman's gift is anyone's ("any man translates"), so the lines equivocate about what translation is. Is it any transmutation performed by the poet as "Answerer," or must the translation be "intralinguistic" (in Roman Jakobson's definition, "a *rewording* [that] is an interpretation of verbal signs by means of other signs of the same language"[25])? If the interpretation is embedded in a new verbal arrangement, rather than a rewording, can this gross change be called "intralinguistic"? Finally, how could the "idiom" of "every existence" be translated into a universal tongue without muting idiosyncratic variants, when even in the rendering of one language into another there is this misgiving (José Ortega y Gasset's): "the enormous difficulty of translation" is that "in it one tries to say in a language precisely what that language tends to silence."[26] Whitman's translation of "all tongues into his own"[27] would extend such a qualm, were it not that his universals are also swept up in continuous fluctuation, in which one formulation presses past another to enumerate (beyond explanation and beyond what even Whitman can "fathom"[28]) an integral whole:

> These are really the thoughts of all men in all ages and lands . . .
> If they are not yours as much as mine they are nothing, or next to
> nothing. . . .

This is the grass that grows wherever the land is and the water is,
This the common air that bathes the globe.
(SM 17:355–56, 359–60)

Here each demonstrative pronoun is subjected to a rethinking of its momentary singularity as when all "thoughts . . . all men" of the first line is refigured in an image that connotes a more comprehensive inclusion: "the common air that bathes the globe"—more comprehensive because "air" and "water" (the latter, introduced in the previous line and reiterated in the metaphor "bathes" to describe the immersive air) are more pervasive than the "thoughts of all men" (or are they?), supposing of course that these shifting ensembles of air, earth, water, and the fire of thought, oddly constituent elements of life as a whole, could be compared. Whitman's *alls*—all men, all thoughts, all objects and persons, all "tongues" and "idiom[s]"—everyone and everything (including what can be incarnated and what, like the "air that bathes the globe" [SM 17:360], cannot) are as ephemeral as the particulars that momentarily constitute them. This transience also touches Whitman's semantic translations to which I now turn.

ii

In section 6 of "Song of Myself," Whitman's word "translate" for the gloss he performs on the "uniform hieroglyphic" of "grass" (SM 6:106) implies both a semantic transfer and a transformation—thus a convergence of, and bridge between, *linguistic* translation and the broader band of Whitmanesque *interchanges* perceptible in the "I/you," "I/all" transfers I've examined. Though "I wish I could translate the hints about the dead" (SM 6:121) expresses an intuitive sense of the hieroglyphic code that does not yet make sense as discursive meaning,[29] several lines later (in an oblique allusion to Isaiah, "All flesh is grass" . . . "the grass withereth" [KJV 40:6]), Whitman hazards this understanding: "The smallest sprout proves there is really no death" (SM 6:126). Whitman's exegesis reveals not only the common truth that the grass dies back each winter and grows again in spring, but also perhaps that the "hieroglyphic" (SM 6:106) is a trope for all understanding as a kind of translation, and for the poet's work as translator of world into revivifying words that are sometimes said to *be* the things that are signified: "flag of my disposition" (SM 6:101); "handkerchief of the Lord" (SM 6:103); "hair" (SM 6:110); "mothers' laps" (SM 6:115); "uttering tongues" (SM 6:119); and more. The seeming inexhaustibility of this polysemous elucidation yields a remainder that can be ascribed to none of the entities drawn together, but that rather hovers between and across them as what Benjamin calls a "supplement."[30]

In the extremely dense passage characterizing the excess that remains beyond sense in translation, Benjamin writes: "In all language and linguistic creations, there remains in addition to what can be conveyed something that cannot be communicated; depending on the context in which it appears, it is something that symbolizes or something symbolized" (TT 261). If "sense" or "information" is the goal, "some ultimate decisive element remain[s] beyond all communication—quite close and yet infinitely remote, concealed or distinguishable, fragmented or powerful" (TT 260–61). For Benjamin, the ultimate "supplement" is "pure language" evacuated of meaning.[31] For Whitman, in "Song of Myself," the "supplement" is precisely the force that reaches outside each phenomenon, entity, or experience to dissolve the fixed boundaries that segregate it. In Benjamin's analysis, "great texts contain their potential translation between the lines" (TT 263). Whitman's translations occur *in* the lines *between* the images that bear its effects. Benjamin's theoretical ideal is language that doesn't signify. Whitman's practice gives us language that does not identify.

Thus when "a child" asks "*What is the grass?*" (SM 6:99), the latter is immediately associated with the self's hope ("the flag of my disposition"), then, correctively, with a divinity ("the handkerchief of the Lord"), even as this whimsical image leads to a question that the determination of letters on the handkerchief was meant to confirm ("Bearing the owner's name . . . that we may see and remark, and say *Whose?*" [SM 6:104]). The grass is nothing that could belong to anyone, and the one with whom it might transiently be associated does not identify it. When Whitman asserts, "Or I guess the grass is itself a child, the produced babe of the vegetation" (SM 6:105), the young grass metaphorized as a child is drawn into the figure of the child who asked: "*What is the grass?*" (SM 6:99). Such a confluence bespeaks a relation that is near tautological: the literal, the subject (the child who asks), and the metaphoric, the object (the grass that is the child), collapse into each other on either side of the "is" as a difference indistinguishable from a redundancy. Say rather that the grass the child asks about and the child the grass becomes cannot be pried apart except insofar as each imperfectly reflects the other. Or rather, the incommensurability on either side of the "is" neutralizes the differential manifestations of subject/object, literal/metaphoric opposition, but not because the two are equivalent. Rather, these manifestations of being that can't be separated but also can't be equated cast light on the "is," the third-person singular indicative of "to be," which exceeds *any* incarnation that could bound it, thus spilling over to what is contiguous (the grass/the child; the child, the grass) and what is not. The "produced babe of the vegetation" (SM 6:105) and the "child who ask[s]" (SM 6:99) about it reflect a vernal aliveness that could not be the property of either, even as it radiates from both—a spark of life, energy, or just the excess of that unbridled "*is*" whose endurance Whitman renders perceptible beyond any specification, a supplement.

In section 6, a like diffusion also extends across the figurative attribution of voiced expression to unequivalent sources. "So many uttering tongues" (SM 6:119) are at once said to come "from the roofs of mouths" (SM 6:120) and from the heteroglossia of grass, both made cognate with *Whitman's* tongue in an affinity established by the enjambed phrases "a spear of summer grass. / My tongue" (SM 1:5–6) placed in apposition in "Song's" first section. The grass-like shape of the human tongue and the tongue-like shape of the blade of grass, evoked as kindred forms that converse, are each accorded an expressive power that Whitman metaphorizes as language. Consequently, Whitman can all but assert he speaks the same tongue as that of the grass he intersemantically translates. Cascading responses to the "*is*" the child asks about do not distill to a homogeneous thing, and neither do its mutations—as when the "curling grass" (SM 6:111) is transmuted into "the beautiful uncut hair of graves" (SM 6:110), which is not the same kind of hair as that which "transpire[s] from the breasts of young men" or "from old people" or "from offspring taken soon out of their mothers' laps" (SM 6:113–16), and it is certainly not the same as "the mothers' laps" (SM 6:114) this "curling grass" (SM 6:111) again becomes in the demonstrations Whitman performs on the "uniform hieroglyphic" (SM 6:106) whose meaning is peripheral even when it is decipherable. The problem raised by these permutations is not what the grass *means*, but what the grass *is*, a question no chiasmus ("a child asked . . . the grass is . . . a child" [SM 6:99, 105]); no antithesis ("the smallest sprout shows there is really no death" [SM 6:126] . . . "Now it seems to me the beautiful uncut hair of graves" [SM 6:110]); and no implicit claim to speak a foreign language as though it were a native tongue ("grass / My tongue" [SM 1:5–6]) could extract.

Because in Whitman's universe no thing possesses identity if the latter means to have a relation of equivalence *only with itself* and with nothing else—a truth that in section 6 also underlies Whitman's treatment of pictographic and linguistic writing—we could apply to Whitman a formulation of Werner Hamacher's about Nietzsche for whom "individuality is so completely determined as incommensurability that no individual could correspond to its concept if it were to be at one with—and equal to—itself. . . . Only the nonidentity of the individual with itself constitutes its individuality." Thus "the impossibility of achieving unambiguous knowledge of a being whose singularity lies in its splitting."[32] Whitman's interrogatives—"To be in any form, what is that?" (SM 27:611)—are enveloped in curiosity that supplants identification, as in section 6 where each manifestation of being could only be serially named across its changes, but not decisively decoded. In distinction to Emerson's bifurcated system, for instance, in "The Over-soul" where the person is rigidly defined in opposition to an impersonal whole and must be sacrificed to secure benefit to a "universal self,"[33] in Whitman's writing there is no uniform "all" that could exact such tragedy and no circumscribed person who could supply it. Since everything is nonidentical with itself, there is no place for suffering to lodge, and no one who could identify suffering as a condition that establishes his destiny. Afflictions—like conditions, like mind states, and like an ostensibly immutable fate—are fugitive. Whitman's expressive non-lament (or is it a celebration?) both trivializes this provisionality and exposes

a truth at its core when he announces: "Agonies are one of my changes of garments" (SM 33:843). As I shall suggest, such a statement is at once a glib dismissal of agony and a profound truth about its superficiality.

iii

The changes that wash over *all* experiences and feelings deprive them of calcification. The vision (or understanding) that enables the "I" to divest himself of agony emerges from a recognition of that freedom. Just as for this speaker there is no agony that could solidify what "So Long," Whitman's farewell poem, calls "the great individual, fluid as Nature,"[34] that same fluidity translates one kind of embodiment into another, as when in "So Long" the unbound "I" is released from his book: "I spring from the pages into your arms" (SL 57). The leap from words into fleshed being that Whitman names one "of my many translations" (SL 67), but only at the moment of incipient death when "decease calls me forth" (SL 57), assaults credibility, not only because of the category transformation, inert object to living being, but also because of the logic that enables it. Why does the condition that will putrefy flesh induce a kinetic image of its vitality in the resilient verb "spring"?—a question that could also be asked of Keats's "This Living Hand," which "reach[es]" toward the reader at the moment of Keats's extinction.

Why in "So Long" does the "I" lavish endearment not on a "you" that he knows, but on one he does *not* know, a question raised by the affectionate expressions "Camerado" (SL 53), "dear friend" (SL 64) that are addressed to an unspecified person—to *any* person: "Whoever you are take this kiss, / I give it especially to you" (SL 64–65). That agony falls away and therefore might not enduringly afflict the person, and that affection bestows itself "especially" (SL 65) on strangers, unsettles everything we think we know about persons—how they might be deformed by an experience like agony and who they might be disposed to cherish. Thus Whitman's "whoever you are" (SL 64) engenders the same kind of love as—or rather more love than—one might experience for an intimate. In the state of affairs Whitman represents, the kiss bequeathed to the stranger is not bestowed out of the wrenching difficulty of heeding an ethical imperative. It is spontaneous.

In Whitman's practice of assembling things that are conceptually incongruent, and then assaulting the intractability of the limits that mistakenly inform each—the fixture of "agonies" (SM 33:843); the fixed line drawn around objects of affection to exclude strangers; words bound in, and fixed by, a book; a vernacular and a common tongue—we are asked to think about persons in a way that rescues them from categorical understandings that sequester stranger from beloved, affectionate words from affection that is incarnated. Such effaced distinctions (the overarching object of Whitman's attention) dissolve classifications, but not from the same vantage or in relation to the same objects: the rigid concept that drives a wedge between stranger and intimate is not the same fixity that associates the intensity of agony with its protraction. Between each of Whitman's heterogeneous and incongruent compoundings, there could be no transition—and none is needed. Whitman's restless visions record what is seen from different outlooks and begin anew. Each moment: a starting over. At the same time, since the discordant pieces of this ontology consistently flow into each other (though not in the same way, or to the same effect), Whitman's lines, stanzas, sections have the paradoxical feel of a starting over that is repetition. Repeated is the assault on expectations of how things are—and on thinking that prematurely grasps how things are—that is ventured beyond, or rather at the edge of, thinking. The edge is not a dead end, but where Whitman's thinking takes place. Whitman is always at that place, which could not be the same place from one moment to the next, or from one problem to another, though the same intention—to shatter the illusion of recognition that identifies what things are before one even sees them—compels his vision. How could an "I" that pushes past the solitude in which it is sequestered not bump up against a question about its relation to any "you"? How could one at the edge of thinking not wonder how affection expressed in words could be released from words and incarnated? This edge precipitates Whitman's mode of thinking and always involves a basic question—not how one gets from one thing to another, but rather at each moment how one gets from nothing to something (which for Christians, and for

Whitman in a comparable register since his is also "death's outlet song of life,"[35] presumes an impossible possible posthumous presence) and is a question about origins (ex nihilo).

Because in Whitman's translations, each moment is, paradoxically, experienced as original, it excites astonishment rather than recognition, astonishment being the response to things coming into being or seen for the first time. For this reason, the "you" singled out in section 19 of "Song" and the intimacy established with the stranger-become-neighbor, potentially at the furthest distance from the speaker—in that the invitation includes "all," anywhere ("I will not have a single person slighted or left away" [SM 19:374])—do not contradict each other, since the truth of *each* being chosen is not compromised by the truth of *all* being chosen. The stranger who is included becomes an intimate with whom Whitman arranges a unique meeting. For Whitman's "appointments with all" (SM 19:374) are not conducted en masse but with each alone—that is the implicit promise of his "affectionate presence," which is as unstinting in its inclusivity as in its avid response to the charm of each sovereign particular. The inconceivable moment in "Crossing Brooklyn Ferry" when Whitman addresses each of us ("Who knows, for all the distance, but I am as good as looking at you now, for all you cannot see me?" [7:91]), and of course the poem as a whole arises out of such sublimities. Just as, earlier in section 19, when Whitman reconceives the relation between the "I" and the "you," he also introduces an unparalleled strategy for establishing similitude among these divergent elements:

> Do you guess I have some intricate purpose?
> Well I have, for the Fourth-month showers have, and the mica on
>   the side of a rock has.
>   (SM 19:382–83)

The ascription of "intricate purpose" to entities that might be unequal in manifestation but which, according to Whitman, all exist or have been created for some reason or end (even if the "mica," the "showers," the "I" called "Whitman" could not be said to share the same degree of purpose or the same kind of purpose). To notice such a disparity, however, is immediately to realize that the "intricate purpose" (SM 19:382) of each remains unknown and unknowable. In this demonstration of alliance with respect to what cannot be fathomed (including whether there is in fact a purpose undergirding elements of existence), Whitman translates questions about differences of kind into congruence discovered in another register—that of the shared ignorance about the purpose behind anything created. In a like manner, in the stanza that follows—

> Do you take it I would astonish?
> Does the daylight astonish? Does the early redstart twittering
> through the woods?
> Do I astonish more than they?
> (SM 19: 383–86)

—"daylight," "the early redstart twittering," the untethered "I," each evoke astonishment, and the last of the questions seems to suggest (or does it contradict the notion?) that astonishment provoked by each could be quantified, as a measure of the value of the discrete things that elicit it. Perhaps the comparative "more than" is a pretext for turning the wonder occasioned by Whitman toward other phenomena, which, if deeply looked at, would also be seen (as he sees himself seen) as marvelous. Understood thus, the final rhetorical question to the reader—lodging the very premise of the discourse—is also an imperative: see "daylight," and hear "the redstart twittering" (SM 19:384), and these will astonish as I do, but absent contrast or resemblance. For if astonishment is anything, it is absolute.

Even so, the stanza retains its difficulty because the insistence that *anything* could astonish is hard to grasp as more than a salutary idea (as is much of Whitman's writing, despite the illusive simplicity across which a reader might glide), because of the enigma of sorting out discordant elements, questions about their relation, and comparatives posed but then dissolved in the absurdity of assigning degrees or amounts to classes of things—like astonishment or purpose—that escape them. In addition, Whitman's constellations contain differences that could dispute his groupings, even as these challenges are ultimately irrelevant to the cohesion of the relations being established. Thus sound, light, and the omnipresent "I" are drawn into one configuration of strangely collated elements, in that the "I" could intend or desire to "astonish," but intent cannot be attributed to the bird or the light. Man and bird are incarnated, but light could never share this attribute, since while objects absorb and reflect light, light itself is not an embodied object. The pressure to puzzle over these—as it happens—irrelevant distinctions arises from a reader's bewilderment about *when* differences count, *how* they count, and the criteria that draw incommensurable elements into relation so that differences apparently *cease* to count (as when the stranger becomes an intimate purely by being identified as such). Most sensational: the criteria that draw incommensurable objects toward each other are themselves incommensurable, as "appointments with all," "intricate purpose," and "astonishment"—denominators that constellate each grouping in section 19—are not categorically comparable.

In these ways Whitman bursts our conception of what kinds of things can be drawn into relation, and also our supposition that criteria which establish those relations must be congruous. Whitman translates experience into forms and arrangements of forms that often seem more radical than the moment in Hebrews 11:15, when God translates Enoch from earth to heaven. For Whitman does not escape death as Enoch is said to do. Thus in "When Lilacs Last in the Dooryard Bloom'd," beyond the "long panoramas" (WL 15:170) of the "battle-corpses" (WL 15:177), Whitman's eyes "unclos[e]" (WL 15:169) also to see: "*In the day, in the night, to all, to each / Sooner or later delicate death*" (WL 14:137–38). That almost inexplicable adjective "delicate"—which abruptly attributes tact, care, and even tenderness to death's ministrations—moves us away from the preceding carnage and, at a distance, permits death's translation to "loud human song" (WL 13:103), an "ever-altering song" (WL 16:188), a "song of the bleeding throat" (WL 4:23). The rendering of "death" into "song" and "song" into "praise" (WL 14:139–44) does not make death intelligible, or ultimately mute the visceral horror Whitman earlier evokes, but rather situates these amid other indecipherables: the "measureless light" (WL 12:95), "the fathomless universe" (WL 14:139), the illimitable "I"—composite parts of the domain of incommensurable things that can't be "tallied" independently. In this way death, the light, the limitless "I" conform to each other, even though the perception of light (the "floods of the yellow gold of the gorgeous, indolent, sinking sun, burning, expanding the air" [WL 11:83]) could not be made cognate with the perception of death. Their convergence in Whitman's poem is the ground of our lived experience of their relation.

According to Benjamin, in a "free translation" there is an "emancipation" from the "barriers" of "language" such that "sense" "pursu[es] its own course . . . in the freedom of linguistic flux" (TT 261). This understanding of "emancipation" is visible in Whitman's translation of flesh into grass that grows again, of death into "song" and "light," and of course of the "I" into the "you" and "all"—the latter being the most arduous. For Benjamin (writing about translation that pertains to the life of language), the aspect of "a translation which goes beyond transmittal of subject matter" is that it "does not lend itself to further translation" (TT 257–58). For Benjamin, this *nothing further* is a language of signifiers with no signified. Pure language is purely language without meaning. For Whitman, *nothing further* opens into the seemingly inaccessible *is* of the real, *that* original—not, as for Benjamin, in Messianic time, but *here*. Yet for the ever-regenerate "you"—there must be something further. For if Whitman translates, announces, instantiates a starting over, a release from thinking as we know it, to read Whitman is barely to understand him. How can affect for a beloved extend to a stranger? How can one slip out of agonies as out of a garment? How could any fragment of experience discover the whole from which it is riven?

iv

Whitman lodges these questions in our minds as "fierce enigmas!" amid the "strangling problems!"[36] identified in "Passage to India," a poem in which transcendence of the status quo ("Have we not stood here like trees in the ground long enough?" [PI 9:245]) resides in the emergence of impediments ("shores . . . strew'd with the wrecks of skeletons" [PI 9: 230–32]), in their becoming visible, and beyond this visible, in a glimpse of what is "more than India" (PI 9:224). In Whitman's poems, a "procreant urge" (SM 3:45), a drive toward a possible real, possible now—now being all there is and in which all is—is made actual through a passage from one kind of understanding governed by rift to another kind of understanding where what is identified could not be disentangled from what is alien: "all these separations and gaps . . . taken up and hook'd and link'd together / The whole earth, this cold, impassive, voiceless earth . . . justified" (PI 5:109–10). The imperative ("farther, farther, farther sail!" [PI 9:255]) in "Passage to India" is the "demand of what is real to become possible"[37]—for being to realize its own immanent possibility in the seeing anew of what is given—a demand that yet points to a privation for us, who do not grasp this now in which everything is at once, and one. In such a calculation, what is unrealized becomes "unforgettable" and thus "the very form of demand" (D 31). In Agamben's reordered words: "The kingdom of heaven is *here and now* for those who are farthest from it." Such a "demand is—in its essence—beatitude" (D 34): "the thing we hope for is already completely present as demand" (D 32). In such spiraling formulations, one can barely understand how "beatitude" could be decoupled from the poverty that keeps it at bay. Whitman fleshes out the bones of that philosophical abstraction so that we see its lure, its risk, and its immediacy.

Done with the Compass, Done with the Chart

OFF-THE-MAP SCENES IN DICKINSON'S POEMS

Scene is what emerges when the eyes detect and process visual detail, turning light that hits the retina into electrical signals that pass through the optic nerve, are delivered to the brain, and then transformed into images. Sometimes the homonyms "scene" and "seen" are inseparable, even synonymous. From another vantage, scene is more than optics. The disposition of scene comes into view through a constellation of objects, stages, or processes within a frame, a context, or a surrounding that can be recognized or identified. But in the topography of Emily Dickinson's poems, scenes often cannot be placed even when the poems appear to be operating realistically. Consider the first stanza of this well-known poem to which I will return:

> Because I could not stop for Death -
> He kindly stopped for me -
> The Carriage held but just Ourselves -
> And Immortality.[1]
>
> (F 479)

The poem progresses through a scene, but the seeing of the scene is by someone who is dead, who is no longer a person, someone who cannot see. As I have shown in *Lyric Time* and *Choosing Not Choosing*,[2] Dickinson wrote many such poems in which speakers inhabit a posthumous state. What is the status and function of scene in such a poem? What happens to the categories on which the poems depend,

or which they evolve, when what is viewed reveals a scene that can't be seen under the conditions the poem stipulates?

My questions are far afield from analyses of Dickinson's scenes consumed by judgments that validate or disparage her poems according to whether the sites they depict are ontologically attainable.[3] Such analyses colonize the poems' strangeness. In distinction, in what follows I regard Dickinson's poems as residing outside of a framework that can be domesticated. The tenacity of my fascination with Dickinson's poems has kept me returning to them over decades, reinvigorated each time from distinct vantages. In the 1970s I observed that when Dickinson's poems sabotage time, they incidentally exaggerate the characteristics of the lyric genre. In the 1980s, facsimiles of Dickinson's fascicles made available in Ralph Franklin's 1981 *The Manuscript Books of Emily Dickinson* raised questions about the identity of Dickinson's texts: Should Dickinson's poems be read as individual lyrics or as variants of each other within the specific fascicle in which she bound them? Should variants to words within and outside the metrical line be read as alternative or combinatory? The present essay does not relinquish concerns with temporality in Dickinson's utterances or with the frames that demarcate them, but it takes a sharp turn away from my initial formulations of these matters to examine scenes in some of her most celebrated poems which transpire in alien territory that resists being categorized or delimited. Such poems cannot be tamed by theoretical paradigms.

Part i begins with Dickinson's posthumous journey poems that posit scene where it is prohibitive to do so, since the death that will be one's own defies access to scene. Yet the speakers in these poems occupy the same uncanny position all humans do. We can only think our death, but in doing so it becomes unthinkable—a predicament played out uniquely in the many poems that engage it. Part ii turns to poems that represent internal states for which there are no good correlatives, even though the psychic states they portray—like that in "I felt a funeral in my brain" (F 340)—are made scenic, and thus efface the distinction between what is internal and external. For instance, in "Like eyes that looked on wastes" (F 693), a scene in the shape of a contemplated face is taken in passively ("So looked the face I looked opon -"), but it then assaults the speaker's vision ("So looked itself - on Me -"). How is such an extrusion possible? At their extremity, the poems examined in part iii move from scenes whose location can't be identified because it is too far out ("I saw no Way - the Heavens were stitched - / I felt the Columns close -" [F 633]) to poems that portend access to what lies beyond scenic representation, gesturing toward "places" called "reportless" (F 1404).

Dickinson's poems vary in the ways in which they bend, fracture, and conflate categories of mortal being and cosmic Being; time and space; inner and outer regions; scene and its vacuity, not least when that emptiness registers as a spectral presence. Yet consistently in these poems, sensation erupts from abstraction, its incongruous counterpart emerging around the edges, or breaking out of the center, of the inconceivable immensities that constitute Dickinson's off-the-map scenes. The reader experiences sensation in the clang of rhymes that couple variants; in phonetic repetitions; in images that both invite and resist hearing and envisaging ("As all the Heavens were a Bell, / And Being, but an Ear" [F 340]); syntactically in chiasms; and of course meaningfully for a speaker in the catastrophic fate endured when, afflicted by sensation, "I dropped down, and down - / And hit a World, at every plunge" (F 340). Through the cumulative analyses of such scenes, I intend the work of my essay to demonstrate a sui generis bond between abstraction and sensation whose ontology is not caught in a binary that drives these modes apart. As with the poems that cross epistemological thresholds, Dickinson does not segregate forms of experience that are incommensurable.

i

The unfolding of scene in Dickinson's journey poems imparts a surprise, but not the same surprise. Consider the following in which a speaker imagines a straight route from being to Being in a movement uncompromised by peril:

Our journey had advanced -
Our feet were almost come
To that odd Fork in Being's Road -
Eternity - by Term -

Our pace took sudden awe - Our feet - reluctant - led -
Before - were Cities - but Between -
The Forest of the Dead -

Retreat - was out of Hope -
Behind - a Sealed Route -
Eternity's +White Flag - +Before -
And God - at every Gate -

White Flag] cool   Before] in front
(F 453)

That "odd Fork in Being's Road -" displaces the metaphysical diagram the speaker has construed, for "Eternity -" is not a "Term -," another *period of time*, but rather the *end* of time. Yet time continues for the speaker until the last stanza. The pun on *terminus* draws a line that "Eternity -" eventually exceeds. "Term -" as *interval*, along with "term" as *name*, "Eternity -" eludes all but belated identification. Similarly, "Before -" also has two meanings, signifying the expanse *behind* the speaker where lie the "Cities -" of the living and the region *in front* of her, "The Forest of the Dead -" through which she must pass. The "White Flag -" also lies ahead. "Before -" thus indicates the micro-differential between dying and eternity and, as Geoffrey Hartman claims, the poem is radically liminal.[4] The splitting within the homonyms finds a corollary in the tension between "sudden awe -" and "reluctan[ce] -," which puts a brake on wonder in the two places ("pace" and "feet -") where the reactions register. These function less as synecdoches that emblematize the speaker than as manifestations of motion that have usurped her emotion and agency. In a like disjuncture, the plural possessive ("Our journey . . . our feet -") is denied by the solitude of a journey that could never be communal. Whether the scene in "Our journey had advanced -" depicts a collective undertaking or whether the speaker merely subsumes in the plural pronouns a surmise that what happens to all only happens to each alone is neutralized in the last stanza, where such distinctions end—thus the disappearance of features that could personalize *or* generalize. In a final rift, "out of Hope -" calls to mind (and displaces) the proximate expression *without hope* by portraying the loss of hope as a process that has concluded, rather than as a static absence. Human being is thus implicitly identified in the poem's serial manifestations of division—one part against another to which it is sutured—whether of the homonym of the contraries ("Before -" / "Before -"), or of a death that is unique and yet common to all. From that splitting, the poem releases its energy in a movement that is an "advanc[e] -" toward a breakthrough.

Yet the "White" of the "Flag -," the color of surrender, demands *the speaker's* surrender. The flag belongs to "Eternity -," where it compels her submission to a stupendous presence that accosts her. She has expected release. But in the surprise twist that links the architecture of "every Gate -" to the twelve gates described in Revelation (KJV 21:12), she encounters entrapment: "Behind - a Sealed Route -." For "God - at every Gate -," a suffusion of "God," an overwhelming excess that is exhaustive and unitary, is too much "God -." The tacit violence of such an exhibition is not perceptible in "Because I could not stop for death," where a cognate journey has no outcome: the structure of the poem is "We passed," "We passed," "We paused":

Because I could not stop for Death -
He kindly stopped for me -
The Carriage held but just Ourselves -
And Immortality.

We slowly drove - He knew no haste
And I had put away
My labor and my leisure too,
For His Civility -

We passed the School, where Children strove
At Recess - in the Ring -
We passed the Fields of Gazing Grain -
We passed the Setting Sun -

Or rather - He passed Us -
The Dews drew quivering and Chill -

For only Gossamer, my Gown -
My Tippet - only Tulle -

We paused before a House that seemed
A Swelling of the Ground -
The Roof was scarcely visible -
The Cornice - in the Ground -

Since then - 'tis Centuries - and yet
Feels shorter than the Day
I first surmised the Horses' Heads
Were toward Eternity -
(F 479)

In the penultimate stanza the speaker lingers before a grave marker ("a House," a "Cornice - in the Ground -"), whose untimely placement precedes her own burial. The transposed sequence (she is outside the grave whose stone will identify her once she is within it) has a vertiginous counterpart in the woozy temporality of the poem's last stanza, established by the incompatible coordinates of *actual* time post-burial (actual within the poem in the passage of "Centuries -") and *experienced* time in which the speaker's transit "Feels shorter than the Day / I first surmised the Horses' Heads / Were toward Eternity -." Here the enjambment turns the noun "Day," as if the last of her life, into the adverbial *day when* the arresting moment of recognition occurs. In the distance between the extremes of "Centuries -" and "the Day" of the "surmis[e]," time seems to swoon, to have progressed and regressed. The impediment of determining how to calculate the time elapsed—hundreds of years or the day they are perceived, which is virtually no time, is augmented by a spatial impasse: "the Horses' Heads" that she can't see beyond. Moving, but never reaching "Eternity -" in the time that has elapsed—no matter how it is calculated—draws attention to the inertia of the preposition *toward*. If there is movement without arrest, it may also be without development, so that "Eternity -" is supplanted by interminable delay ("'tis Centuries -"). Where is she?

In "Our journey had advanced" and "Because I could not stop for death," Dickinson drives apart "Death -" and "Eternity -." The mood of one poem is auspicious and then ominous; of the other poem, placid. Both speakers pass through death while being denied its finality. They continue. In the speaker's novel relation to death, and in death's novel severance from eternity—also in the separation of "Immortality" (endless time, like that experienced by Tennyson's Tithonus) from "Eternity -" (the end of time, like that prophesied in Revelation 10:6)—we see that these states are conceptually linked because both have left human time behind, but in Dickinson's poem they remain incommensurable. For "Immortality" is a passenger in Death's "Carriage," while "Eternity -" is a destination. In this tension of conflicting cues, the terms escape taxonomy. Similarly, the torque in the twisted idiom "Because I could not stop for Death - / He kindly stopped for me -" raises the question of what it means to stop or end. Stopping is inevitably referenced to time, as in the expressions *Stop dead. Stop now.* Or, as in Dickinson's "Life like This - is stopless - / Be Judgment - what it may -" (F 698). In "Our journey had advanced" and "Because I could not stop," there is no stopping. "Could not stop" implies the speaker is so busy that she can't give death the time of day, and is thus a figurative expression (though its basis, agitated haste, is a corporeal experience, her last before she is carried beyond somatic manifestation). Therefore "Death" "stop[s]" for her and, in a manner of speaking, stops her. But is it only a manner of speaking, since death does stop one? Being stopped, but not stopping, is the aporia that haunts both poems. In Dickinson's poems, not stopping happens in a visionary sequence outside of mortal time.

Like the two periods of time, "Centuries -" and "shorter than the Day," in which contradictory understandings of how to measure duration disable an answer to a question about the time span of the journey,[5] sequence is inverted when the body is buried after rather than before the commemorative marker is placed in earth. The poems throw weight on single words ("Before -" in one poem, "toward" in the other) whose meanings divide sense; install recognizable symbols to whose conventional significations they adhere (the "White Flag -" of surrender, the "Gate[s]" of heaven), but reconstrue major religious tenets, like immortality and eternity. In eliciting traditional associations attached to these words but contextually redefining them, Dickinson releases their connotations from recognizability.

Her scenes are not built on empirical ground, but they establish a gripping reality outside that ground, where they play havoc with tags like before and after, inside and outside, standing and moving, stopping and not stopping, abstract sense and raw sensation, and the literal and the figural. In Dickinson's poems, what transpires between these antitheses is less a boundary crossing than a volatile movement in which one can't trace the dividing line that would affiliate aspects of each poem with one pole or the other.[6] Is "God - at every Gate -" (F 453)—the poem's breakthrough experience—figural? In Revelation those gates, each made of a single pearl, are miraculous, supernatural. Yet in Dickinson's allusion to those gates, nothing seems more literal within the contrasts the poem establishes between the speaker's fanciful expectation of a smooth transit to eternity and the intervening obstacles that chastise her idea ("The Forest of the Dead -," her reluctance, the surrender), of which the superfluity of God is the ultimate correction—depicted as a veritable actual that discloses God's excess.

The following poem anatomizes "Eternity -," "Immortality -," the Father, the "Son" not in eschatological extremes, but rather in the temporal and spatial nomenclature of a person who establishes herself as a mere "Term between -" cosmic immensities:

Behind Me - dips Eternity -
Before Me - Immortality -
Myself - the Term between -
Death but the Drift of Eastern Gray,
Dissolving into Dawn away,

Before the West begin -
'Tis Kingdoms - afterward - they say -
In perfect - pauseless Monarchy -
Whose Prince - is Son of none -
Himself - His Dateless Dynasty -
Himself - Himself diversify -
In Duplicate divine -

'Tis Miracle before Me - then -
'Tis Miracle behind - between -

A Crescent in the Sea -
With Midnight to the North of Her -
And Midnight to the South of Her -
And Maelstrom - in the Sky -
(F 743)

The archetype proposed in the first stanza collapses into glib phrasing (in the "they say -" of the second stanza and the flip reference to a conception that identifies Christ as "Son of none -"); into redundancy ("Himself - . . . Himself -"; "Miracle . . . Miracle"; "Midnight . . . Midnight"; "between - . . . between -"; "Duplicate divine -"); into inversion ("Behind . . . Before" . . . "before . . . behind -"); and finally into chaos. In Charles R. Anderson's reading of the poem's last stanza, in which the moon is perceptible in the ocean ("A Crescent in the Sea -") while the "Maelstrom -" (a vortex in a body of water) is transferred to "the Sky -,"[7] the poem ends by turning everything upside down into the opposite of the system at which the intoxicating scheme aims. No spatial or temporal specification could chart how "Eternity -" and "Immortality -" are affiliated, notwithstanding the linear diagram of the poem's first line. Nor could it be deduced how a person mediates these realms except schematically. In claiming to decipher the imponderables, the speaker loses her bearings, as registered in the third stanza by the transformation of an implicit "I" into a "Her -." Given Dickinson's practice of objectifying the "I" by a shift of pronoun to the dative case of "she,"[8] the "Her -" does not refer to a nautical "she," the feminization of Nature, but rather to a speaker whose calculations have alienated her from subjectivity. For the reader, "Eternity -," "Immortality -," "Death -" dissolve into placeholders that lack detail and depth. The speaker can juxtapose these terms and insert herself as a commensurate "Term between -," thus placing herself at the center of a grandiose thought experiment, but that strategy is foiled by the impotence of thought. Yet something breaks through the blockage with the blunt force of redundancy: specifically, "Miracle" calls attention to what that word repeats. The repetitions are touchstones that bypass calculation. What is "Behind" (prior to), "Before" (ahead of), and "between -"—where the speaker locates herself—is "Miracle." "Miracle" defines human being, also suffusing the infinites she sought to place. Dickinson can't write what the poem proposes to glean and no human could read it.

"Prayer -" seems a more refined form of calculation than the metaphysical charting sabotaged in the previous poems. Below it is employed as an "Art -," or rather a set of emboldened "Tactics" to hunt down the Creator to beseech an intercession in the crisis with which the poem begins:

My period had come for Prayer -
No other Art - would do -
My Tactics missed a rudiment -
Creator - Was it you?

God grows above - so those who pray
Horizons - must ascend -
And so I +stepped upon the North
To +see this Curious Friend -

His House was not - no sign had He -
By Chimney - nor by Door -
Could I infer his Residence -
+Vast Prairies of Air

Unbroken by a Settler -
Were all that I could see -
Infinitude - Had'st Thou no Face
That I might look on Thee?

The Silence condescended -
+Creation stopped - for me -
But awed beyond my errand -
I worshipped - did not "pray" -

stepped] stood see] Reach-touch Vast prairies] Wide prairies
Creation stopped] The Heavens paused

(F 525)

The greater the detail about how to plot a course—to step "opon the North" as on a platform to locate God—the more unintelligible the project, since God could only be omnipresent. The prepositions "opon," "above -"; a verb like "grows" (nonsensical in this context since growth implies change, while a "rudiment -," like a first principle, is unalterable); and finally, the noun and adjective that identify the object of the quest ("this Curious Friend -") estrange the idea of encounter, of relation, and of deity itself. The serial misnomers that insinuate, concretize, and even flaunt an implausible intimacy imply that this pilgrimage could only be figural—though figural with qualification, since to "Reach -" or "touch -" have an actuality inscribed in the corporeal metaphor of revelation. The poem's spatial terms raise a question of what counts as proximity and communion. Simultaneously, the shifting denominations in the speaker's discordant nouns—"Creator -," "Friend -," "Infinitude -," "Silence"—betray uncertainty about what is pursued. Is God a "you" (as in the cozy nudge "Creator - Was it you?") or a "Thou" (as in the reverential penultimate stanza)? Is the speaker addressing a begetter (a "Creator -") or an abstraction (a "rudiment -")? Though she asks for a "sign" that would illuminate the inscrutable presence whose nature is indeterminable, she comes up with nothing. *Nothing* takes the form of "Vast Prairies of Air," prairies being generally uncultivated and treeless, while air is transparent. The assonance and embeddedness of "Air" in "Prairies" encloses the tenor in its own vehicle. "Air" is stretched uninflected, like a prairie, begging the question whether what mediates the gulf between the human and divine is a quasi-material substance like air. The speaker can locate an extent that is an immensity, but it is evacuated of qualities. The reality that she would particularize can't be particularized. At issue is how to perceive her relation to an essence without qualities—a query seared into the cry: "Infinitude - Had'st Thou no Face / That I might look on Thee?" If "Infinitude -" had a "Face," an embodied shape, or even a "sign," it would be the ultimate catachresis, since "Infinitude -" is a figure for what can't be delimited. Once infinitude is understood as a pure abstraction with no concrete determinants, its lack of attributes is as factual (literal) as its facelessness is metaphoric. That "Infinitude -" could never be anything but faceless is the poem's recognition. When this shock registers, the "Silence" that overtakes supplication is given a contour and texture in the speaker's changed perception. She can't see or apprehend—but is apprehended: that is the "condescen[sion]." In these ways Dickinson's poem unbuilds the recognizable.

Dickinson's journey poems dismantle truisms about "God -" (F 453), "Death -" (F 479), and "Eternity -" (F 743), revealing them as unknowns that the pursuit invigorates within a real beyond what is "surmise[d]" (F 479)—as in the lived torment of not knowing how endless time is related to a beyond time and also to *our* time (F 479); as in the fear that God is no benignity, but rather a mighty glut (F 453); as in the sense that death does not extinguish but strands one in an enduring nowhere, a tangible nothing that can be narrated but not felt, for the perceptible void of feeling in "Because I could not stop for death" is among that poem's most confounding features. The poems break down the distinction between what is seen and, in one instance, a reverse optic in which scene stares back ("We passed the Fields of Gazing Grain -" [F 479]), underscoring the inefficacy of categorical boundaries undone by each poem's complexity. They plumb ignorance, inscribe "Curious" (F 525) scenes only to revoke them. They are works without a script, venturing beyond significance, heuristic to the end, sometimes apophatic. They have inertial force. They begin without orientation and discover none. "Worshi[p]," not "Prayer -" (F 525), is the act of bearing witness to a divine scale of things, and takes place in a sceneless immensity based on a mere inference without a reference, nothing that could be described or circumscribed. Poems that efface scene as initially contemplated ("Our journey had advanced," "Behind me dips eternity") or that unwrite scene entirely ("My period had come for Prayer -") raise a question to which I will return: What survives the negation of scene in these enigmatic poems? (Enigmatic because the dissolution of scene often seems immanent in its very constitution.) What grounds the metaphysic of scenes that have no roots in our world? But I turn now to examine an inverse imperative within Dickinson's poems which discover scenes that counterintuitively incarnate and exteriorize mental states, even though the latter intrinsically resist visual and dramatic representation. Just as what is posthumous and numinous, thus temporally inaccessible, is rendered scenic, so interior experience, spatially inaccessible to view, is also rendered scenic in Dickinson's poems. These poems, too, erupt in surges of sensation.

ii

Though for the reader the structure of the following poem is implicitly framed by the first and last lines ("It was not Death," it was "Despair"), the speaker caught in "Chaos -" can only define her experience by negation ("not Death," "not Frost," "not Night"), by analogy, and by synthesis ("And yet, it tasted, like them all"—taste being the most interior of the senses):

It was not Death, for I stood up,
And all the Dead, lie down -
It was not Night, for all the Bells
Put out their Tongues, for Noon.

It was not Frost, for on my +Flesh
I felt Siroccos - crawl -
Nor Fire - for just +my marble feet
Could keep a Chancel, cool -

And yet, it tasted, like them all,
The Figures I have seen
Set orderly, for Burial
Reminded me, of mine -

As if my life were shaven,
And fitted to a frame,
And could not breathe without a key,
And 'twas like Midnight, some -

When everything that ticked - has stopped -
And space stares - all around -
Or Grisly frosts - first Autumn morns,
Repeal the Beating Ground -

But, most, like Chaos - Stopless - cool -
Without a Chance, or spar -
Or even a Report of Land -
To justify - Despair.

Flesh] Knees   my] two
(F 355)

The living death that is despair pervades all aspects of the speaker's perception, while resisting her capacity to name it. The images in the last stanza suggest that "Despair" can't be named because its opposite, hope—metonymically figured as a "spar -" (the piece of wood or metal used to support a ship's rigging)—which would carry the speaker away from turmoil toward a "Report of Land -," cannot be discovered. "Despair" would be "justif[ied]"—the speaker would be absolved from it in a theological sense, and the designation "Despair" would be recognizable in a commonplace sense—if hope, its antithesis, were perceptible. Hope and despair must be conceived in relation to each other without one collapsing into the other, but in this poem obverse criteria that might orient cannot be differentiated. Thus while bell clappers derisively "Put out their Tongues, for Noon," they also chime twelve times at midnight; while "Night" is ruled out as temporally situating in the first stanza, it is reinstated in stanza 4 with "And 'twas like Midnight, some -." A specific point on the continuum we call time, the measure of heat and cold we call temperature, the properties that distinguish being from nonbeing, cannot be discriminated by the speaker. The combinatory quality of antithetical sensations, including "Frost" and "Siroccos -"—states that should be opposite—melt into each other, rendering identification impossible.

Each term of these paired correlatives must be understood within a stable antithesis (like that of Freud's sense of antithetical words or like Hegel's sense of a double consciousness[9]), the absence of which defeats the speaker's ability to render her impressions legible. The poem's correction to the bewilderment that suffuses her is rendered *scenically* in the figure of that "spar -," that "Report of Land -"

in the poem's conclusion, thus permitting recognition of the state the speaker can't name—of the "It" initially without an antecedent. Though the externality of scene seems incompatible with despair or with any internal experience, the extrusion of mental experience into scenic development is repeated in "I felt a funeral in my brain" (F 340), where scene, or rather a series of scenes, exposes the incongruous trope with which the poem begins—even though funerals are ceremonies, not mental events, nor are mental events inhabited by "Mourners":

I felt a Funeral, in my Brain,
And Mourners to and fro
Kept treading - treading - till it seemed
That Sense was breaking through -

And when they all were seated,
A Service, like a Drum -
Kept beating - beating - till I thought
My mind was going numb -

And then I heard them lift a Box
And creak across my +Soul
With those same Boots of Lead, again,
Then Space—began to toll,

As all the Heavens were a Bell,
And Being, but an Ear,
And I, and Silence, some strange Race,
Wrecked, solitary, here -

And then a Plank in Reason, broke,
And I dropped down, and down -
And hit a World, at every plunge,
And +Finished - knowing - then -

Soul] Brain   Finished] Got through –
(F 340)

In Dickinson's *Lexicon*, the "brain" connotes "imagination; cognition; sensory perception" and is also described as "the center of emotion."[10] Thus "brain" is not differentiated from "mind" in any sense that would identify one as an organ, the other as a mental phenomenon. Dickinson uses the words interchangeably in the first two stanzas. What resides in the brain to be submerged are thoughts, perceptions, feelings. After Freud, this burial would be called repression. How then should we understand figuration that externalizes the entombment of an immaterial thought or feeling by a ceremony marking the burial of a coffin? Though the incongruity of the conceit is startling, it is not unique, since analogous complements—"Ear" and "Being"; "I and Silence"; the genitive-like "Plank in Reason"—that differently yoke material and immaterial phenomena are also tethered. As a consequence, the annihilation of sense is fully open to view; that is what renders the poem scenic. It begins by personifying those aspects of the brain ("Mourners") that lament the extinction and burial of sense, and unfolds as a narrative that transmits an instantaneous event as a sequence: resistance; "Silence"; and oblivion—the speaker psychically passes out. Yet while the poem does not segregate levels of significance (as in an allegory), there is more than one scene, or more than one way of understanding the devolution of the scene in the second part of each stanza into auditory sensation—repetitive, rhythmic, stultifying—that creates the story of unknowing. It's hard to locate the speaker in this psychomachia. It seems she has been expelled from the conflict that is registered in the first stanza and drawn inward toward a single point, the "Ear"—that receptacle for auditory sensation that collects, amplifies, and vibrates sound into which all of "Being" distills. At the same time, she can't be located in a single place, for in these interlocked scenes, she is both the object of the splitting we associate with repression and a witness to it.

This mixed sense of being at once outside and inside the plunging, the finishing, and above all the hearing has a counterpart: sound, too, is nomadic. The "treading -" and "beating -" initially ascribed to "Mourners" close in on and inhabit the speaker ("I heard them . . . creak across my Soul"), who becomes the visceral medium through which sound travels and disappears. The penultimate stanza proposes an apparent solecism in the affinity of "I, and Silence," a pairing perceived as a "Race"—aberrant, because race refers to one or more people classified together on the basis of genealogy's shared characteristics. But when the speaker is divested of all but hearing ("Being, but an Ear"), and when in a second reduction, the "Ear" is deprived of ambient sound, "I, and Silence" emerge as kindred, one bred from the other, even though they are taxonomically incommensurable, since the depersonalized "I" is still an entity, while "Silence" is the remainder that survives sound's extinction. The conjunction of such correlatives that pull agonistically in discrete directions precipitates the breakdown—as when what is deafeningly heard ceases and nothing can be heard; as when spheres of unknowing ("hit a World, at every plunge") energize the speaker's mere perception that still to be conscious is, with each "plunge," to be somewhere new that is uncharted; and as when the breakdown of "Sense" is linked to an assault of sensation.

A like onslaught of sensation is palpable in the third stanza of the following poem, which also documents a crack-up:

> The first Day's Night had come -
> And grateful that a thing
> So terrible - had been endured -
> I told my Soul to sing -
>
> She said her strings were snapt -
> Her Bow - to atoms blown -
> And so to mend her - gave me work
> Until another Morn -
>
> And then - a Day as huge
> As Yesterdays in pairs,
> Unrolled it's horror in my face -
> Until it blocked my eyes -
>
> My Brain - begun to laugh -
> I mumbled - like a fool -
> And tho' 'tis Years ago - that Day -
> My Brain keeps giggling - still.

And Something's odd - within -
That person that I was -
And this One - do not feel the same -
Could it be Madness - this?
(F 423)

Scene that applies itself to the eyes—occluding all that could be seen outside its widening scope—explains the rhetorical question of the poem's last line: "Could it be Madness - this?" A past to the "terrible -" event is anticipated, but the past never arrives. Rather, there is a "snap[ping]," and then an amplification of the darkness inherent in the "first Day's Night." Because the augmentation is repeated in the plural of "yesterday" and the plural of "pair" ("Yesterdays in pairs"), the magnification, beyond mere doubling, intimates an excess that can't be figured—half simile, half metaphor: the proliferation disseminates horror everywhere. For though "As Yesterdays in pairs" initially looks like a simple comparative clause, it does not quite make realist sense as such. For this reader, it shifts into a simile of temporal impaction that interrupts a sustained metaphor ("a Day as huge / . . . Unrolled it's horror in my face - / Until it blocked my eyes -"), interposed between the parts of an overarching conceit. Unlike Donne's "all my pleasures are like yesterday,"[11] which identifies pleasure as being as finished as yesterday is finished, this "horror" won't stay finished, but replicates "Yesterday" more than two times over; its residue lingers and then aggrandizes in those plurals that attack the eyes. A state of affairs that isn't right, noted in the first stanza, in the third becomes a state of affairs that is irrecoverable.

The first two stanzas of the following poem record a blow that also deranges vision:

It struck me - every Day -
The Lightning was as new
As if the Cloud that instant slit
And let the Fire through -

It burned Me - *in* the Night -
It Blistered *to* My Dream -

It sickened fresh *opon* my sight -
With every Morn that came -

I thought that Storm - was brief -
The Maddest - quickest by -
But Nature lost the Date of This -
And left it in the Sky -
(F 636; italics mine)

The jolt of energy, metaphorized as a bolt of lightning initially in the atmosphere, bursts onto the speaker's body ("It burned Me -") and into the mind, penetrating "My Dream -" so that there is no place the fiery violence fails to register. In the second stanza, the prepositions "in . . . to . . . opon" perform the omnipresent agency of an "It" whose unspecified antecedent, averted by successive metaphors ("Lightning," "Fire," "Maddest" "Storm"), is abstracted into an inclusiveness that exceeds a single source, which, even identified, could account for the profusion of bodily and mental injury. A burn infects scenes that the mind's eye projects in sleep ("Blistered [in] to My Dream -") and also seeps into waking sight, plaguing not only what the eyes take in, but what they crowd out, blinding the speaker to everything but that initial vision whose immediacy does not wane ("Nature lost the Date of This -") while each time experienced with novelty at a shock that does not exhaust itself. In the harrowing "It struck me every day" and "The first day's night had come," a visual surplus emerges from a psychic trauma, while the poem below concludes with a deviant simile—deviant because it optically heals the ruptures whose consequences it is also called on to express:

I felt a Cleaving in my Mind -
As if my Brain had split -
I tried to match it - Seam by Seam -
But could not make them fit -

The thought behind, I +strove to join
Unto the thought before -

But Sequence ravelled out of +Sound
Like Balls - opon a Floor -

strove] tried   Sound] reach -
(F 867)

The poem records a psychic split ("Cleaving"), a material split (fabric that pulls apart "Seam by Seam -"), a conceptual split (in which the mind cannot hear itself think), and a grammatical split, in which the syntactic inversion of object before subject in the choppy predication of "The thought behind, I strove to join / Unto the thought before -" has more than the enjambment to overcome in enacting the very gap of its failed juncture. These rifts leave in their wake a surplus of acoustic and visual sensation. The poem concludes with an image for the mental silence that—unlike the preceding ruptures—visually coheres. "Balls -," presumably of yarn, soundlessly unwinding, or fraying like sanity, do not figure the absence of temporal connection so much as its consequence: auditory deprivation, the mind struck dumb. Yet the simile for this devastation—for a standstill in which one thought does not succeed another—is an optical supplement to, and thus an escape from, the poem's multiple schisms. The strands of yarn twisted together "Cleav[e]" to each other intact as they unroll, proposing an antithetical primal word, and an antithetical sense—"Cleaving" as joining rather than as sundering—to that of the poem's first line: a scene in miniature that paradoxically figures the breakdown through an image of continuity denied the mind when thoughts cannot be unified and do not *make sense*. In this poem, visual sensation is a compensatory plenitude that replaces sense.

In Dickinson's poems of breakdown, thought and feeling are consistently expelled to a field of vision, into an appearance, an "outside," that thought, feeling, and the abstraction, existence itself, do not possess—as when "Mourners" walk "to and fro" in "I felt a funeral in my brain" (F 340); as when the incalculable depth of being is epitomized, extrapolated, and installed in an organ of hearing ("Being, but an Ear" [F 340]); as when mental "fire," affixed to the eyes, "sickened fresh opon my sight -" (F 636). What are these if not the mind's immaterial occupants reshaped, embodied, and figuratively released—*seen* within a *scene*? Ejected from interior space—from the "Corridors -" of "The Brain" (F 407)—and placed within an external setting, often advanced by a sequence, mental experience is open to view in scenes that are a prolonged catachresis figuring unpicturable references that are intrinsically ineffable. Thoughts and feelings extruded into scene are at once estranged from recognition because they have been rendered visible, and are simultaneously identifiable because they have been manifested. Such a double sense, and for the reader a related double take, attends the following poem, an allegory of sexual fascination and fulfillment that unfolds in a narrative—or rather in the sharp disparity of two narrative settings—in which we witness experiences each scenically out of view of the other:

I started Early - Took my Dog -
And visited the Sea -
The Mermaids in the Basement
Came out to look at me -

And Frigates - in the Upper Floor
Extended Hempen Hands -
Presuming Me to be a Mouse -
Aground - opon the Sands -

But no Man moved Me - till the Tide
Went past my simple Shoe -
And past my Apron - and my Belt
And past my +Boddice - too -

And made as He would eat me up -
As wholly as a Dew
Opon a Dandelion's Sleeve -
And then - I started - too -

And He - He followed - close behind -
I felt His Silver Heel

Opon my Ancle - Then My Shoes
Would overflow with Pearl -

Until We met the Solid Town -
No +One He seemed to know -
And bowing - with a Mighty look -
At me - The Sea withdrew -

Boddice] Bosom. Buckle One] man -
(F 656)

With the flick of a detail—a dog walk to the sea—the poem's first lines summon a peopled world, even if the people are not yet stirring, within a realistic scene in which the throng of workaday arrangements, still in abeyance, are signaled as backdrop to the quotidian walk. In a second scene, no less real, but with differently persuasive coordinates, the speaker is visually drawn toward the surface of the water by ropes ("Hempen Hands -") that extend from "Frigates" and simultaneously toward its depth by nymphs who rise up: they "came out to look at me -." When the "Solid Town -" gives onto the flowing "Sea -," the waves of water merge with waves of desire; the garb of the speaker with a "Dandelion's Sleeve -" (a trope for the leafy receptacle bearing the blossom head); the desire of a "Man" with that of the speaker: he "made as He would eat me up - / As wholly as a Dew / Opon a Dandelion's Sleeve - / And then - I started - too -."[12] All fluid and fluent. All but the diction—the puerile "Mouse / Aground -" . . . "Basement" for ocean bottom—that awkwardly marks the shift to a scene that shares no common tongue with dog-walk parlance.

The poem's conceits reveal a polarity more subtle than that of the juxtaposed scenes. A conceit enacts a transport in which one thing is enlisted to express another. But in Dickinson's "I started early took my dog" (F 656), tropes simultaneously ensure and resist identification, as when "Then My Shoes / Would overflow with Pearl -" names the man's ejaculate, seen through the froth of sea foam, even as the glamour of that image surpasses what it figures. In the same way, the poem's concluding personification—"And bowing - with a Mighty look - / At me - The Sea withdrew"—plainly alludes to the curl of the retreating wave, but no less to the lover's postcoital withdrawal, yet in diction so grand that it presumes an import in excess of what is imparted. The sensuous eroticism even of the phrase "would eat me up -" elicits both less and more than a figure of desire. If the "Sea" swells into a tumescent lover, "He," too, is a mere metaphor for the superfluity that engulfs this poem in which scene is continuously forced from mere sensation—into which it again dissolves. "And then - I started - too -" might be construed as the speaker's response to the lover's spasm. But in "He - He followed - close behind -" we hear, outside of any scene, one distended latently sensuous syllable trailing itself, a bliss almost purely auditory. From these moments of surfeit—and this sublimity—the splendor of sexual transport breaks free of agency (whether of the "Sea," a "He," or a she), rewriting the communion of "Sea" and she into a vision that exceeds both. The scene of the "Silver Heel" is not just erotic as distinct from routine—that is, distinct from the poem's first line—it also transmutes the routine of the erotic into a *look* that partakes of neither: august, opaque, and immediate, reflecting something beyond contrast or encounter.

In distinction to the scenic incarnation of out-of-body transport to such numinous goals as "Eternity -" (F 453) or "Immortality -" (F 743), whose contact with these immensities swallows up sensation in voids like God (F 525), "I felt a funeral in my brain" constructs a scene for mental breakdown in which sensation overwhelms "Reason" and, in the plummet downward ("hit a World, at every plunge"), "Being" itself (F 340). A similar glut affects "the Sky -" and the eye in "It struck me every day" (F 636), when a fiery charge leaves an optic "Bliste[r]" that hinders vision. That occlusion then itself becomes a scene, the only one a speaker can behold. In "I felt a cleaving in my mind" (F 867), scene breaks through material, temporal, and conceptual splits, into a cohesive image of these breaches—picturing the ruptures (strands of yarn unfurling) while repairing them in a counterimage (since the remainder yarn retains its unified spherical shape). In these poems, Dickinson repeatedly employs a scene that can be envisioned as a metaphor for, or as a fitting site of, states of mind or being that cannot be. Sensation is the cause and sometimes the effect of optic damage, mental derangement, and of bliss that spills out of range of the scenic confinement that would shape it. In poems to which I now turn, sensation has neither a symptomatic nor a compensatory presence, but rather supplements abstractions that are bereft of situating particulars.

iii

The following poem occludes a context that would account for a scene in which a speaker is imprisoned and then released from one domain to its slant antithesis, from confinement to a periphery:

> I saw no Way - The Heavens were stitched -
> I felt the Columns close -
> The Earth reversed her Hemispheres -
> I touched the Universe -
>
> And back it slid - and I alone -
> A speck opon a Ball -
> Went out opon Circumference -
> Beyond the Dip of Bell -
> (F 633)

Though the speaker is liberated to a "Circumference -" (the line around the circle that marks distance from a center), this freedom, or expulsion, does not imply a breakthrough of the columns that enclosed her laterally, nor a piercing through the stitches that restricted access to "The Heavens" above. Rather, deliverance materializes in another region by a flip of the earth's two spheres, which, dislodged, leave an opening. For notwithstanding the shifting movements (closing, reversing, sliding) and the incommensurable forms ("Columns," "speck," "Earth," "Universe -") they set in motion, there is no inherent relation between the "Heavens" that constrict and the "Hemispheres" that subvert the impediment. Moreover, liberty has the feel of bondage, since solitude is enforced by an exploit undertaken involuntarily when the "Universe -" deposits the speaker on its verge. Or does her "touc[h]" impel freedom? But how could the cosmos surrender to a touch? How could all matter and space considered as the whole that is the "Universe -" *be* touched? The poem has no interest in engaging questions of agency, or revealing a cause for these colossal shifts. Rather the sudden transmutation of one plight to an antithesis itself becomes the scene.

The cool objectivity of Dickinson's restraint governs not only the unnerving description of the speaker's fate but also the omission of any response to her extravagant delivery. That reserve is punctured by a burst of sensory detail in the poem's final images. The juxtaposition of the "speck" that is the speaker to the "Ball -" that is the "Universe -" reiterates the antipodal principle introduced by the swing from bondage to liberty, a transfer repeated one more time in "Beyond the Dip of Bell -," a "Dip" that figures the clapper's movement from one side to the other and, in its decreasing acceleration as the vibrations die away, its silence. In this fluctuation, "Dip of Bell -" explodes with a palpability that grounds abstraction in sensation, and then extinguishes both. That extinction is the "Beyond" where the last line strands the speaker. Yet something is grasped from the stillness—a resonance of what can no longer be heard that sounds against the stringent aesthetic shaping of the poem's sparse details. Dickinson's renditions of occluded scene cannot be captured by any single predicate or any single relation between scene and what is seen. In the first stanzas of the following poem, the negations of scene are embedded in what is viewed by one and inflicted on another who reciprocates the assault:

Like Eyes that looked on Wastes -
Incredulous of Ought
But Blank - and steady Wilderness -
Diversified by Night -

Just Infinites of Nought -
As far as it could see -
So looked the face I looked opon -
So looked itself - on Me -

I offered it no Help -
Because the Cause was Mine -
The Misery a Compact
As hopeless - as divine -

Neither would be absolved -
Neither would be a Queen
Without the Other - Therefore -
We perish - tho' We reign -
(F 693)

Though the poem omits the source of the "Misery" that precipitates the first line's simile, what is "Like Eyes that looked on . . . Nought -" if not the "Compact" of this lethal, mutual looking? The novel rendering of "Infinites of Nought -" is augmented by "Blank - and steady Wilderness - / Diversified by Night -"—additions that might be thought gratuitous since the plural "Infinites" form an omnitude. But "Nought -" has a heterogeneity that emerges from nowhere recognizable. The constellations of "Nought -"—nothing that constitutes scene in the nihilistic gazes, and the absence of sound and movement that can neither be heard nor seen in "Beyond the Dip of Bell -"—withhold the logic that would press their contrary parts into intelligibility. Yet the poems are august and mysterious in their sonic and conceptual rhyming of stratospheric opposites, as when in "Like eyes that looked on wastes," "Ought"[13] (anything at all, everything) is drawn into intimate contact with "Nought -" (nothing at all). Or as when celestial and planetary spheres, though categorically riven, are contrasted in the cryptic sequence of the abstruse unfolding of "I saw no way." The sensory flood issuing from that profusive "Dip" entangles bell and clapper within a play of graphic and phonic equivalences—as when "Bell -" visually rhymes with "Ball -," and in "Like eyes that looked on wastes" as when "Night -" echoes "Nought -," constituting an aberrant opulence. Such scenes lure and alienate when, as in the poem below, they materialize incandescent spots of nothing that can be grasped:

The Tint I cannot take - is best -
The Color too remote
That I could show it in Bazaar -
A Guinea at a sight -

The fine - impalpable Array -
That swaggers on the eye

Like Cleopatra's Company -
Repeated - in the sky -

The Moments of Dominion
That happen on the Soul
And leave it with a Discontent
Too exquisite - to tell -

The eager look - on Landscapes -
As if they just repressed
Some secret - that was pushing
Like +Chariots - in the Vest -

The Pleading of the Summer -
That other Prank - of Snow -
That +Cushions Mystery with Tulle,
For fear the Squirrels - know.

Their Graspless manners - mock us -
Until the Cheated Eye
Shuts arrogantly - in the Grave -
Another way - to see -

Chariots - in the Vest -] Columns - in the Breast -
Cushions Mystery with Tulle,] Covers Mystery with Blonde –
(F 696)

The objectification conferred by all those *The*s ("The Tint . . . The Color . . . The . . . Array - . . . The Moments . . . The . . . look - . . . The Pleading") locks the instances into a sum total. Everything seen, all the surfaces evoked—whose diversity stands for a more enveloping all that does not require further exemplification—reveal a sublimity that balks vision and expression. The scenes that register "on the eye," "in the sky -," across "Landscapes -," within seasons, "on the Soul" are surfaces that do not yield up the elusive phenomena whose existence they augur. They allure and enchant, but do not impart. They engulf (as the seasons do), engross (as color does), beckon (as the "Landscapes -" do), almost avow (like the "Moments of Dominion") but then withhold. These different forms of resistance to disclosure, and even to manifestation, would seem to drive the scenes apart as categorically unassimilable. Thus the display of gaudy color personified by analogy to the opulence of "Cleopatra's Company -" briefly incarnates the incorporeal "Tint," while the "Moments of Dominion / That happen on the Soul"—an idiom for *happen by surprise*, rather than the superficial *take place on*—have no heft and do not linger or penetrate the soul. Yet the intangibles have the same value—they are rare, resplendent, sovereign, fleeting, and leave this residue: "Discontent / Too exquisite - to tell -." By an arcane economy, "Discontent" (which tacitly contains traces of these fugitive encounters) is hoarded—as though the "Tint" in the unintended slant rhyme "tint" / "tent" (latent in "Discontent") has escaped the speaker's relinquishment of it. Though the last stanza alleges that intimations had in bodily life will be divulged only after death, soul-knowing is imperfectly glimpsed *while embodied* within crossover inklings whose insufficiency torments. The poem charts a more enveloping sense of sweeping loss than of what slips away. When in "The tint I cannot take is best" (F 696) the speaker sees the "eager look - on Landscapes -" look back at her "As if they just repressed / Some secret - that was pushing / Like Chariots - in the Vest -," she gleans, but cannot extract, the object of the urgency. How landscapes "look" to the speaker is certainly meant to indicate the gaze she casts upon them. But there is an implied second sense of the "look on [*the face of*] Landscapes"—how they look in a personification introduced by the verb "repressed" to signal the burial of a "secret - . . . in the Vest" (a near displacement of "Breast -," one of the variants), not in the West that the spirited "Chariots -" lead us to anticipate. This evocative "look" is one the speaker can't penetrate.

Such barriers emerge across the journey poems ("God - at every Gate -" [F 453]), the trauma poems (where parallel vantages refer to a spectacle a speaker witnesses when an unconscious thought is transported across her "Soul," but also to *her* unconsciousness when she loses the capacity to witness anything [F 340]), and poems that are virtually stripped of content as in the baffling reflexive looking that defines an expenditure of waste (in "Like eyes that looked on wastes -" [F 693]) whose ravages reduce "Ought" to "Nought" (F 693). In the lines "Behind Me - dips Eternity - / Before Me - Immortality -" (F 743), profusive sound foils sense when the *m* phoneme, that bilabial nasal, is heard even in the silently uttered words "Immortality," "Me -," "Monarchy -," "Miracle," "Midnight," "Maelstrom -." When *m* blocks air through the mouth, the vocal cords vibrate in a diffusive hum that is more persuasive than the attempt to schematize the categorical notions of "Eternity -" and "Immortality -," whose references in Dickinson's poems are inventive and tentative. By one means or another in Dickinson's poems, sensation overtakes abstraction. In "I saw no way," taxonomic sites ("Heavens" and "Hemispheres -" [F 633]) are engulfed in the immersive "Dip of Bell -," whose effects surpass the solid classifications of the poem's first lines. We hear the furor of breaking . . . "creak[ing] . . . toll[ing] . . . drop[ping] . . . plung[ing] . . . finish[ing]" throughout "I felt a funeral in my brain" (F 340) that almost drowns out the "treading" of the ephemeral "Mourners" in the poem's first stanza. In "It struck me every day" (F 636) and "The first day's night had come" (F 423), sensation rages in the "burn[ing]," "Blister[ing]," "sicken[ing]" that vitalizes shock from the "Storm" that "struck me - every Day -" (F 636) and from "Yesterdays in pairs" that "Unrolled" its "horror in my face -" (F 423)—extremities that swell to occupy the space left void by the undisclosed source of these derangements. The sterility of generic abstraction (what kind of storm? struck by what?) is rectified in each by an onslaught of effects that sting, sear, and blind. The question "Infinitude - Had'st Thou no Face . . . ?" (F 525) directly anatomizes that void—no bearing and no features, nothing from which sensation could emanate, even as the word "Face" awakens a visceral hunger that momentarily breathes life into an All without attributes. In "I started early took my dog" (F 656), the humdrum scene of a dog walk segues into a scene of erotic pleasure. Then, in another transposition, that pleasure (grounded where?) is surpassed by a superfluity of sensation that almost submerges the tenor in the surfeit of the vehicle which slides free of scene and sense. These poems dilate on violent perturbations, on effects divorced from causes. They lodge on surfaces. In "The tint I cannot take is best"

(F 696), rapture reclaims the treasure lurking within the penury the poem celebrates—awakened by savoring what dwells below the surface forever out of sight. By distinction, in the following lines, John Ashbery *gives face* to the unseen "core"—the referential ineffable—by equating it with the "surface": "your eyes proclaim / That everything is surface. The surface is what's there / . . . The surface . . . is not / Superficial but a visible core."[14] But Dickinson sustains the impasse between surface and core when she futilely coaxes the apostrophized "Infinitude" to reveal—or rather to possess—a reference or a "Face" (F 525).

iv

Examining the rhetorical figure of "prosopopoeia"—the trope that personifies how what has no face is given face—Paul de Man writes: "Rather than being a heightened version of sense experience, the erotic is a figure that makes such experience possible. We do not see what we love but we love in the hope of confirming the illusion that we are indeed seeing anything at all."[15] To gloss the last sentence, objects we see and love recede before something more essential that their existence validates: a world *with* objects that *can be seen* (and loved). De Man's claim that "the erotic" is a figure that "makes [sensory] experience possible" bears on the flood of sensation that succeeds the dog walk and the ocean wave, revealing something primary that antecedes and underlies all scenic configuration. In de Man's larger claim, "concepts"—akin to what I have been calling abstractions—are without "material reference" and therefore require sensory impression to validate them:

> As most philosophers well know, the very concept of certainty, which is the basis of all concepts, comes into being only in relation to sensory experience. . . . If there is to be consciousness (or experience, mind, subject, discourse, or face), it has to be susceptible of phenomenalization.[16]

I will return to de Man's point that postulates what I have particularized in Dickinson's poems when abstractions are made palpable by the sensory impressions that overtake them. But first, consider the following two poems—one rooted in time and space, and one divested of both, even as each moves beyond the *there is* that differently constitutes it. "There's a certain slant of light" (F 320) reaches past the temporal-spatial coordinates that anchor it to dilate on something seen whose effects escape manifestation:

> There's a certain Slant of light,
> Winter Afternoons -
> That oppresses, like the Heft
> Of Cathedral Tunes -
>
> Heavenly Hurt, it gives us -
> We can find no scar,
> But internal difference -
> Where the Meanings, are -
>
> None may teach it - Any -
> 'Tis the Seal Despair -
> An imperial affliction
> Sent us of the Air -
>
> When it comes, the Landscape listens -
> Shadows - hold their breath -
> When it goes, 'tis like the Distance
> On the look of Death -
>
> (F 320)

The "certain Slant of light" is deictic, singling out *this* one, mirrored in a series of identifiable effects. It has a source (the adjective "Heavenly Hurt" specifies agency as well as origin: "Hurt" dispensed from Heaven as well as deriving from that location); an immaterial consequence, "internal difference -," without embodiment or display ("no scar"); an intractability ("None may teach it - Any[thing]"); an incommunicability ("None may teach it [to] Any [one else]"); and a fatality (it precipitates "Despair -" and "Seal[s]" it in). The "imperial affliction," like the "Hurt" that leaves "no scar," could never be evinced, though it is transmitted by pellucid "Air -." The "Slant," the "Heft," the "Hurt," the "internal difference -," the "Seal Despair -," and finally "the Distance / On the look of Death -" flow into each other. They are "of" each other in the way the "imperial affliction" is "of the Air -." Though not grammatically in apposition, "Slant," "Heft," "Hurt," "Despair," "Distance / On the look of Death -" read as synonyms rotated toward each other from discrete perspectives revealing consequences of that "Slant." And although the genitive "of" in "the Distance / On the look of Death -" proximately associates the extinction of the "light" at day's end with the "look of Death -"—with what death looks like seen from a distance and by analogy—the poem more inclusively also yokes "the look of Death -" to the initial vision of the "light." It does so by coupling "When it comes" with "When it goes," even though a personification intervenes to disrupt the syntax. We read across the divide to see the immediate course into the ultimate. The "look of Death -" is not only what death looks like at a distance from its experienced actuality, but also what death looks like, through a glance backward, *within* the "Slant of light." That confluence—not the clang of "Cathedral Tunes -"—is what makes this a religious poem without the content of traditional religion.[17] The mere beholding of the "Slant" is angled to permit relations discerned across phenomena that could not be seen straight on. Even the personifications ("the Landscape listens - / Shadows - hold their breath -") are opaque. What one sees in landscape and shadow is surface: one looks at, rather than through, them. The "look of Death," however, is not a personification. "Look" does not mean "face." The "Slant of light," pitched across the scene of these particulars that give onto each other, reveals conjoined opposites—"of the Air -"/"of Death -"; "breath -"/"Death -"—matching what is essential with what voids essence.

The following groundless scenes record a visitation that, like "the Slant of light" (F 320), ranges over everything:

In many and reportless places
We feel a Joy -
Reportless, also, but sincere as Nature
Or Deity -

It comes, without a consternation -
+Dissolves - the same -
But leaves a +sumptuous Destitution -
Without a Name -

Profane it by +a search - we cannot -
It has no home -
Nor we who having once +inhaled it -
Thereafter roam.

Dissolves -] abates -. Exhales. sumptuous] blissful
a search] pursuit inh*aled it*] wayl*aid it*
(F 1404; italics mine)

A residue survives the elusiveness recorded in "reportless places." The "places" are "reportless," the "Joy -" is "reportless," and the "Destitution -" is "reportless"—a word that one might have thought had a coinage tending toward the ineffable, but which Dickinson's *Lexicon* glosses as "not well known, without repute." Yet something has been reported. An intimation unexpectedly traverses the "Slant of light" and "the look of Death -" to link them in the decisive action recorded in that poem, while in "reportless places" "Joy -" that seemed intangible becomes weighty—as when, internalized, it sweeps through and infects its witnesses, who mimetically themselves become nomadic. We also hear the internalization resounding from a phonetic chiasmus at the poem's end when, in an encounter with "Joy -," an echo arises mid-variant as "*'aid/'t*" answered in uptake by the fuller breath of "*'aled/'t.*" In that effect there is a synthesis of the phonetic sensation embodied in sounding the words and the feeling that their semantic content can never quite name. Although the bare scene in "Slant" could be regarded as routine—a light that might always be observed under conditions stipulated by the poem—while the scenes in "reportless places" are unique, the poems share a transport that carries one extreme into the arms of its antithesis. Thus the impossibility of extracting "Destitution -" from the modifying adjective "sumptuous" (or from its variant "blissful"). In that congruence, "Destitution -" is saturated with opulence, with a plenitude of bliss that the *Lexicon* calls "grand." Both poems evoke an impersonal "we" that orients vision to a shared intensity ("We can find no scar" / "We feel a Joy -"), just as the source of their composure is fostered by the consonance of "Nature / Or Deity -," implied in one poem and specified in the other. The two converge obliquely in the "light" imbued with "Heavenly Hurt" (F 320) and specified in "reportless places" (F 1404) where "Joy -" is avowed "*sincere* as Nature / Or Deity" (italics mine)—*sincere* from the Latin "clean, pure, sound"; in the *Lexicon*, "undeceiving"; in Webster's, "unmixed," "being what it appears," "real," complete—as when one part of experience flows from another; as when the "look of Death -" issues from "the Slant of light"; as when "Joy -" arises amid the "Destitution" it cannot temper; as when perception and opacity lean into each other within these emerging visions of improbable wholes.

In such scenes of disclosure and concealment, Dickinson marks the place where vision is occluded: "Midnight to the North of Her - / And Midnight to the South of Her - / And Maelstrom - in the Sky -" (F 743). There is a thrill in these failed vision poems that locate suspense not in any unusual discovery, but in the speakers' absorptive looking. While the poems insist on the illegibility of certain scenes ("Vast Prairies of Air . . . all that I could see -" [F 525]), the act of looking itself becomes arresting. The domestic objects that block supernatural vision—the "fly" in the celebrated "I heard a fly buzz when I died" (F 591); the "Horses' Heads" in "Because I could not stop for death" (F 479); the "Sheets of Place -" (F 901), whose categorical vacancy denies the epiphanic vision sought at that poem's beginning—are themselves invested with wonder that has rubbed off from the act of looking at these mundane objects. In the poems that aspire to preternatural vision, the goal is uncanny, the obstacles are uncanny, and the looking is uncanny. Poems like "There's a certain slant of light" (F 320) transform what is recognizable, while the quest poems dismantle our assumptions about what could never be recognized. Although a poem like "I saw no way" (F 633) is unhooked from situating coordinates, it is perfectly legible in identifying a visual and audible curve—a "Dip" (F 633), an edge, an outer limit, in which release from a mystifying imprisonment is more terrifying and more exhilarating than the state from which the speaker has been liberated. Dickinson's speakers desire a breakthrough experience that would open to ubiquity. But ubiquity, like "Infinitude" (F 525), has no face, though the region beyond the precarity of that "Dip" (F 633) has a look, or perhaps just a "feel," like the "Stars about" another speaker's "Head" (F 926) in a poem—with which I conclude—in which geographic pathways block out scene, both map it and mark it as indecipherable:

> I stepped from Plank to Plank
> A slow and cautious way
> The Stars about my Head I felt
> About my Feet the Sea -
>
> I knew not but the next
> Would be my final inch -
> This gave me that precarious Gait
> Some call Experience -
> (F 926)

At the end of the first stanza, there is a mimetic chiasmus (one scale up in syntax from the phonetic chiasmus in F 1404) where "About my Feet the Sea -" is a circumambience more normatively specified by a syntactic rhythm: "Stars" above me, below me "Sea -." The poem concretely evokes a walk on a plank bridge with dangerous waters splashing up around a speaker's feet in bad weather. But the details that would flesh out the circumstances of her experience are incommensurate, and so is the poem's scale. While in rough weather it would be physically possible for the sea to swirl around the speaker's feet, it would not be physically possible for her head to abut the stars, or for her to *feel* the stars, rather than to *see* them. Perhaps the speaker is recounting a nightmare in which *feeling* the stars is a dream distortion of *fearing* that the stars will press down upon her as the water rises up from below. But why is the past tense of the word *feel* used to indicate both an experience that is perfectly imaginable if she is walking on a plank bridge and one that could never be imagined as literal? Why does the personally apocalyptic vision (the step that would be the speaker's last) expand to include what surpasses the personal? The site graphs a set of coordinates—"Plank/Plank": "Stars/Sea -"—that constitute horizontal and vertical expanses, while omitting the mid-world of legible phenomena that might orient the speaker. Put differently, a chiasmus governs the coordinates above/below: about/about, thus revealing there is no *there* in the precarity "Some call Experience -." Such syntactic and phonic chiasms read as an immediate felt substitute for an impalpable vividness of feeling. At the same time, or rather elsewhere, from within the modest word "felt" that haunts the intermundane space separating "Stars" and "Sea -," the poem transmits the queasy specificity that is Dickinson's signature. Across her poems, unfigurable sensation and slant abstractions combine to mediate scenelessness in an approach to feeling with a sensory dimension all its own.

Finally, because chiasmic relations govern not only the interiors of Dickinson's poems, but also overarchingly the alternate abstraction and sensorium between which the poems vacillate, I touch one last time, now in a broader context, on how the relation between the tangible and the visible (and their inverses) might be construed outside of the deconstructive terms proposed by de Man, for whom "the claim of all poetry to make the invisible visible is a figure to the precise extent that it undoes the distinction between sign and trope."[18] In contrast, the cultural theorist Leela Gandhi considers the problem in philosophical and historical terms. Gandhi writes: "Abstraction . . . is long situated at the confluence of idealism and materialism as something concurrently sensory and extrasensory. Such an outlook points to the chiasmatic quality of abstraction. By that I mean a crisscross arrangement in which adversarial elements (mind/matter, spirit/flesh, visible/invisible) are placed in an intersectional relationship, and through which they partake in a shared state of reversibility."[19] She adds: "A true abstraction is manifest and intelligible. It has a breakthrough quality."[20] For Dickinson, however, the breakthrough quality of "intelligibil[ity]" that Gandhi describes never quite happens. Within her poems, abstraction and sensation do not achieve the concurrence posited by de Man in the coupling of trope/sign, and by Gandhi in that of abstraction/sensation. Nor in Dickinson's poems do antagonisms disappear as in the "axial" paradigm at the heart of Gandhi's analysis.[21] Perhaps this is because Gandhi is exploring a categorical concept, like that of Number, or God, or Justice, whereas Dickinson's poems trace alienating experiences of shifting cognitive states, like that of ecstasy, or existential anxiety, wonder, or mortal trepidation. In her poems, abstraction and sensation could not squeeze into the narrow model offered by de Man, and their unique interactions would get lost within Gandhi's exhaustive model. Nor could any theoretical paradigm reflect the frontier encounters in which in these poems sensation and abstraction cross, always in motion around each other, along with the shifting mental states they register.[22] A simple chiastic reversal operates in the homonyms in "Our journey had advanced" (F 453), where "before" initially means *behind* and then *ahead of*. These antitheses are mere placeholders (like "about/about" [F 926]) that don't tangibly situate, though the speaker is caught between them in a constriction that prohibits escape. More complexly, chiastic relations in Dickinson's poems also redefine the positions of sensation and abstraction tout court, as when in "I started early took my dog" (F 656), a poem that frankly defies categories as such, the contrasted scenes of dog walk and sexual commerce are weighted down by solid details, while the sensation that exceeds both scenes so that no site grounds it is oxymoronically abstract. In another manifestation of their torqued relation, in "My period had come for prayer," the metaphor that corporealizes the invisible *air* in "Vast Pr*air*ies of Air" (F 525) literally contains the word that ostensibly required troping. Where, here, does abstraction end when what is sensory and what is extrasensory can't syllabically be extracted from each other?

I reiterate these examples to stress that Dickinson's poems never relinquish the pull between incommensurate pieces of world which emerge in each poem anew, as when the "Slant of light" that can be seen and "the look of Death -" (F 320) that cannot be seen are drawn into the same space, but don't give onto each other, even as one seems to mark the inception of the other. In the same way stopping and not stopping (F 479), mourning and relishing (F 696), sensation that exceeds the boundaries of scene and sensation defined by those boundaries (F 1404), the "Stars" and the "Sea -" (F 926), the

"Dip of Bell -" and "Beyond" (F 633), abstraction and sensation—are all folded upon each other; their distinct idioms may not merge or even meet, yet they can't be torn asunder. Such poems stop short of meaning but are redolent of it, like a strange kind of proto-writing whose sense is too far off or too close-up, beyond calculation; sublimes that lean toward or away from each other to form unsituated wholes—illegible, yes, but thick with lived experience whose cohesion cannot be breached.

Something like Nebraska and Something like Virginia

CATHER'S INCOMMENSURABLES

At the end of Willa Cather's *The Professor's House*, Professor Godfrey St. Peter is awaiting the return of his wife Lillian, daughter Rosamond, and son-in-law Louie, who are unexpectedly returning early from a vacation in France.[1] Reading the letter announcing the homecoming, St. Peter's first thought is that "there must be some way in which a man who had always tried to live up to his responsibilities could, when the hour of desperation came, avoid meeting his own family" (*PH* 274). His sudden aversion is understood as a change of heart: though "he loved his family" and "would make any sacrifice for them," St. Peter now "wanted to run away from everything he had intensely cared for" (*PH* 274, 275). Contemplating the impassivity that has displaced his feelings not only for his family, but for his own past ("He did not regret his life, but he was indifferent to it" [*PH* 267]), St. Peter thinks: "If his apathy hurt [his family], they could not possibly be so much hurt as he had been already" (*PH* 283). Cather never specifies the source of that "hurt," even though the word is provocatively introduced three sentences before the novel's end (*PH* 283). Thus the reader must think back to discover what precipitated an affliction whose extremity—notwithstanding the flat, smooth, affectless language that seems to express it—is punctuated by the extraordinary psychic calculation in which St. Peter assesses that he has endured more anguish than his family. Cather treats "hurt" as a psychological matter ("apathy," "hour of desperation" [*PH* 283, 274]) that morphs into an ontological one, concerning questions about being rather than questions about mind, as in Professor St. Peter's belated realization that a man's "first nature" could return to him (*PH* 267).

There is more than one candidate for the source of St. Peter's distress. Is its origin his discovery that the "life with this Kansas boy"—the young St. Peter—"was the realest of his lives," was essential, while everything that followed "had been accidental and ordered from the outside? His career, his wife, his family, were not his life at all, but a chain of events which had happened to him" (*PH* 264). Is its impetus St. Peter's sudden realization that despite "the fifteen years he had been working on his *Spanish Adventurers in North America*" (*PH* 25), he was not a "scholar" but "a primitive . . . only interested in earth and woods and water" (*PH* 265)? Does his distress arise from the belated insight that a "first nature could return to a man, unchanged by all the pursuits and passions and experiences of his life" at the very time "that he was nearing the end of his life" (*PH* 267)? Is the injury instigated by grief at the death of Tom Outland, who sparked a "romance" of "the imagination" that restored the grown man to "a kind of second youth" (*PH* 258), and by dismay at the use to which Tom's inheritance is put by the acquisitive Rosamond—St. Peter's daughter and Tom Outland's wife—her avarice being the opposite of Tom's "religious" feeling for the "value of . . . objects" discovered at Cliff City (*PH* 251, 245)? Of course, impassivity is itself a misery: "he knew that life is possible, may be even pleasant without joy, without passionate griefs. But it had never occurred to him that he might have to live like that" (*PH* 282). Or does injury more focally arise from the loss "of something very precious" ("he had let something go—and it was gone" [*PH* 282]), relinquished along with consciousness the moment St. Peter passes out in his study from the gas leak of an old stove that almost asphyxiates him?

The "something very precious" (*PH* 282) St. Peter lets go, like the unrivaled "hurt," eludes specification, even while the two are placeholders for what has no separate or static denomination. At the end of *The Professor's House*, there could be no isolated source of "hurt" and no one name for the loss of "something very precious" (*PH* 282). Were we to focus on these calamitous states, we would see that what apparently constitutes each is an aggregate of things that swarm into and out of each other, overlapping, diverging, fusing, with a fluidity that divests entities (whether "precious" things or sources of "hurt") of boundaries. While the kindred particulars materialize potential sources for the "hurt" (*PH* 283) and the loss (*PH* 282), the uncertainty about which one, or ones, constitute either afflictive state simultaneously disables any but a tenuous relation to these near abstractions, thus holding what can be identified and what resists identification in a queer suspension.

The radical indeterminacy of St. Peter's "hurt" in an open semantic field is more typically in Cather's writing dynamized by obvious tropes of transmutation and interchange, rather than mere multiplicity. Sometimes even at the level of an image or sentence, Cather's universe is Heraclitean and Ovidian, constituted by flux and metamorphosis, respectively. In *My Ántonia* a gesture and a posture before an ordinary Christmas tree ("there had been nothing strange about the tree before") converts not the tree but the aura that surrounds it—"but now . . . Grandfather merely put his finger-tips to his brow and bowed his venerable head, thus Protestantizing the atmosphere"[2]—even as the connotations of "Protestantizing" restore familiarity to the ambience transiently made alien. Such animation is the apparent antithesis of the momentarily gorgeous still life in *My Ántonia* of a "plough [that] had been left standing in the field. The sun was sinking just behind it. Magnified across the distance by the horizontal light, it stood out against the sun, was exactly contained within the circle of the disk; the handles, the tongue, the share—black against the molten red. There it was," personified, "heroic in size, a picture writing on the sun" (*Á* 181) whose beauty is caught in a figural stasis. Writing here seems to be a kind of motionless imprinting, an impress of momentary form burnished by the sun. And even this iconic image is immediately dimmed by the descent of light when "our vision disappeared. . . . The fields below us were dark . . . that forgotten plough had sunk back to its own littleness somewhere on the prairie" (*Á* 181).

Like the fugitive origins for St. Peter's "loss" and "hurt" (*PH* 282) and the fluctuating mood around Jim Burden's Christmas tree, mercurial sensations color the recitation of a story in its several recountings, and these differences meld when they do not supplant each other. The story from *My Ántonia* is introduced by Pavel, who, along with his comrade, Russian Peter (two immigrant Bohemian farmers, who live close to the children Jim and Ántonia), recounts a harrowing memory of a sledge ride in Russia late into the evening after a wedding celebration, when the party, "the worse for merrymaking," sets out in six sledges for home. Before they reach the village, they are chased by wolves—"bad that winter"—"that ran like streaks of shadow . . . there were hundreds of them" (Á 42). When the wolves overturn all but one of the sleds, Pavel tells the groom they must "lighten" the load "and pointed to the bride"; a "struggle" ensued and "Pavel knocked [the groom] over the side of the sledge and threw the girl after him" (Á 44). That is not the terminus of this thrilling but awful story of "the two men who had fed the bride to the wolves" (Á 44). Though Pavel and Peter arrive home safely, "they were run out of their village," and "wherever they went, the story followed them" (Á 44). With a like momentum, the story is transferred to the children's rehearsal of its titillating horror: "For Ántonia and me," the narrator recounts, "the story of the wedding party was never at an end," "as if the wolves of the Ukraine had gathered that night long ago, and the wedding party had been sacrificed, to give us a painful and peculiar pleasure" (Á 45). The tirelessly rehearsed anecdote is then adapted for private delectation in Jim's hypnagogic vision: "At night, before I went to sleep, I often found myself in a sledge drawn by three horses, dashing through a country that looked something like Nebraska and something like Virginia" (Á 45). The transit across the sites in which disaster unfolds and is relished—the catastrophe itself, its delicious recitation, its upbeat alternative to humdrum life, the bounty of enjoyment replenished from an undiminished resource—conflates revulsion and fascination, marrying and dying, serenity and crisis such that the tale abrades its frame, and the power wielded by the story cannot be attributed to any one of the scenes or the affective responses they elicit that become entangled in each other.

Though the site of the story's violent horror is initially Russia, it is mobilized in a sickroom in Nebraska, where in bed from a fall "as if . . . having bad dreams or . . . waking to some old misery"—a misery that has not yet been narrated for the reader—Pavel cries out in terror at the "whining howl" of the coyotes that he mistakes for "wolves." Ántonia explains: "in his country . . . they eat men and women"

(*Á* 40). Is it only long ago? So the Russian wolves have a spectral reappearance on the Nebraska prairie in Pavel's reexperiencing of his terror of them. The story drifts from "the dead of winter" (*Á* 42) in Russia to fall in Nebraska, where, in the dark at "the little house on the hillside . . . so much the color of the night" (*Á* 39), the narrator Jim—and where is he located?—retrospectively devours Pavel's story. Of course Pavel's story, as he unburdens himself of it to Mr. Shimerda, must first be translated by Ántonia before Jim can understand it. Though she elaborates details on the ride home, the story is revisited: "we talked of nothing else for days afterward" (*Á* 41). What Ántonia divulges in the bedroom—"It's wolves, Jimmy. . . . It's awful, what he says" (*Á* 41)—is, as noted, itself rescripted in the children's gleeful rehearsal of it, and in Jim Burden's dreams. Thus there is no single place, time, or affective hue that tinges the unfolding tale. It flows from one site to another, never exhausted, a rich repository of elements, with one crucial emotion ostentatiously banished from acknowledgment: that feeling would be guilt—a countercharge to Pavel's terror and the children's exhilaration. Guilt over the deaths of the innocent bride and groom—whose horrific sacrifice is the cost of Pavel's and Peter's survival—is the part of the story that has no place in anyone's recitation of it, even as its averted presence lingers around the story's edge, inescapably part of the anecdote, nowhere to be found in any of the accounts but in ghostly intimations, tingeing all the tale's incarnations.

The charge of that sublimated force is akin to what Cather called "the thing not named" when she famously wrote: "whatever is felt on the page without being specifically named there—that, one might say, is created. It is the inexplicable presence of the thing not named" (above, the source of the "hurt" [*PH* 283], the guilt, the loss of "something very precious" [*PH* 282]) "that gives high quality to the novel or the drama, as well as to poetry itself."[3] Cather attributed this elusiveness to the role of intimation, to "the overtone divined by the ear but not heard by it, the verbal mood, the emotional aura of the fact or the thing" (*NUF* 50).[4] "The thing not named" (*NUF* 50) in Cather's writing is not a particular thing, but rather evolves and mutates into heterogeneous transformations that resist classification.

In the following pages, I deploy the word "transposition" and its synonyms for shifts in emphasis, mood, and subject. The flux that couples incommensurate states and often does so in abrupt changes is the very method of Cather's storytelling in which energies that cannot be specified or acknowledged sweep through the writing, appearing and disappearing without warning or explanation. These transmutations are at the heart of Cather's writing and affect the construction of the image, the sentence, and the depiction of character, ontological state, and thus generically category. Metamorphosis is also conspicuous in the juxtapositions and vibrations of Cather's phrases. The passages in which these conversions predominate are essentially, though unsystematically, anti-narrative, registering insights that do not drive the story forward: they disrupt and subordinate straight-line continuities of narrative that divide things into units in a compulsively linear way.[5] In her assessment of *Death Comes to the Archbishop*, Cather wrote: "the essence of such writing is not to hold the note, not to use an incident for all there is in it—but to touch and pass on,"[6] a characterization applicable to the passages I consider, which pull away from the main narrative. One premise of the following pages then is that although Cather's plots can be gripping (as in the artistic growth of the Scandinavian American singer Thea Kronborg, whose musical career takes her from a small town in Nebraska to the Metropolitan Opera), sensational (as in Tom Outland's fate or Lucy Gayheart's), or tragic (as in "Paul's Case"), their stories momentarily fade in dominance before passages that loom at the edges of their portraits and compel attention. Transpositions occur in every register of Cather's writing—as when features that define individual characters also surpass that individuality so that what is "personal" and "impersonal" can't be disengaged from each other (examined in part i). Metamorphosis also dissolves the boundary lines across points where individual properties begin and end, as well as the breach that conceptually divides one mind from another. Other passages relax the border between the living and the dead, which is rendered permeable, as when in *O Pioneers!* Alexandra and her dead brother meet in a graveyard and share a memory neither can be said to have had (considered in part ii). And transmutation permeates Cather's style as when rhythm subtends, when it does not counter, the sense it helps convey (part iii). Part iv considers the ways in which unmoorings that drift across so many regions of Cather's writing constitute a special case of "the thing not named" (*NUF* 50).

Cather read Henri Bergson's *Creative Evolution* in 1912 and was especially struck by the first two chapters, in which Bergson insisted that "reality appears as a ceaseless upspringing of something new"[7]—specifically "a new form of consciousness, incommensurable with its antecedents" (*CE* 27). Bergson's "upspringing" embodied as "intuition" is elsewhere described in terms of transition and "becoming," in which "forms are no longer snapshots taken of the change, they are its constituent elements" (*CE* 317). In fact "form is only a snapshot view of a transition" (*CE* 302). Moreover, though "intuition," like these "forms," is "fugitive and incomplete, it is, in each system, what is worth more than the system and survives it" (*CE* 238).[8] Cather did not indicate the particulars that stirred her interest in Bergson's "intuition," but it is certainly the case that his characterization of "every pulsation of life" as "discontinuous" (*CE* 307) describes the volatile changes in Cather's transpositions. Yet for Bergson, "evolution" is a matter of radical, but simple, and continual change in which the "something new" (*CE* 47, 313) is detached from what precedes it. What is prior to the new reality can only be thought of as external to it—to suppose the two infuse each other or are alternatively related is a mistake of "mechanism" and "finalism."[9] For Cather, there is not this kind of subtraction amounting to a reduction in the transmutations she represents. The diverse elements or aspects of a thing are rather obliquely combinatory even when they are antipodal or more subtly deviate from each other—as when Ukraine, the site of the story's inception where "two men had fed the bride to the wolves" (*Á* 44), cannot be extracted from its transplantation "to a country that looked something like Nebraska and something like Virginia" (*Á* 45), a federation of places whose union is discoverable in the alloy of the mind's compounding. Such commingling is more abstractly perceptible in Cather's representation of the tensile edge that separates the singular and the universal; the natural and the preternatural;

incommensurable value-bearing attitudes; and the materializing and dematerializing of phenomena—states and conditions that might be the obverse of each other, but that traverse and seep into each other.

i

Cather's central characters become who they are not only through novelistic development, but also through a transposition to a region outside of individual and even bodily confines, as in *O Pioneers!*, where Alexandra is said to be domiciled in nature: "You feel that, properly, Alexandra's house is the big out-of-doors, and that it is in the soil that she expresses herself best."[10] Consanguinity with the earth might begin as a metaphor for Alexandra's stewardship of the natural world (for planting, cultivating, protecting), but it anticipates a more intimate kinship that links the life of "the soil" outside her to the growth of its life within her: "There were certain days in her life . . . when she was close to the flat, fallow world about her, and felt, as it were, in her own body, the germination of the soil" (*OP* 105) in one mode of organicism transposed to another. The "as it were" of Cather's sentence hedges on how the growth within the soil is incarnated in Alexandra, drifting over from idiom to subjunctive, from *so to speak* to a more ontological *as if it were*, thus a kind of latent transposition in phrasing itself. What is *hers* and *not hers* (her and not her) is definitively glossed by the analysis supplied by Jim Burden of Alexandra's sighting of a "wild duck," recalled by her "years afterward" as "one of the happiest [days] in her life" (*OP* 105–6). In his exegesis: "Most of Alexandra's happy memories were as impersonal as this one; yet to her they were very personal. Her mind was a white book, with clear writing about weather and beasts and growing things" (*OP* 106).

In the next paragraph, that static inscription comes to life as sensation which intermeshes the natural and the human, the physical and the mental, in Alexandra's "reverie" of "being lifted up bodily and carried lightly by some one who was very strong. It was a man, certainly, who carried her, but he was like no man she knew . . . and he carried her as easily as if she were a sheaf of wheat. She never saw him, but, with eyes closed, she could feel that he was yellow like the sunlight, and there was the smell of ripe cornfields about him" (*OP* 106). Though immediately identified as human, he is also impersonal—"yellow like the sunlight"—a perception that involves substitution of something seen (color) for something felt (warmth), since color, unlike warmth, cannot be transferred when the eyes are closed, whereas heat is energy in transit from one object to another, independent of vision. That same "sunlight" provides generative heat that ripens the cornfields and is the source of the corn's maturation then fathomed as scent. Cather's synesthetic tropes disable a clear separation of the senses and even a manifest distinction between what is couched as a manner of speaking (the subjunctive "as if she were a sheaf" or the simile "like sunlight" [*OP* 106]) and what ostensibly does not require figurative language, since ripeness is immediately experienced as fragrance. In such exchanges "growing things" migrate from "her mind['s] . . . white book" to bodily sensation that could only be personal, even as the feeling of "being carried swiftly off across the fields" must be impersonal, since "no man on the Divide could have carried" Alexandra—or, rather, "her gleaming white body"—"very far" (*OP* 106). Cather's complex sentences cross the personal and the impersonal, which can't be extricated from each other, much as the bundle or "sheaf" that is the "wheat" can't be separated from the bundle or "sheaf" that is Alexandra—each behaving like parts of a homology.

The etymology of metaphor from the Latin *metaphora* (carry over), from the Greek *metaphorá* (transfer), and from *meta* (beyond)—figuratively, to carry something into another realm[11]—describes the conveyance of a word to an object or action to which it is not literally applicable. The "carry[ing]" of Alexandra "across the fields" by a man who is "like no man she knew" doubles the idea of a crossing or transfer. At one level transfer pertains to how any metaphor works; at another, it pertains to the specific content of this metaphor (simile being a subset of analogic transfer) when in Alexandra's "reverie" she is "carried" from one place to another (*OP* 106). The metaphor also contains a transmutation in which the decorporealization of the "man" ("like the sunlight, . . . the smell of ripe cornfields," a reverse personification of nature incarnate) is transferred to Alexandra's near-weightless experience of herself as also decorporealized (a sheaf of harvested grain). The transport of Alexandra and the transmutation of his bodilessness into hers instances a special case of metaphoric transfer that becomes transposition. The point bears emphasis, since even without the circumstantial doubling particular to this example, Cather's use of metaphor to signal transposition is overdetermined. What metaphor does in general (transfers, transports) and the service it often performs in Cather's writing—echoing that transposition in its content—coincide in a rare alliance.

In *My Ántonia*, Jim Burden's description of that novel's title character exemplifies how such interweavings of the personal and impersonal reveal an intuition about how to see the world—that surrounds and constitutes the vision of any particular. Ántonia, a human particular, exemplifies a specific disposition beyond any frame of mind that might personally be hers (hence the word "lent" in the passage below). What she exemplifies is oxymoronically the omnipresence of "attitudes" shared by everyone, but not immediately recognized by anyone until she renders them palpable:

> She lent herself to immemorial human attitudes which we recognize by instinct as universal and true. . . . She was a battered woman now, not a lovely girl; but still had that something which fires the imagination, could still stop one's breath for a moment by a look or a gesture that somehow revealed the meaning in common things. She had only to stand in the orchard, to put her hand on a little crab tree and look up at the apples, to make you feel the goodness of planting and tending and harvesting at last. (Á 252)

"Attitudes" might at first seem to denote classic poses or physical stances, as in Jim's recollections of Ántonia that reside in "images in the mind that did not fade" (Á 252). But "immemorial . . . attitudes" also suggests something manifest from within—whether frames of reference; generous principles; or expansive understandings that can't be pinned to a gloss, however they might be timelessly shared by all—that are never remembered and never forgotten. They abide in Cather's placement of them in Ántonia's "look or gesture" (Á 252), sans language and formula, and convey a discernment that, in its inclusiveness, has more than one manifestation. The *all* implicit in "attitudes" that are "human," hence shared by everyone, though not immediately recognized, because requiring modeling to elucidate them assumes another reference when it diversely applies to every stage whereby something comes to be what it is, as in the encompassing parts of a process in which "apples" are planted, ripen, and are harvested. All-inclusive is what "universal" (*Á* 252) means, whether it pertains to the attitudes of all persons or to all the stages of apple life. Cather's segue from "attitudes" to "apples" occurs in the object of "a look or gesture" that "somehow revealed the meaning in common things"—thereby implicitly yoking incommensurables ("attitudes" and "apples") beyond the logical strictures that would dictate a single context they could share. The passage thus couples objects that equally exemplify those *all*s but that possess no categorical similarity.

Unlike the figuration that transmutes Alexandra's bodiless experience of herself into a reflection of the discarnate man who bears her across the fields, the value-bearing "attitudes" that define Ántonia (the "universal," the "meaning in common things," "the goodness" of "planting/tending/harvesting" [*Á* 252]), while positionally equivalent, are not logically comparable. "Meaning" is not coextensive with the "universal"; the genitive "of" that links "goodness" to "planting . . . harvesting" embodies only one instance of the "meaning in common things" (which is not the same as the "goodness" of labor, or of the care that dictates its necessity) and, in its finite inclusiveness, such goodness is only a limited "universal." Yet in Jim's vision of Ántonia, nothing could be alien to the spirit of Cather's construction in which diverse values inhabit a space where each particular flows into a whole, whether of "apple" being or "attitudes" that represent the core of human being. Another chapter analogically couples Ántonia's bearing of sons to the progeny of forerunners whose birth she could not have engendered. She is a "natural-born mother" (*Á* 231) and, by resemblance, she is a preternatural one: the "rich mine of life" that is Ántonia is "like the founders of early races" (*Á* 252), modeling in her "attitudes" exemplars that precede her own transient moment in time.

Then is Ántonia an archetype? According to Jim, she is "anything that a woman can be to a man" (*Á* 233). We should add that she also exemplifies a child's intuition, since Jim identifies her with "the country, the conditions, the whole adventure of our childhood" (*Á* xi), not only because the "early accidents of fortune which predetermined for us all that we can ever be" (*Á* 265–66), but also because very like a child, but also like a pioneer who prepares the way for others, she grasps what is true: "a child's attitude toward everything is an artist's attitude"; "artistic growth is, more than it is anything else, a refining of the sense of truthfulness."[12] And, like Alexandra, Ántonia is a businesswoman. Perhaps she is nothing but pure becoming—now one embodied ideal, now another, but not in a Bergsonian way, because each transposition adds to the aggregate that exemplifies her genius. The ideals she incarnates do not fall away when they appear to be succeeded but are compounded. Similarly, the metamorphoses that constitute Alexandra are reinvigorated in the proleptic claim that at her death "the fortunate country" will "receive hearts" like hers "into its bosom" to be reborn in sensory particulars: "in the yellow wheat, in the rustling corn, in the shining eyes of youth" (*OP* 159). Thus she will be incorporated in the fruit of the earth, but also be intangibly present as light and sound. The dissemination of Ántonia, like that of Alexandra perceived everywhere, has a corollary breadth in the attention she lavishes on her apple trees: "I love them as if they were people. . . . I could n't feel so tired that I would n't fret about those trees when there was a dry time. They were on my mind like children" (*Á* 243). "On my mind like children" might then be another gloss of the passages in which the limited "goodness of planting . . . harvesting" (*Á* 252) becomes a "universal" because it does not segregate manifestations of life that deserve exhaustive care from those that require less vigilance, an equality not neutralized by the claim's analogic scaffolding. The mere frequency of such figuration in Cather's writing obscures how mobile her propositions are, effacing distinctions across categorical divides. This is the point, as well as the effect, of all literary conceits that pair incommensurables while also driving them apart from the literal ideas on which they depend. But Cather's metaphors drift and transpose not only the personal and the impersonal, but also the flux of phenomena unconstrained by classification, in which the characteristics of one thing migrate to converge with those of another.

ii

Thus Jim Burden's description loosens the boundaries around what a natural phenomenon is deemed to be when he views "rough, shaggy, red grass, most of it as tall as I":

> The little trees were insignificant against the grass. It seemed as if the grass were about to run over them. . . . As I looked about me I felt that the grass was the country, as the water is the sea. The red of the grass made all the great prairie the color of wine-stains, or of certain seaweeds when they are first washed up. And there was so much motion in it; the whole country seemed, somehow, to be running. (*Á* 9)

"Grass" covers the land in Jim's sight and, by extension, envelops land out of his sight, until, in that spread, grass becomes an omnipresence. When the root of the idiom "to run over" (describing how the wind-blown grass bends trees to the ground) shifts to "running" the mutation captures a motion whose speed no longer applies to grass, but to what the country—or, rather, its velocity—has become. Grass is a continuum across different domains and, by the logic of a second analogy ("as the water is the sea"), also an essence that is ubiquitous so that what is not grass becomes grass-like: "the red of the grass" is like "the color . . . of certain seaweeds when they are first washed up" on rocks or shore (*Á* 9). The effect of this metonymic transposition[13] is to build grass into a totality whose extent is "prairie," "country," and "sea." Grass is also inseparable from a force epitomized by "motion" when grass, one entity, passes over the surface of another entity ("little trees") to morph into "the whole country" that "seemed, somehow, to be running." "Running" is a participial adjective that mutates into an effusion of movement without destination or end.

When Jim muses that "perhaps the glide of long railway travel" to the Nebraska prairie "was still with me, for more than anything else I felt motion in the landscape" (*Á* 10), his lingering sense of mobility from being transported on the train is recast as attention to other kinds of locomotion. The latter includes the proprioceptive sense of his own walking as a propulsion forward when his body is perceived as a kindred mass in transit: "I wanted to walk straight on through the red grass and over the edge of the world, which could not be very far away," "only the ground and sun and sky were left, and if one went a little farther there would be only sun and sky, and one would float off into them" (*Á* 10). The passages that attune Jim to "running," "walk[ing]," and "float[ing]" perform a series of transformations in a lower key than that in which Cather describes the climactic magnificence of late afternoons when "the miles of copper-red grass were drenched in sunlight. . . . The whole prairie was like the bush that burned with fire, but was not consumed. That hour always had the exultation of victory, of triumphant ending, like a hero's death—heroes who died young and gloriously. It was a sudden transfiguration, a lifting-up of day" (*Á* 29–30). The epiphanic ("transfiguration"), and the pathos-laden evocation of "heroes who died young" to describe the burning and fading of light could not be employed to represent a mobility that has no sensational, or any apparent, finish, and thus is not melodramatically punctuated.

The historical evolution predicted in the passage below more radically assaults the partitions that divide phenomena into discrete categories when Jim Burden sizes up the "breathless, brilliant heat which makes the plains of Kansas and Nebraska the best corn country in the world" (*Á* 99):

> The cornfields were far apart in those times, with miles of wild grazing land between. It took a clear, meditative eye like my grandfather's to foresee that they would enlarge and multiply until they would be, not the Shimerdas' cornfields, or Mr. Bushy's, but the world's cornfields; that their yield would be one of the great economic facts, like the wheat crop of Russia, which underlie all the activities of men, in peace or war. (*Á* 99)

The passage records a way of seeing the world through the lens of a category transformation that hypothesizes a common fate underlying all things—no matter how each element of the whole is independently classified. From this perspective, the expansion of one cornfield into another is not only construed in terms of a commingling of property and thus joint ownership, but to a possessive that aggregates all the fields into "the world's cornfields" (*Á* 99), pushing the idea of proprietorship beyond intelligibility. Even if all beings could be designated communal landowners of planet Earth, this commonality would contradict a proposition fundamental to the meaning of ownership: the possession of exclusive rights over property. Yet the proposed collectivity shifts attention to the outcome—the value of the produce that would issue from the conglomeration of plots of land amounting to "great economic facts, like the wheat crop of Russia," which are the foundation of "all the activities," even those that transpire in conditions as contrary as "peace or war" (*Á* 99). These *alls* are nested in each other and are part of the same burgeoning whole, even as the cosmic perspective arises from a lone point of view—"grandfather's" "clear, meditative eye" (*Á* 99)—whose expansive field of vision not only rivals the inclusivity of those *alls*, but generates them.

In *The Professor's House*, Tom Outland, on the mesa, discovers amplitude of a different order when, studying Latin, he found he "was reading too fast" (*PH* 252),

> so I began to commit long passages of Virgil to memory—if it hadn't been for that, I might have forgotten how to use my voice, or gone on to talking to myself. When I look into the *Aeneid* now, I can always see two pictures: the one on the page, and another behind that: blue and purple rocks and yellow-green piñons with flat tops, little clustered houses clinging together for protection, a rude tower . . . —behind it a dark grotto. . . . Happiness is something one can't explain. . . . [T]here was that summer, high and blue, a life in itself. (*PH* 252–53)

The passage draws coexistent but categorially distinct artifacts into a single vision: "two pictures" of ancient civilizations, one conveyed by an epic poem, the other by a history inscribed in stone by the Anasazi, who left behind rich archaeological remains, Cliff City, that Tom Outland discovers. These pasts also converge in his voice, which sounds Virgil's words by inhabiting not only the Latin tongue, but also the "filial piety" (*PH* 251) of the poetic culture that infuses it—so that physically Virgil's words in Tom's mouth become his words. The process of incorporating the piety of Latin poets into Tom's ardor for the mesa, Virgil's epic on the page and the stone city behind it, provide a reversal that is an opening: "I wakened with the feeling I had found everything, instead of having lost everything" (*PH* 251). This "everything," unlike the diverse *alls* of the cornfields passage, does not accrue by aggregation but by an ontological leap beyond sequence that adds up to what Cather variously names "happiness unalloyed" (a "religious emotion" rather than an "adventure" [*PH* 251]), and most liberally "a life in itself" (*PH* 253). The ontological leap not only springs over sequence but also over enumeration ("Happiness is something one can't explain" [*PH* 253]), recalling the inscription on Cather's gravestone: "that is happiness; to be dissolved into something complete and great."[14] In an actual leap in "Paul's Case," when Paul "jumped" in front of an "approaching locomotive," he "dropped back into the immense design of things" (*W* 488). "Things" plural, when singularized as "something," or "itself," are experienced within an "immense design" beyond shape or specification.

Cather's transpositions can also be located in a narrator's (rather than a character's) limited, if migratory, vision of "life in itself" (*PH* 253). In the passage below from *The Song of the Lark*, life is what elicits absorptive interest experienced as glamour and meaning for one object of attraction at a time. One Wednesday night Thea Kronborg, at home in Moonstone, attends a tedious "prayer-meeting" where "the prayers and the talks went on and on" (*SL* 117) and returns home to read "a poor translation of *Anna Karenina*" that was "one of the 'line' of paper novels the druggist kept to sell to traveling men" (*SL* 118). When she "fixed her eyes intently on the small print," "the hymns, the sick girl, the resigned black figures [of the prayer meeting] were forgotten. It was the night of the ball in Moscow":

> Thea would have been astonished if she could have known how, years afterward, when she had need of them, those old faces were to come back to her, long after they were hidden away under the earth; that they would seem to her then as full of meaning, as mysteriously marked by Destiny, as the people who danced the mazurka under the elegant Korsunsky. (*SL* 118)

The lure of the passage is not that the wearisome prayer meeting is displaced for Thea by the thrill of "the ball in Moscow" in Tolstoy's novel. Rather the transport moves in the other direction when "those old faces" prospectively captivate Thea's attention with the same fascination as that which, years earlier, compelled her interest in Tolstoy's characters to deliver her from Moonstone doldrums. Yet in that imagined future, there is an illusory redress of Thea's initial judgment, since it is the narrative voice that ponders the change in perspective, and only subjunctively: "if she could have known" (*SL* 118). For Thea, there is never a compensatory reassessment, and thus no irony at what could only retrospectively be judged a deficiency from the vantage of a future insight—were she to have had it—about the stature of lives she once dismissed as colorless. What it would mean for Thea to have "need of them, those old faces" (*SL* 118) would be something like what it would mean for her to value them, and to see retroactively that she failed to prize them in the same way that she once esteemed the characters in the magnificent *Anna Karenina* when she supposed Tolstoy's characters were "marked by Destiny" (*SL* 118) while her Moonstone acquaintances were deprived of it. This transport takes place in the narrator's flight of fancy—one could not even call it omniscience—since the narrator's conjecture is spectral and does not happen to Thea in the ruminative terms proposed. Thus there is a subtle drift in the proposition that transposes as an appositive what the narrator knows to what Thea could never know in these compensatory, formally regulative terms.

A parallel migration between states that are ostensibly closed off from each other, at least at one end, is represented in the path by which the living access the dead, even as its discovery does not annul the boundary that ontologically separates the two states. After Mr. Shimerda commits suicide (lying on a "bunkbed, close to the ox stalls" in the "barn" [*Á* 70], "he pulled the trigger with his big toe" [*Á* 71]), Jim Burden watches Grandmother and Grandfather set off to Mrs. Shimerda's: "Then, for the first time, I realized I was alone in the house" (*Á* 73). But Jim is not alone thanks to a visitation from the dead man's "released spirit" (*Á* 74) and, more queerly, from the dead man's memories, which, in distinction to Thea's fascination with the characters in *Anna Karenina* are, for Jim, more alive than is the fictional *Robinson Crusoe*:

> The quiet was delightful, and the ticking clock was the most pleasant of companions. I got "Robinson Crusoe" and tried to read, but his life on the island seemed dull compared with ours. Presently . . . it flashed upon me that if Mr. Shimerda's soul were lingering about in this world at all, it would be here, in our house, which had been more to his liking than any other in the neighborhood. . . . I knew it was homesickness that had killed Mr. Shimerda, and I wondered whether his released spirit would not eventually find its way back to his own country. I thought of how far it was to Chicago, and then to Virginia, to Baltimore,—and then the great wintry ocean. No, he would not at once set out upon that long journey. Surely, his exhausted spirit, so tired of cold and crowding and the struggle with the everfalling snow, was resting now in this quiet house. . . . Outside I could hear the wind singing over hundreds of miles of snow. It was as if I had let the old man in out of the tormenting winter, and were sitting there with him. . . . Such vivid pictures came to me that they might have been Mr. Shimerda's memories, not yet faded out from the air in which they had haunted him. (*Á* 73–74)

Jim's surmise that if Mr. Shimerda's "soul were lingering about in this world at all," he "would be here, in our house," hardens to a certainty. When Jake, a hired hand of the Shimerdas', claims: "it will be a matter of years to pray [Mr. Shimerda's] soul out of Purgatory, and right now he's in torment," Jim contradicts him: "'I almost know that is n't true.' I did not, of course, say that I believed he had been in that very kitchen all afternoon, on his way back to his own country" (*Á* 75). In these avowals, there is no distance between the "vivid pictures" that come to Jim from "all that Ántonia had ever told me about his life before he ever came to this country," his own additions to those images, and what "might have been Mr. Shimerda's memories, not yet faded from the air" (*Á* 74). The omnipresence of "air" is a placeholder for what cannot be singularized, directing attention away from the spectral nature of the visit, where the subjunctive routes it toward a collaborative sense in which the details of Mr. Shimerda's memories before he came to this country haunt Ántonia and Jim, and perhaps initially Mr. Shimerda. Cather draws attention away from the idea that the apparition is Jim's projection toward the question of who is haunted by the details of Mr. Shimerda's life as they are passed back and forth in a transit whose boundaries Cather leaves indefinite.

What counts as intimacy with the dead is specified in a more decisive encounter in *My Ántonia* when Ántonia tells Jim:

> Look at my papa here; he's been dead all these years, and yet he is more real to me than almost anybody else. He never goes out of my life. I talk to him and consult him all the time. The older I grow, the better I know him, and the more I understand him. (*Á* 233)

The comparatives ("more real . . . than . . . anybody else"); the absolutes ("never . . . out of my life"); the prodigious understanding ("all the time . . . the better . . . the more"); and, mostly, the verb "consult" ("I . . . consult him")—which supposes a back-and-forth exchange, not a monologue, and thus can't be reduced to a memory of what he did say, but rather in Ántonia's mind is based on fresh evidence of her father's responsive presence—materialize in this passage with a Jamesian multidimensionality that animates Mr. Shimerda, resurrecting him not to life but to Ántonia's experience of a bond that deepens after his death. Unlike the access to his memories by which Jim establishes the soundness of Mr. Shimerda's "lingering" (*Á* 73) posthumous presence, Ántonia offers testimony to the comparatively more plausible dialogue with her father—the barrier between the living and the dead being more permeable than that between one mind and another, since the former is a line that will ultimately be crossed by all, while the latter is one that can never be crossed. Cather contests the ossified boundaries between the living and the dead—never more powerfully than when Alexandra in *O Pioneers!*, grieving her brother, the slain Emil, intuits a respite experienced by both the living and the dead that pulls them into shared space:

> When you get so near the dead, they seem more real than the living. Worldly thoughts leave one. Ever since Emil died, I've suffered so when it rained. Now that I've been out in it with him, I shan't dread it. After you once get cold clear through, the feeling of the rain on you is sweet. It seems to bring back feelings you had when you were a baby. It carries you back into the dark, before you were born; you

can't see things, but they come to you, somehow, and you know them and are n't afraid of them. Maybe it's like that with the dead. If they feel anything at all, it's the old things, before they were born, that comfort people like the feeling of their own bed does when they are little. (*OP* 145–46)

In Alexandra's reverie, she is transported regressively into a "baby['s]" "feelings," then further back to a pre-birth "dark" without visible features but also, in its inscrutability, benign and revelatory ("things . . . come to you . . . and you know them" [*OP* 145]), while, she muses, the dead might travel directly to "the old things, before they were born," a comfort recognized by an affinity to children's ease in "their own bed" (*OP* 146). The trajectory to places of solace from opposite conditions constitutes a crossing that draws the living and the dead backward and further backward and then forward in memory of that "comfort" of "their own bed" "when . . . little," here shared by the living and the dead until they could be said to intersect. While the boundary on either side of the mortal limit remains intact, the balm perceived by each from converse vantages draws them together.

A like transposition that effaces classificatory distinctions between kinds of reality is recalled by Alexandra once she lies down to rest after her visit to Emil's grave when a figure who, in her youth, appeared to her as nature incarnate (*OP* 106) reappears in "the old illusion of her girlhood, of being lifted and carried lightly. . . . [S]he saw . . . him clearly, though . . . his face was covered. . . . His shoulders seemed as strong as the foundations of the world. His right arm . . . was dark and gleaming, like bronze, and she knew at once that it was the arm of the mightiest of all lovers" (*OP* 146). The "mightiest" lover could only be a providential one. Like the knowledge gleaned in the pre-birth "dark," "she knew . . . where he would carry her" (*OP* 146). No criteria rise up to identify the basis of Alexandra's epistemology, her "she knew." Nor could any acumen identify the spectral figure in a uniform way (no matter whether identity is understood as numerical or qualitative, equivalent or relative), since the amalgamation that visits Alexandra is human, but also natural, and then again divine, at once material and immaterial. Thus the aggregate that transports her has no discrete identity—unless identity is loosely defined as a composition in which the parts of a whole are literally identical with the whole itself.

The metamorphosis of one state of being crossing into another is a paradigm glimpsed across Cather's writing: in Alexandra's "memories" that are at once "impersonal" yet "very personal" (*OP* 106); in Jim Burden's experience of "the glide of long railway travel" awakening him to the "motion in the landscape" (*Á* 10) that contracts into his own locomotion; in individually owned cornfields that mutate into "the world's cornfields" and then into a vaster totality divined by an analogy to "great economic facts" contingent on the sale of Russian wheat that affects "all the activities of men, in peace or war" (*Á* 99); in the "two pictures," Virgil's Latin and the purple rocks of Cliff City that Tom Outland sees as one (*PH* 252); in a narrator's perspective that almost migrates—but stops short of doing so—into a character's perspective (*SL* 118); and in the discrete passages in which the dead and the living (*Á* 73, 233; *OP* 145–46) are released from the rigor of a defining imprisonment by the perception of realities that incline toward and into each other in a sphere far removed from what Alexandra calls "worldly thoughts" (*OP* 145). These instances of mobility cannot be further parsed. If such metamorphoses are marked by hyperbole as implicit in the sequential *alls*—all the fields; "all the activities" (*Á* 99); "all the time" (*Á* 233); implicitly all the "people" (*OP* 146); "the whole country" (*Á* 9)—the extravagant "all" arises from absorbed attention to the undulation of experiential particulars, not from dreamy or abstract fantasy. Nor are these interchanges frozen in emblematic relief like the "three footprints" of thirteen-year-old Lucy Gayheart, who had run across "wet slabs" of "a sidewalk" being laid,[15] thereby imprinting a paradox of movement in stasis, whose moral is italicized when in that novel's last sentence Gordon reflects on those iconic "light footprints" (*LG* 195) of Lucy, laid to rest, but eternally "running away." Rather these swells capture the fluidity within acute perceptions of routine experience in which categories dissolve or merge in any context whatsoever if one looks as Grandfather, Ántonia, Jim Burden, Alexandra, and Willa Cather do with a "meditative eye" (*Á* 99). The inclusive *any* also pertains to the transpositions within Cather's prose, to which I now turn—specifically to those that occur at certain pressure points evident in the internal shaping of phrasing itself, the foundation of Cather's style.

iii

In Cather's prose, feeling and sensation are dematerialized and rematerialized across a range of affective states, as in *One of Ours* where diverse responses to opposite regions of Mrs. Wheeler's life move between composure that can't be ruffled and unbridled emotion:

> Her personal life was so far removed from the scene of her daily activities that rash and violent men could not break in upon it. But where Claude was concerned, she lived on another plane,—dropped into the lower air, tainted with human breath and pulsating with poor, blind, passionate human feelings.[16]

The contrastive syntax—the straightforward exposition of the first sentence in its full subordinate closure and the next, released in a fall into past and present participles—marks the difference between a life that is secreted and then involuntarily revealed. When Mrs. Wheeler's son contemplates his mother's hands, there is an opposite trajectory from what is perceptible to what is apparently impalpable: "Her fingers arched back at the joints, as if they were shrinking from contacts. . . . They were sensitive hands, and yet they seemed to have nothing to do with sense, to be almost like the groping fingers of a spirit" (*OO* 232). "Shrinking" and "groping" name a strict disparity, but "fingers of a spirit" punctures the opposition—intact with respect to retreating and advancing, but not with respect to formation, for the oxymoron suggests that "spirit" also has a substantiality that can make "contacts" (*OO* 232) across a divide where matter leans into what refines it.

In a more developed polarity, fervor characterizes the "two lives" of St. Peter's—"university work" and the days spent in his study when he "worked like a miner under a landslide"—"both of them very intense" (*PH* 28), even as these activities are dwarfed by a more consuming ardor: "The great fact in life . . . was the lake. The sun rose out of it, the day began there; it was like an open door that nobody could shut. . . . [I]t ran through the days like the weather, not a thing thought about, but a part of consciousness itself" (*PH* 30). Comparisons of the lake to other bodies of water count for nothing, since the lake "was altogether different" from "*le Michigan*" (*PH* 31) even when they share attributes: "Yes, there are clouds and mists and sea-gulls, but—I don't know, *il est toujours naïf.*" The lake "was itself, as the Channel and the Mediterranean were themselves" (*PH* 31). In the surprising formulation that the lake is "not a thing thought about" but, in effect, "a part of" thought "itself" (*PH* 30), Cather inhabits thought in its own texture, even as the negated thing thought ("not a thing thought") relaxes into a more diffuse and capacious body of water, that is at once object and idea.

In another exorbitant reckoning, we see Tom Outland's passion for Cliff City, the "little city of stone, asleep" that he stumbled upon "hidden away, in this inaccessible mesa for centuries" (*PH* 201, 202).[17] When Tom learns that Blake has traded the curios found in the rooms of the pueblo villages for "real money" (*PH* 241), he chastises Blake: "You've gone and sold your country's secrets, like Dreyfus" (*PH* 243). But there is a stylistic shift that recuperates Tom's clichéd feeling that he has "lost everything" to a less idiomatic, more internalized "feeling that I had found everything" (*PH* 251), a transformation that has nothing to do with objects (bowls, water jars, fiber mats in the villages [*PH* 208]), but with a joy that surpasses any wellspring to which reference could confine it. The surfeits in which the profusion of affect turns feelings upside down (loss to gain) and outside to inside (object to idea) are rooted in semantic oppositions. But in their asymmetry, they exceed them: what Tom has lost harks back to artifacts, but the joy he has "found" (*PH* 251) cannot be explained by any rarity or any other thing (*PH* 250); St. Peter's work worlds of "university lectures" and "creative work" (*PH* 29) share an intensity, but the "lake" is matchless. The asymmetries resonate voicelessly beyond the semantic containers of language as do the two superlatives (different manifestations of "everything"), perceptible across 200-plus pages in which Tom's joy is "happiness unalloyed" (*PH* 251), while for St. Peter reading Tom Outland's story, "happiness" is derivative. In their phrased reoccurrence, these asymmetries in which categories are interwoven produce an aspect of narrative so unique as to become a kind of structural idiolect in Cather, to which local stylistic effects gravitate. Similarly, no model could capture the mobility in which the awakenings of each (at the mesa for Tom, "all of me was there" [*PH* 250], while for the professor, "outward bound" [*PH* 281], there will be no "all") turn back to inequivalences in this crucial juxtaposition that Cather instigates at a distance. When the awareness in which the world as each knew it is replaced by something unrecognizable (kindled for Tom by the loss of the relics [*PH* 241], for the professor by the loss of "something very precious" [*PH* 282]), their slant insights resound, albeit so subtly as to count as something like style degree zero, an abstruse relation that shrinks from enumeration. For like Mrs. Wheeler's fingers "that seemed to have nothing to do with sense, to be almost like the groping fingers of a spirit" (*OO* 232), Cather's style can seem intangible.[18]

Cather's judgment of her own style calls attention to its divergent features.[19] In *Death Comes to the Archbishop*, the modesty of the prose matches the homogeneity of experience held up to something higher: "it is as though all human experiences, measured against one supreme spiritual experience, were of about the same importance. . . . [O]ne must use language a little stiff, a little formal" (*W* 960–61). Conversely, William Heinemann, publisher of *McClure's Magazine*, "declining [to publish] *The Song of the Lark*," described its "method" as "full-blooded" because it "told everything about everybody" (*W* 965), a practice more demographic than novelistic. The handling of "detail" (*W* 965), emotion, drama, reserve—expression tamped down or revved up—define what could be called Cather's conceptual style: a way of thinking conveyed through odd juxtapositions which elicit the conclusion that for all Cather's lucidity, sense often lies outside or to the side of what is enunciated. While Cather singles out the expressive characteristics of her novels in differential terms, these extremes also play out within a single novel.

In *My Ántonia*, there is an abrupt segue from breezy writing that pans across a gamut of entertainments—including the music of d'Arnault, a "mulatto" pianist, leading "men gathered round him" who "sang one negro melody after another" (*Á* 135)—at Mrs. Gardener's

Boys' Home Hotel, where Jim and Ántonia go to visit their friend Tiny—to a close-up of the pianist's young life: "He was born . . . on the d'Arnault plantation, where the spirit if not the fact of slavery persisted" (*Á* 136). His mother "named him Samson because he was blind, but on the plantation he was known as 'yellow Martha's simple child.' . . . [W]hen he was six years old he began to run away from home, always taking the same direction" to "the 'Big House,' where Miss Nellie d'Arnault practiced the piano every morning" (*Á* 136). In *The Song of the Lark*, Professor Wunsch explains that musicality is not acquired by training: "there must be something in the inside from the beginning. . . . [*D*]*er Geist, die Phantasie.* It must be in the baby, when it makes its first cry, like *der Rhythmus*, or it is not to be" (*SL* 71). Samson's encounter with the sound that spontaneously draws him toward it vibrates with his own spirit and is embedded in writing as foreign to anything in the chapter that has preceded it as the strange object that looms before him. One day after Miss Nellie had left the room:

> He crept up to the front windows and stuck his head in. . . . He put one foot over the window sill and straddled it. . . .
>
> [H]e pulled in his other foot.
>
> Through the dark he found his way to the Thing, to its mouth. He touched it softly, and it answered softly, kindly. He shivered and stood still. Then he began to feel it all over, ran his finger tips along the slippery sides, embraced the carved legs, tried to get some conception of its shape and size, of the space it occupied in primeval night. It was cold and hard, and like nothing else in his black universe. He went back to its mouth, began at one end of the keyboard and felt his way down into the *mellow thunder*, as far as he could go. He seemed to know that it must be done with the fingers, not with the fists or the feet. He approached this highly artificial instrument through a mere instinct, and *coupled himself to it*, as if he knew it was *to piece him out*, and make a whole creature of him. . . . [H]e began to *finger out* passages from things Miss Nellie had been practicing, passages that were already his, that lay under the bones of his pinched, conical little skull, definite as animal desires. (*Á* 137–38; italics mine)

. . .

> Several teachers experimented with him. They found he had absolute pitch, and a remarkable memory. As a very young child he could repeat, after a fashion, any composition that was played for him. No matter how many wrong notes he struck, he never lost the intention of a passage, he brought the substance of it across by irregular and astonishing means. . . . He could never learn like other people, never acquired any finish. He was always a negro prodigy who played barbarously and wonderfully. As piano playing, it was perhaps abominable, but as music it was something real, vitalized by a sense of rhythm that was stronger than his other physical senses. . . . It was as if all the agreeable *sensations possible to creatures of flesh and blood were heaped up on those black and white keys,* and he were gloating over them and trickling them through his yellow fingers. (*Á* 138; italics mine)

Cather gives us the piano from the child's alien experience of it ("the Thing . . . its mouth"); the inchoate darkness his discovery mitigates ("the space it occupied in primeval night"); and the range of tones as his fingers move down the keyboard and explode at the deep end in an oxymoron of pleasure ("*mellow thunder*"). In the last sentence of the first excerpt the boy's ecstasy at sound is inseparable from the feel of the fingers that release it. In narrowly stylistic terms, "*piece him out*" is a metaphor with undertones of a *piece of music he fingers out,* so that vibrations move inward from the invisible keys to the "flesh and blood" thrill of his own integrity: he knew it would "make a whole creature of him" (*Á* 137; italics mine). In an opposite trajectory in the second extract, the "sensations . . . heaped up on" the piano are a transfer from what is within Samson to what is outside of him. Such phrases reveal the correlative movements in which person and instrument are "coupled" (*Á* 137). Samson is deprived of the dignity Cather novelistically accords to Mexicans and immigrants. He wakes up out of his black universe to the white lady's piano, but not so far as to lose his barbarity until he learns to perform by playing dance music. The passage implicitly reflects on its own stereotype, since "*black and white keys*" so near the epithet "agreeable sensations possible to creatures of *flesh and blood*" (*Á* 138; italics mine) suggests a synthesis of the two phrases that, were their order flipped, would be almost continuous. Their shadow inversion aims a question at the denigration of Samson—"He was always a negro prodigy . . . enjoying himself as only a negro can" (*Á* 138)—without negating it.

At the end of the previous passages, Cather's narrative switches from Samson's pounding (a retrospective account of the day he creeps up to the house and tries "all the sounds . . . on the big and little keys" [*Á* 137–38]) to another mood entirely that he coaxes from the piano in accord with the present night's gaiety. The swerve is signaled through a shift in musical tempo ("in the middle of a crashing waltz d'Arnault suddenly began to play softly" [*Á* 138]) that accentuates by lighthearted contrast the mind-blowing transformation that narratively precedes it. When d'Arnault "began to draw the dance music out of it" (*Á* 140), Cather's prose buoyantly orchestrates the appearance of jollity. The intensity of the former and the frivolity of the latter, augmented by their proximity, never develop thematically or structurally and thus could never dissipate. Rather, without further mention, like the incidental story of the bride thrown to the wolves, in all its incarnations, d'Arnault and the piano vanish from the novel's scrutiny, even as for the reader they linger—counterparts that do not jibe. A touch transforms Samson's "docili[ty]" (*Á* 136) to genius while, in a twist of the children's minds, violence that kills the bride kinetically flips to benignity. Cather coerces a weird consonance from these jangling aggregates that, without further development, could not be construed as meaningful. Oscillation locks such antipodes into a cadence until they become rhythmically unthinkable apart from each other.

Sensation that is amplified, as in Samson's discovery of the piano, can also be downplayed to a striking effect as when Cather lowers the pitch and clears the stage[20] in the short story "Old Mrs. Harris," where the characters are almost incidental to what they typify: the incomparable ways that hardships are calculated. Toward the end of that story, we see the teenage bitterness of Mrs. Harris's granddaughter Vickie, as reported by the narrator in free indirect discourse: "she had only two weeks" to get ready for school, and "no trunk and no clothes"[21]—adversities that swell to this lament: "my whole life hangs by a thread" (OMH 312). Victoria, Mrs. Harris's daughter, expresses a kindred bitterness—"why must she be forever shut up in a little cluttered house with children and fresh babies?"—while her operatic refrain ("life hadn't used her right") half rhymes with her daughter's (OMH 308). Such agitations of desire and disappointment are juxtaposed to Mrs. Harris's affinity with Victoria's ten-year-old twins of whom she thinks: "she and the twins were about the same age; they had in common all the realest and truest things. The years between them and her, it seemed to Mrs. Harris, were full of *trouble* and unimportant" (OMH 311; italics mine). What she shares with the twins is knowledge of a reality that isn't compromised by fluctuating convulsions of happiness and misery.

Style lies behind the cues that link elements by apposition—the text in which Mrs. Harris feels her attunement with the twins and one that elaborates another form of concord: "In her mind she was repeating a passage from the second part of *Pilgrim's Progress*, which she had read aloud to the children so many times; the passage where Christiana and her band come to the arbour on the Hill of *Difficulty* [italics mine]: '*Then said Mercy, How sweet is rest to them that labour*'" (OMH 311). The accord that entwines the two passages crosses more than the words "trouble" and "difficulty," conceptual rhymes, for in their proximity "realest" and "truest" have been permeated with Bunyan's "sweet[ness]." The interchange is also reciprocal, vested in adjectives that implicitly cross over in the other direction, so that "real" and "true" belatedly characterize Bunyan's "Hill of Difficulty" and thus the "trouble" prematurely dismissed as trivial (OMH 311). Such undertones suggest that what is difficult and not difficult cannot be pulled apart, as the isolated passages divide them. The Bunyan passage conciliates them in the syllabic rhyme "arbour" and "labour" (OMH 311), an echo that Cather's stylistic, as well as spiritual, disposition means us to hear, since she weaves *Pilgrim's Progress* into her text. When Mrs. Harris died, she

> slipped out of the Templetons' story; but Victoria and Vickie still had to go on, to follow the long road that leads through things unguessed at and unforeseeable. When they are old, they will come closer and closer to Grandma Harris. They will think a great deal about her,

> and remember things they never noticed; and their lot will be more or less like hers. They will regret that they heeded her so little; but they, too, will look into the eager, unseeing eyes of young people and feel themselves alone. They will say to themselves: 'I was heartless, because I was young and strong and wanted things so much. But now I know.'" (OMH 313–14)

"Still had to go on" and "But now I know" are flat, almost toneless phrases that downplay the difference between *going on without knowing* and *knowing but not going on*. Yet "now I know" and "still had to go on" mark the antinomy in the double meaning of "still" (a now that cannot change and the unremitting change of "go[ing] on") by Cather's ascription of irreconcilable temporalities to plights that cannot countenance each other. The disparity is stressed by the vowel rhyme in "the *ea*ger uns*ee*ing eyes of young p*eo*ple" who think nothing "unfores*ee*able" will overtake them, a blindness whose presumption of invincibility renders them (in the irony of another dead anatomical metaphor) "heartless" (OMH 314; italics mine), a cliché the narrator predicts they will invoke to reflect on their own cruelty. Thus, at the end of "Old Mrs. Harris," the equipoise of Cather's prose throws into relief vantages that succeed each other but that could never be reconciled.

Upheavals in Cather's style in which one kind of treatment (Samson's pounding) flips into another (Samson performing); or in which the coupled visions of "life in itself" (*PH* 253)—Tom's, Professor St. Peter's—are offset by the contrast of prose that registers vigor and prose that registers melancholy to portray the disposition of each; or in which Cather gives us a double take (racial bias and its latent qualification) are sometimes so abrupt that they seem not to have come from the same pen or voice. For Cather, style is a mercurial use of voice. Not a use of the speaking voice that often fails—as for the minor figure "Silent Irv," so-named "because nobody could ever get a word out of him. He had almost no voice at all" (OO 171). And not as for Jason Royce, Claude's father-in-law, who "had no words, no way to make himself understood. . . . What he wanted was to hold up life as he had found it, like a picture, to his young friend; to warn him, without explanation, against certain heart-breaking disappointments" (OO 138). Also not a singing voice that abounds in overtones and undertones. But more like a singing voice that can be felt as well as heard when in *The Song of the Lark* Mr. Harsanyi, Thea Kronborg's teacher, literally feels her voice: "He put his hand back to her throat. . . . He loved to hear a big voice throb . . . and he was thinking that no one had ever felt this voice vibrate before. . . . A relaxed, throat, a voice that lay on the breath, that had never been forced off the breath" (*SL* 171). For Professor Wunsch, Thea's "was a nature-voice . . . breathed from the creature and apart from language, like the sound of the wind in the trees, or the murmur of water" (*SL* 70).

Style is not a "nature-voice" but an author's phrasal register—a picture of life, but a moving picture. Cather's style draws together, disjoins, underscores, minimizes, and reverses. Its transmutations drive down deep while evading any formulation that would circumscribe a pattern within a radius of semantic fixture. Yet the following exchange exhibits a structure that almost resonates as a paradigm across the pages of *The Professor's House* when Professor St. Peter asks Augusta, the German Catholic woman who sews for his wife and children, about "that passage in the service about the Mystical Rose, Lily of Zion, Tower of Ivory—is that the Magnificat?"

> "Why, Professor! Did you receive *no* religious instruction at all?"
>
> "How could I . . . ? My mother was a Methodist, there was no Catholic church in our town in Kansas, and I guess my father forgot his religion. . . . What is the Magnificat . . . ?"
>
> "The Magnificat begins, *My soul doth magnify the Lord*; you must know that."
>
> "But I thought the Magnificat was about the Virgin?"
>
> "Oh, no, Professor! The Blessed Virgin composed the Magnificat."
>
> St. Peter became intensely interested. "Oh, she did?"[22] (*PH* 99–100)

The exchange seems aimless, except to contrast Augusta's faith—strong, like that of her namesake—with St. Peter's derision of it. Yet it corrects a mistake (the Virgin is not the object of praise but the subject who offers it) and oddly sticks in St. Peter's mind as a marvel: "Surely she had said that the Blessed Virgin sat down and composed the Magnificat!" (*PH* 100). His stammering ("Is that the Magnificat . . . ?"; "What is the Magnificat . . . ?"; "But I thought . . .")

suggests surprise at being told he has rotated subject and object. In *The Professor's House*, that rotation also describes less parochial reversals that more dynamically turn things around, redefining St. Peter's assessments, his values, and his categories, as in the upending of his sense of the possible: "He had not known" a "first nature could return to a man" (*PH* 267) when "the original, unmodified Godfrey St. Peter" (*PH* 263) floods back to him in his sudden recoil from his family (*PH* 275). And as when his revulsion for Augusta, who "was like the taste of bitter herbs" (*PH* 280), suddenly dissolves: "he would rather have Augusta with him just now than anyone he could think of" (*PH* 281). Nothing further tells us how this exchange is related to the novel as a whole. Cather defaults on explicit connections even as her presence lingers in the tacit suggestions that replace the cinch of a verbal harness with vibrations whose undercurrent declines to identify the fictive logic that constitutes such affinities. Unlike "love"—the one word that is never uttered in Edith Lewis's memoir *Willa Cather Living: A Personal Record*[23] but that a reader hears suffuse every sentence, and so is never absent from Lewis's book—Cather's reader is not provoked to guess what *she* leaves unspecified.

In similar elusive terms, Cather constellates characters when what is irrelevant to character grips the novels' focus—as in *My Ántonia*, where the heroine's idealized, even mythic, often incommensurable qualities are fashioned into an aesthetic whole that affirms the value of a character who is "just a figure on which other things hang" (*L* 492), an "antonomasia"[24]—while in *O Pioneers!* all characters take a supporting role to "the country itself [which] is frankly the hero" (*L* 169). The kindred episodes I've examined—the tale of the bride and the wolves that provokes terror and relish; the pounding that is the ecstatic genesis of Samson's public performance but that also predicts the impossibility of public acceptance; the subject/object confusion about the "Virgin" in the "Magnificat"—are also sui generis and have a murmuring resemblance to each other through their transport to a space outside the novels' progressions. Like the possible sources of Professor St. Peter's "hurt," which are indicated but never identified, the confluences in these passages can be presaged by language but, being themselves other, only experienced without names, on its far side. In an equally conspicuous characterization, stressing the idiosyncratic compositional elements of that novel, Cather described *The Professor's House* as an "experiment" that "was very much akin to the arrangement followed in sonatas in which the academic sonata form was handled somewhat freely" (*W* 974). In the sonata form, technically, there is a three-part organization: an exposition, a development, a recapitulation. In Cather's novel, there are rather enmeshed contrasts, not continuities. She exemplified the counterpoints: the professor's "house rather overcrowded and stuffy with new things" and "the fresh air that blew off the Blue Mesa" (*W* 974).

The passages I've considered are contrasts of another kind and glancingly call to mind Theodor Adorno's portrayal of music as reaching past names, meaning, and intention: "pure sound" being "the opposite of every act of meaning, every intention toward meaning."[25] Since language could never condense to "pure sound," the pertinence of Adorno's remarks on the nature of music for Cather's writing best comes into focus in his essay on punctuation marks when he asserts that "music's contact with the punctuation marks in language" is "bound up with the schema of tonality."[26] Such an account stresses the relation between notes, chords, key, and scale, as these illuminate the contrapuntal impact of rhythms and their variations that inflect the episodic passages whose interludes are breathers of sorts—pauses—from the rush of plot across Cather's writing. Adorno continues, "To the person who cannot truly conceive anything as a unity, anything that suggests disintegration or discontinuity is unbearable: only a person who can grasp totality can understand caesuras" (TA 93). Though the intermittent episodes suspend, and thus disrupt, the momentum of the main story, they have their own propulsion—not of action but of access to what Cather in "Two Friends" calls an "out-flowing," a "melt[ing] together"[27] that only a "totality" can absorb (TA 93). Throughout Cather's writing, the blending of one thing into another—whether of entities (Samson and the piano keys), qualities, or phrasal registers—is caught up in a rhythm in which a thing is no longer identical with itself, but with the cadence of its changes and with the lacunae between states they negotiate but never quite bridge. "Cadence" indicates "how sharply music and language diverge from each other" (TA 92). Such "out-flowing" (TF 330)—with no melting or merging—is also palpable in Cather's figuration.

When Thea Kronborg beholds an eagle fly away, she "sprang to her feet as if she had been thrown up from the rock by volcanic action," exclaiming, "O eagle of eagles!" (*SL* 288), an apostrophe that erupts into a sweeping vision of all that the eagle symbolizes—"endeavor, achievement, desire, glorious striving of human art," "she saluted it"—features that migrate past rather than into each other, but whose beat is no less defined by transposition.

The changes modeled by Cather's writing may occur internally at unthinkable velocity, as evoked by Grenfell in "Before Breakfast," up all night, contemplating the planet: "What a dreadful night! The speeds which machinists had worked up in the last fifty years were mere baby-talk to what can go through a man's head between dusk and daybreak."[28] Or their rhythm may be leisurely, even languorous, as when Lucy Gayheart muses, "If only one could lose one's life and one's body and be nothing but one's desire; if the rest could melt away, and that could float with the gulls, out yonder where the blue and green were changing!" (*LG* 86). When desire flows outward, it "float[s] with the gulls, out yonder" toward the shifting colors and shapes of the waves from which it becomes virtually inseparable, but it also flows inward with the adverb internalized as part of an interrupted verb phrase "float . . . out [yonder]." "Float" is the operative word in the passage—and in Cather's writing generally—establishing a cadence of the two motions. Cather's stylistic charge of a hovering, floating sense is consonant with our seeing the waves' colors as merely shifting with the light ("where the blue and green were changing") and seeing the colors turn into each other. Both senses are implied. In a like transposition, St. Peter's lake reflects the "blue" of its color and "quite another blue" (*PH* 31) that is also "part of consciousness" (*PH* 30), a "blue" beyond "itself."

iv

Cather's 1932 short story "Two Friends" embodies the transpositions in Cather's novels that have been my subject. The story chronicles the breach over a political disagreement that separates Robert Emmet Dillon, a banker, and J. H. Trueman, "a big cattleman . . . from Buffalo" (TF 316). "Mr. Dillon . . . was a Democrat" and

"Mr. Trueman was a Republican" (TF 321). Yet each has an intuitive understanding of what the other describes "quite irrespective of words" (TF 326), which cements their bond, until the intimacy is shattered by Mr. Dillon's support of the populist William Jennings Bryan, for "Trueman looked down on anyone who could take the reasoning of the Populist party seriously" (TF 330). When the "quarrel of 'principle'" (TF 329–30) turns nasty, it busts up a friendship mourned by the young narrator, who thinks of these two men as "aristocrats" (TF 321), because their friendship represented "some law of balance . . . like that between the earth and the moon" (TF 330). The tale of the friendship is also told in kindred images that extend to a visual register of the insubstantiality of differences while their friendship endures, here envisaged transiently in the simile of the "silence between" them that "was as full and satisfying as the moonlight" (TF 330). Yet, oddly, these images (ostensibly the story's subtext) depict not "some law of balance" (TF 330), but rather of co-option when one visible form engulfs another, here the moon, a star:

> Sitting there on the edge of the sidewalk one summer night, my feet hanging in the warm dust, I saw an occultation of Venus. . . . That big star certainly got nearer and nearer the moon . . . until there was not the width of your hand between them—now the width of two fingers—then *it passed directly into the moon at about the middle of its girth; absolutely disappeared. The star we had been watching was gone.* (TF 323–24; italics mine)

While below, solid structures are obliterated:

> These abandoned buildings, an eyesore by day, *melted together into a curious pile* in the moonlight, became *an immaterial structure of velvet-white and glossy blackness.* (TF 323; italics mine)

But in the following passage, there is no splitting of what is embodied and what could never be:

> The road, just in front of the sidewalk where I sat and played jacks, would be ankle-deep in dust, and seemed to drink up the moonlight

> like folds of velvet. It drank up sound, too; muffled the wagon-wheels and hoof-beats; lay soft and meek like the last residuum of material things—the soft bottom resting-place. (TF 323)

In the crossing of mixed metaphors, light, though substance-less, is also textured, since the simile ("seemed to drink up the moonlight like folds of velvet") refers to how the light is imbibed by the dusty road and to the seeming density of light that "folds" on itself, while the dust, though shapeless but also "ankle-deep" (TF 323), has bulk and thus drifts between material embodiment and its mere "residuum." Another strain governs the relation of the adjectives "soft" and "meek." Both attributes refer to "dust," the amorphous remainder of matter. Of course dust is also the "last residuum" of living beings, and this fleeting but extraneous hint at personification (gratuitous in that persons are not implicated in the thrust of the sentence) is animated, but also suspended, so that the association almost doesn't count but can't be dismissed. A word like "meek" can't mean submissive (as would pertain to a person) so it must mean featureless (as would describe particles of matter). But how might any connotation of "meek" chime with the voraciousness of the earlier description in which the dust of the road "seemed to drink up the moonlight . . . drank up sound, too," unless we hear something like a rhythm not only between substance and its effacement, but also between passive and active verbs ("drank up . . . lay") and between the adjectives ("soft . . . meek"), which transpose sense toward and then away from materiality and personification so that any gloss of the passage leaves some part of it unaccommodated? The rhythms have a tempo which departs from the neat formulations that otherwise govern Cather's short story—and this is the point of my apparently digressive analysis of "Two Friends," whose tidy conceptions are the inverse of the transpositions I've described throughout these pages. These transpositions defy an either/or logic, as well as the narrator's piety in evoking concepts like "truth" (TF 331), "harmony" (TF 330), "balance" (TF 330)—"unalterable realities . . . at the bottom of things" (TF 315) whose superficial moralism complements such logic.

When Cather wrote of "getting the material, coming up against the surfaces of things" (*L* 170), she might have been thinking, though she wasn't, of formulations that can't be reduced to the kinds of simplifications characteristically exemplified by the plot of "Two Friends," because in distinction to that story, in the passages I've examined, elements converge, pull apart, and compel questions about the integrity of aggregates in which incommensurate parts are constellated. In Cather's aggregates, there is often something that can't be accommodated because it lacks applicability or congruity—as in the personification that hangs over "soft and meek" which can't be smoothed into the sense of the formulation that embodies it. The stray element could be something left out of the tangle that constrains an assemblage—like guilt at the cruelty of the story of the bride "fed . . . to the wolves" (*Á* 44), missing from all its versions, or like the unspecified source of Professor St. Peter's "hurt" (*PH* 283). Or it could be something that sticks out as empirically impossible, as when—to return again to the passage in which Alexandra visits Emil's grave and discovers the no-place where the dead feelingly meet the living ("if they feel anything at all" [*OP* 146])—they are linked by a shared recollection of "the old things, before they were born, that comfort people like the feeling of their own bed does when they are little" (*OP* 146). The site is so contingent on legible conditions to gloss what is illegible that in its substitution of a "bed" that can be remembered for a womb that cannot be, it almost domesticates what it displaces. In this way the phantasmal notion that the dead and living could meet anywhere is usurped by the dreamlike place where they are said to meet—in effect, crossing two inconceivables, as though one element of the compound to which each belongs could make the other sensible. Or elements break loose from each other when an adherent that binds them together doesn't hold—as in the "religious emotion" (*PH* 251) that almost glues the *Aeneid* and the cliff dwellings into a unified picture, but splits into two registers, the visual and the audible, when Tom reads the *Aeneid* aloud (*PH* 252). Or they press against the logic that assembles them, as in Ántonia's characteristics which raise a question about how such comprehensive features could be attributes of a single person. Or they constellate an expansion that cannot be demarcated, as when Mr. Shimerda's "cornfields" morph into "the world's cornfields" (*Á* 99), into a universal beyond Mr. Shimerda's experience of his own land. Cather's transpositions admit of no boundaries to the wholes they compose, but we also see the edges of the elements that shape them. In these transpositions, we have a sense of elements floating one way toward the totalities they become, and then the other, away from these assemblages. The elements brought into relation are identical neither to themselves nor to the wholes into which they are drawn, but move between them, even as the flux and the whole coexist in each shift as a simultaneity and a succession.

One could theorize these pulsings—rhythms that sometimes go through meaning and sometimes bypass it—by looking at them through the lens of Lacoue-Labarthe's transmission of Benveniste's distinction between "*skhema*" and "*rhuthmos*": "If *skhema*" designates "'a fixed, realized form posited as an object' (a *stable* form, therefore a figure or *Gestalt*), *rhuthmos*, on the other hand, is 'the form at the moment it is taken by what is in movement, mobile, fluid, the form that has no organic consistency.' It is, Benveniste adds, 'improvised, momentaneous, modifiable' form."[29] Cather herself theorizes a mode of writing that is cryptic, in which predicates slip away from reference, or never had any in the first place. Something like reference and its erasure permeates Alexandra's divination of what the dead feel that is parallel to, but asymmetrical with, her own feeling, because the pre-birth "comfort" is known by the dead through analogy, whereas she has direct access ("things . . . come to you, somehow and you know them" [*OP* 145]). Moreover, the "comfort" of the dead, ventriloquized by Alexandra—thus also her "comfort" since she deciphers by remembering it—is expressed by the simile of a *singular* "own bed" that "people" recall when "*they* are little" (*OP* 146; italics mine), depicted in a sentence that mixes the possessive, singular noun and plural pronouns, the individual and the collective. In this way, Cather characteristically juxtaposes the personal element and the aggregate impersonal reference, the certitude of feeling-knowing and the omission of any source that would validate the conviction. Cather renders unique but inseparable death, life, and "the dark, before you were born" (*OP* 145). When these states converge, they abolish all time and all states of being. Such junctures are perceptible not as meanings, but as points of contact that move in and out of each other in a rhythm, transposing their own conditions reciprocally. One does not need high theory to understand what Cather identifies as "the thing not named" (*NUF* 50), because it is unmoored—drifts, floats, and "somehow" (*OP* 145) registers in "the overtone divined by the ear but not heard by it" (*NUF* 50)—to which Cather's writing "as if unconsciously"[30] testifies. "As if unconsciously" are Cather's words for the way such writing comes to shape itself in "overtone[s]" (*NUF* 50), and perhaps for how her reader absorbs such writing.

Wallace Stevens's Entangled Objects

Any reader of Wallace Stevens might be struck by the throng of enlargements and multiplications in his poems, by how many things "bulg[e]" or "boo[m]," are "big" or are an "utmost," "the largest, bulging still with more." Such magnitude suggests a leveling point: that all things rightly seen are overflowing with themselves in a unique way. Stevens's poems dwell on what it is "to be large in space / . . . to be part / Of sky, of sea, large earth, large air."[1] Such amplifications not only depend on how anything is justly seen; they also emerge when differences of scale and kind cross or engulf each other, when their accord or even interpenetration, however transient, divulges the inclusive vision of "Things of August" in which "differences lost / Difference and were one" (*CP* 494). In "Chocorua to Its Neighbor," the New Hampshire mountain apostrophizes the person who strives for that mountain's "large air" (*CP* 296), rather than the other, Shelleyan way around (e.g., in "Mont Blanc," where the magnitude of the mountain depends on the power of the imagination to conceive its sublimity). For persons—in Chocorua's reflection—the mountain is not only a model of physical and mental stature, "power" and "thought" (*CP* 299), but also a template for their own prodigiousness, purged of their defects: "They wanted him by day to be, image, / But not the person, of their power, thought, / But not the thinker, large in their largeness, beyond / Their form, beyond their life, yet of themselves / Excluding by his largeness their defaults" (*CP* 299). In this equilibration of category ("*beyond* their life, yet *of* themselves" [italics mine]), "beyond" marks an impasse that separates the mountain's capacity and the person's, while the partitive "of" punctures the blockage. The convergence of the two characteristics (boundary and its effacement) may be taken to illustrate the way in which in Stevens's poems' discrepant entities with unlike measures are drawn into each other, while still retaining their distinct properties.

"Looking Across the Field and Watching the Birds Fly" also posits "a pensive nature" that is "larger and yet a little like" our own (*CP* 517–18): "No doubt we live beyond ourselves in air, / In an element that does not do for us, / So well, that which we do for ourselves, too big, / A thing not planned for imagery or belief" (*CP* 518). But though vast air is "a transparency through which the swallow weaves, / Without any form or any sense of form" (*CP* 518), form—whether embodied in the materiality of a mountain or disembodied in the invisible gaseous substance of air surrounding the earth—when held up against the comparatively dwarfed human being, disappears before a more elastic bond: "We, think, then, as the sun shines or does not. / We think as wind skitters on a pond," while "what we think [is] a breathing like the wind" (*CP* 518). In these convergences, sun, wind, breath, thought, air, all flock, flow, and are reflected in each other in Stevens's metaphor of a "glass aswarm with things going as far as they can" (*CP* 519). The metaphor for the teeming migration of incommensurables into each other—in which "the mannerism of nature caught in a glass . . . become[s] a spirit's mannerism"—reaches past identity, difference, and even comparison, since it is not clear that "spirit" could have a "mannerism" or what it would mean to say nature does. Both are drawn together by a term whose connotations apply to neither. Stevens's strange similes, metaphors, and appositions, like the ones exampled above, equivocate on how the inherent features of one category (nature, phenomena of the physical world) are homologous to those of another category (thought). In addition, the reflective mental activity, initially juxtaposed to "nature," is depicted in the poem's last stanzas as tantamount to "spirit" (*CP* 519), the vital principle of conscious life, even though restrictive "thought" and diffusive "spirit" are not interchangeable. In Stevens's poems proximate things, here modes of being, are at once drawn together and thrust apart in a polarity that mutes and even extinguishes reference, as variously described by critics from the 1930s to the present.[2]

To briefly restate the argument of my explorations in the previous essays: In Emerson's writing paratactic images—"the rose of beauty on the brow of chaos"[3]—are nonidentical in logic but inseparable in context and conjoin the personal and the impersonal in a contact that is momentary and nonteleological, a compact that emerges beyond statement and polemic. Whitman's assemblages burst our conception of what kinds of things can be drawn into relation, as well as our assumption that the criteria governing such constellations must be congruent—as when one quality or entity routinely allies itself with another from which it is presumed to be alien—whether in the enumerated identifications of the "grass" in section 6 of "Song of Myself"; the "I" repeatedly transposed into the "you" in section 47; or in the discordant sources of astonishment that are nonetheless deemed parallel in section 19, since in Whitman's flow of universals, nothing has independent identity. Dickinson conjoins abstraction with an upsurge of sensation in poems that allure and enchant but do not impart or explain. Though Stevens never read Dickinson, in "Like Decorations in a Nigger Cemetery," he would write of opacities ("the mask that speaks / Things unintelligible but understood" [*CP* 156]) like those that glimmer from her poems, as in "The tint I cannot take is best" where "The fine - impalpable Array - / That swaggers on the eye . . . leave[s]" us "with a Discontent / Too exquisite - to tell -"[4]—with a non-narratable dis/content. In Cather's novels, antipodal states coincide, wedged deep in experience but outside understanding—as when in *O Pioneers!* the dead and the living meet in the shared recollection of "the old things, before they were born, that comfort people like the feeling of their own bed does when they are little."[5]

In distinction, Stevens's oeuvre presents an extreme case of incommensurables that are not contrasted in pairs (as in the verse and prose described above), but that flow liberally through his poems. This conjoining and amassing of discordant objects and entities that seem to repel obvious association is especially apparent in poems that do not even hew to a logic of scale, but rather move past all that could be situated to evoke breadth under infinitesimal compression in the instant and the "fidge[t],"[6] in the moment and the mood of mind, in which one thing opens into another beyond like-form or kind, drifting free of context. "Even in the case of [an] object," John Cage writes, "the boundaries are not clear. . . . The Indians knew long ago that Music was going on permanently and that hearing it was like looking out a window at a landscape which didn't stop when one turned away."[7] Reading through the vast stream of incommensurables that pass through Stevens's poems, things not like each other that are affixed to each other, I have the sense that life in these poems expresses itself precisely in the problematic relationship among the objects themselves, as well as in perspectives and foci, which stick together so that their boundaries are not clear. In the effaced margins between resemblance and difference, a dazzling interplay of objects and orientations often linked by appositives that cannot be pulled apart emerge and disappear—erratic, spontaneous, strange beyond accounting—in a spectacle we might see before us if, in Cage's words, we had not "turned away."[8] Such conjunctions arise within what Roger Gilbert called "a virtuosic command of syntax,"[9] where proximate noun elements have different references—as in this series from "Things of August": "The voluble intentions of the symbols, / The ghostly celebrations of the picnic, / The secretions of insight" (*CP* 492). They arise in states described by Stevens that explicitly reach beyond boundaries—as in the plumbing of "a later reason" (*CP* 399) in "Notes Toward a Supreme Fiction" or of what in "The Creations of Sound" is discovered as "intelligent / Beyond intelligence" (*CP* 311)—whereas in "Like Decorations in a Nigger Cemetery," "things unintelligible, yet understood" (*CP* 156) emerge outside of coordinates that govern them.

My essay explores such incommensurables and examines the ways in which, in Stevens's poetry, across chronology and poetic development, objects and the perception of objects embody diverse ways of rendering what he described as "the likeness of things unlike."[10] These objects and objectives are sometimes discernible entities, sometimes entwined perceptions, now coordinated, now wholly disproportionate. Their entanglement is the very act of cognitive adjacency, even without material correlation. In addition, the junctures of objects and the perception of objects are enmeshed in each other from distinct vantages that are themselves incommensurable. For instance, the aesthetic patterning that coerces affinities throughout "An Ordinary Evening in New Haven" could never envelop what the poem calls "everything come together as one" (*CP* 482). "Everything," an abstraction, can only be realized at the poem's conclusion by spontaneous movements of mind that evoke a torrent of images whose flux escapes prediction and final form. The zones of incommensurability that I examine manifest "value"[11] in Charles Altieri's terms since Stevens's likenings are prized in excess of the very grounds of comparison that seem to set them free from ethical and empirical considerations. However, my emphasis is not on their value but rather on the representational differences that, from example to example, mirror whether, and what kinds of, congruences are compelling and even ontologically possible in the transformation of "unlike" to "like."

I consider some of these representative vantages from which phenomena flow together outside of paradigms that could restrict or even decipher them. They do so in unique ways: in "Domination of Black" (*CP* 8) through a *turning* that spins discrete objects into a unity, while in "Woman Looking at a Vase of Flowers" (*CP* 246) a dissolution breaks down the unified contours of an abstract vision by novel acts of *becoming* (both discussed in part i); in the discordant phenomena of nature and mind, and the near-anagrams "heaven" and "New Haven," which resist the aesthetic yokes of counterpoint and counterpart that constrain them (discussed in part ii); serially in sequences in which tangentially related objects propelled by impromptu movements that Stevens in "An Ordinary Evening in New Haven" calls "fidget[s]" and "flickings" (*CP* 488), which flow through or along each other having only passing contact (discussed in part iii); and throughout, in neologisms, solecisms, chiasms, and the "sounds of sound" (*CP* 332) of "The Pure Good of Theory." Part iv glances at passages Stevens copied in "A Collect of Philosophy" that bear on how he understood the "everything" variously described above. My essay's title comes from an extravagant analogy that suggests the interaction of Stevens's unlike objects and unlike perceptions about objects (in "Things of August" called "particles" [*CP* 494]) that cannot be described independently, even though they reside at a *conceptual* distance from each other, can be likened to the entanglement of particles in quantum physics that reside at a *physical* distance and yet are correlated. I will return to this point.

Stevens was following the scientific discoveries of the 1920s, and his relation to them helps orient us to the radical analogical relativism of his poetics. The interlocking of diverse conjunctions, orders, and arrangements—sometimes mental, sometimes material—depends most on what in "Effects of Analogy" Stevens called "the discipline that comes from appositeness in the highest degree,"[12] whose grammatical correlates gather far-flung objects, different in kind, quality, and content but possessing "univocal Being" so that the objects in these appositions reside within "equal being." "Equal being is immediately present in everything, without mediation or intermediary, even though things reside unequally in this equal being. . . . [A]ll things are in absolute proximity, and whether they are large or small, inferior or superior, none of them participates more or less in being."[13] In "The Irrational Element in Poetry," Stevens wrote: "The slightest sound matters. The most momentary rhythm matters. You can do as you please, yet everything matters" (*CPP* 789). The sense of "everything" mattering—because all things are equivalent in being—is that while incongruous things can logically be assembled together, it is the disparity of objects within that "everything" which provokes tensions that rile and confound the equilibrium of Stevens's poems.

i

In these poems, vastness beyond the scale of singular objects emerges from formulations that renounce depictive statement, as in the infinitive of "The Latest Freed Man": "to be without a description of to be" (*CP* 205), an imperative of sorts that throws off elucidation for the intensity of lived experience. Such vigor is apparent in "Domination of Black" (the first poem cited below), where turning melds finite entities with those in infinite space, while in "Woman Looking at a Vase of Flowers" (cited second), the formlessness of abstraction sharpens into thingness, into materiality. In both poems, perception flows through boundaries of what something is deemed to be:

> At night, by the fire,
> The colors of the bushes
> And of the fallen leaves,

Repeating themselves,
Turned in the room,
Like the leaves themselves
Turning in the wind.
Yes: but the color of the heavy hemlocks
Came striding.
And I remembered the cry of the peacocks.

The colors of their tails
Were like the leaves themselves
Turning in the wind,
In the twilight wind.
They swept over the room,
Just as they flew from the boughs of the hemlocks
Down to the ground.
I heard them cry—the peacocks.
Was it a cry against the twilight
Or against the leaves themselves
Turning in the wind,
Turning as the flames
Turned in the fire,
Turning as the tails of the peacocks
Turned in the loud fire,
Loud as the hemlocks
Full of the cry of the peacocks?
Or was it a cry against the hemlocks?

Out of the window,
I saw how the planets gathered
Like the leaves themselves
Turning in the wind.
I saw how the night came,
Came striding like the color of the heavy hemlocks
I felt afraid.
And I remembered the cry of the peacocks.

(*CP* 8)

Stevens wrote of *Harmonium*: "This group of poems is not meant to be a collection of epigrams or ideas, but of sensations." Of "Domination of Black," in particular, he elucidated: "I am sorry that a poem of this sort has to contain any ideas at all, because its sole purpose is to fill the mind with the images & sounds that it contains. A mind that examines such a poem for its prose contents gets absolutely nothing from it. You are supposed to get heavens full of the colors and full of sounds, and you are supposed to feel as you would feel if you actually got all this."[14] In the first stanzas, to get "all this" requires the reader, like the speaker, to turn these colors and sounds over in his mind, until he experiences the objects they modify ("leaves," "boughs," "flames," "the colors of [the peacocks'] tails," and "the wind" that has no color because it has no incarnation) subsumed into one by that swirling, while in the last stanza, what turns outside the room ("the planets") is swept into the same perceptual mobility, and thus into the same domain as the earthly objects that also "turn." In this way the subject of the poem—or what Stevens called "the content"—is submerged in the ubiquity of "turning," of which the decisive "striding," another verb of "transport," is a variation. The past tense of "gathering" (in the last stanza) not only applies to the assembly of the planets, but also indirectly to the pileup of all the entities that are caught in the whirl the poem sets in motion which draws them into relationship. Any attempt to designate what motivates the "cry" is foiled by a proliferation of possibilities: "Was it a cry against the twilight / . . . against the leaves themselves / . . . against the hemlocks?"—or is it the cry of the poem itself that can't be extracted from these possibilities? In the end, it does not matter what turns, cries, or gathers, because the poem nearly effaces the distinctions that would make such specifications meaningful. This is what Stevens must mean when he insists the "prose content" does not matter. And this is what I would mean by suggesting that radically different scales held in the same affective balance empty the poem's material description into the pervasive immanence of mood.

In "Woman Looking at a Vase of Flowers," abstraction is fractured by the propinquity of the diverse forms that break out into sumptuous particulars:

It was as if thunder took form upon
The piano, that time: the time when the crude
And jealous grandeurs of sun and sky
Scattered themselves in the garden, like
The wind dissolving into birds,
The clouds becoming braided girls.
It was like the sea poured out again
In east wind beating the shutters at night.

Hoot, little owl within her, how
High blue became particular
In the leaf and bud and how the red,
Flicked into pieces, points of air,
Became—how the central, essential red
Escaped its large abstraction, became,
First, summer, then a lesser time,
Then the sides of peaches, of dusky pears.
Hoot how the inhuman colors fell
Into place beside her, where she was,
Like human conciliations, more like
A profounder reconciling, an act,
An affirmation free from doubt.
The crude and jealous formlessness
Became the form and the fragrance of things
Without clairvoyance, close to her.
(*CP* 246)

The metamorphoses are enacted through similes governed by differently tensed verbs as the fixed shapes of those flowers emerge from nondistinction whether by the deepening of an ascendant color that clusters in a single space ("how / High blue became particular / In the leaf") or by the dispersion of color ("how the red, / Flicked into pieces, points of air, / Became—how the central, essential red / Escaped its large abstraction") in a series of radical transpositions emerging within a field of awareness imbued by that red: "First, summer, then a lesser time, / Then the sides of peaches, of dusky pears." In the permutations that individuate and vitalize the "large abstraction," "became" is a linking verb, not an abstract intransitive (like came into being) and is ambiguously chiasmic: "High blue *became* particular / . . . how the red / Flicked into pieces, points of air, / *Became*" (italics mine). In this strange verbal formulation the *cen*tral, the es*sen*tial that red and blue become is actually the *sensory*, the *essensual*, even an immanence, that "escape[s]" the vaporized abstraction in the poem's beginning, signifying "A profounder reconciling." "Profounder" because, as in the word's etymology, deeper than abstraction, grounded in the weight of those forms (as "the inhuman colors fell / Into place beside her"). The same unchecked malleability—across seemingly incompatible zones of magnitude and abstraction, temporality and objecthood—expressed in "Domination of Black" by "turning" and in "Woman Looking at a Vase of Flowers" by "becoming"—is at once demonstrated and theorized in the first stanza of "The Glass of Water": "That the glass would melt in the heat, / That the water would freeze in cold, / Shows that this object is merely a state, / One of many, between two poles. So, / In the metaphysical, there are these poles" (*CP* 197).

In both poems things come to be, and then come to be something particular, this or that, and then to be something else through a process of inclusion (the "peacocks," the "hemlocks," the "fire," the "planets") or through a transformation said to be "the form and the fragrance of things / Without clairvoyance" established by the senses, whose confines are a limit experienced as a perfect surfeit. "Form" can be trusted—even when its diversity is experienced as an arrangement without hierarchy—because no preconception displaces the immediacy of perceptions that shock and resound (like "thunder"), soothe (like the sweetness of "fragrance"), and elicit credibility (as something brought to mind that is close enough to be regarded, though not palpably touched, like the season of "summer" or like the tangible hue on "the sides of peaches, of dusky pears"). If the woman is enjoined to "Hoot" in a Whitmanian manner to punctuate the profusion of sensual excess whose vitality is dispersed from the immensity of the atmosphere to the immensity of sensory experience, it is perhaps because these two rivalrous types of plenitude can't be detached from each other, even if only because one is the experience of the other. In "Woman Looking at a Vase of Flowers," the broad category of "becoming" is tethered by iterative completion as a linking verb to the epiphenomenon of its own abstraction so that red becomes itself, first by manifestation not in space but in time, a season, and then in "a lesser time," finally to the blush of "peaches" and "pears" as actual spatialized color.

ii

Yet up close there are rifts that strain against the couplings of the objects in Stevens's poems as in this analogy from "Notes Toward a Supreme Fiction": "The weather and the giant of the weather, / Say the weather, the mere weather, the mere air: / An abstraction blooded, as a man by thought" (*CP* 385). In the crisscrossing of macrocosmic weather and microcosmic thought, each becomes a type of what is without and within. Both are erratic, sometimes turbulent, uncontrollable. In Arden Reed's characterization, weather is "aleatory": "The weather is not so much beyond formalism as before formalism. It is 'situated' prior to the appearance of forms or things on the horizon of being."[15] Stevens's formulation bestows on atmospheric conditions an immensity growing out of intoned repetitions drifting forward to exalt the "air," the barest aspect of weather, and backward to legitimate the hyperbole ("the giant of the weather"), while a personification of giantism recurs in the image of "a man [blooded] by thought." Perhaps a man full of thoughts—with thought flowing through his veins—is a trope for the swollen scape of weather. Yet a fissure is right there within the figurative discrepancy of the analogy itself, where the materiality of blood does not sort well with abstraction. Stevens's simile enacts a compositional fusion that we call mixed metaphor ("blooded . . . thought") to erase the categorical distinction that drives apart "weather" and "thought." But the analogy is as static as the stilled life of "weather by Franz Hals / Brushed up by brushy winds in brushy clouds" (*CP* 385) introduced at the beginning of that section of the poem that could never "realiz[e]" "the giant of the weather" (*CP* 385) in the inertia of a painted composition. By comparison, in "The Pure Good of Theory," we see the true blooding of abstraction in the muscular thrust of air itself as embodied breath:

The day in its color not perpending time,
Time in its weather, our most sovereign lord,
The weather in words and words in sounds of sound.
(*CP* 332)

Here the interface of magnitude and internal amplitude—in which weather that exceeds both hyperbole ("the giant of the weather" [*CP* 385]; "our most sovereign lord" [*CP* 332]) and semantic expression—is directly pieced out as the sound of blown air.

In "Two Illustrations That the World Is What You Make of It," sound also prevails but symptomatically in an abortive attempt to harness "a wind that seemed large and loud and high and strong" (*CP* 513) to the flow of a man's breathing:

And as he *th*ought wi*th*in the *th*ought
Of *the wind*, not knowing *th*at *th*at *th*ought
Was not his *th*ought, nor anyone's,

The appropriate image of himself,
So formed, became himself and he breathed
The breath of another nature as his own.
(*CP* 513; italics mine)

Shifting atmospheric pressures regulate the flow of wind. Respiration is also a flow. Each is driven by a motility that does not respire in the same place, thus each is of another "nature." One kind of flow is changed into another in a modulation regulated by "thought." Yet the contorted syntax ("*So formed, became himself* and he breathed / The breath of another nature as his own" [italics mine]) taxes us to determine how a vagrant "image"—"his," "not his," "nor anyone's"—could be taken as "the appropriate image of himself." In the end, the acrobatic turns of phrase are flattened by the concession that what "he" construes as "an image of himself" is only the wind's "momentary breath . . . that never could be animal" (*CP* 513). To think "within the thought / Of the wind" (objective genitive rather than just subjective genitive) is to probe—but not identify—one's own thought in and of the wind as all that alliterative aspirate phonation imitates, spiraling out of control almost to the point of parody: *thawh thih, thawh, thwi, theh, thawh.*[16] In the same acoustic vein, "Page from a Tale" records the "miff-maff-muff of water, the vocables / Of the wind, the glassily-sparkling particles / Of the mind" (*CP* 423). Here the sound of the wind finds its only speech through the nonsemantic lapping of the waves that mirror "the glassily-sparkling particles / Of the" articulate "mind," or of the wavelike brain signals that precede the surge of that brilliance. Such counterparts recall Coleridge's "The Eolian Harp," in which "the desultory breeze" and "all of animated nature / Be but organic Harps diversely framed / That tremble into thought," in "the one Life within us and abroad."[17]

Rethinking the last examples, one might ask of their dissolving oppositions often made phonetically whether Stevens is engaged in trivial sound-play that masks obscurantist metaphysics. The poetics in these lines seem to arise from the strained avoidance of cliché by contorted figuration that could be glossed as the *mind's inner space*, the *spirit's weather*, *the seasons of vitality*, *the voice of nature*: the late Romantic dodging of the obvious with complications at the micro/macro level of a vestigial sublime. Figurative and analogical oddness are the flip side of the commonplace, as for instance in the phrase "blooded . . . by thought," which sidesteps the more banal *lifeblood of consciousness*. Even the equivocation about the "nature" of "breath" (*CP* 513) could be parsed in a way that routinizes the extravagance of these conjunctions: we breathe in (both senses) the world's weather and give it back in embodied thought, the mind enlarged by the circulatory system of a shared sensory atmosphere. In "Evening Without Angels," such projections are chastened: "Air is air, / Its vacancy glitters around us everywhere" (*CP* 137). In "The American Sublime," "the sublime comes down / To the spirit itself, / The spirit and space / The empty spirit / In vacant space" (*CP* 131), a spiritual descent, not a logical reduction, that can't be interpolated or figured.

In the following stanzas from "It Must Be Abstract, III," to voice or say anything about our relation to nature is gestural, more sound than sign ("*Say* the weather" [*CP* 385]; "We *say*: at night" [*CP* 383; italics mine]), a way of channeling things larger than life (cliché again), and often in regard to nature's own inarticulate sounds. Below, nonsense syllables that embody the very *sense* of the incommensurable get measured out by the insufficient reach of words. Nonsense reveals an affinity more enveloping than sense:

> We say: At night an Arabian in my room,
> With his damned hoobla-hoobla-hoobla-how,
> Inscribes a primitive astronomy
>
> Across the unscrawled fores the future casts
> And throws his stars around the floor. By day
> The wood-dove used to chant his hoobla-hoo
>
> And still the grossest iridescence of ocean
> Howls hoo and rises and howls hoo and falls.
> Life's nonsense pierces us with strange relation.
> (*CP* 383)

What is "an Arabian" here if not an exotic power (if the moon, then more force than figure)[18] whose unintelligible sounds and shadow-shapes flung down from space antagonize with illegibility, like that which permeates dreams. As in a dream, star- not moonlight inhabits the room as a visible saturated with sound that is cadenced gibberish. "By day" the din of "wood-dove" and "ocean" diffuse the babble of the night. In "the grossest iridescence," light and water waves blend in a crude display of color, sound, and luster, in pure sensation. The last line lodges the source of the preceding tumult in this genitive: "Life's nonsense," an attribution as fantastic as that of the "Arabian," identifying something vast that eludes containment and deciphering. This something also invades us. In the etymology of "pierce,"[19] "nonsense" bores through us to reveal a cognate within. "Strange relation" is singular; it isn't lateral relations that are grasped, but rather a global relationality (vis-à-vis the Other, and by inference perhaps the Large). Stevens's name for such melding is "A matching and mating of surprised accords, / A responding to a diviner opposite" (*CP* 468), to an affinity we can't anatomize and can't repel.

The introspective couplings of weather and thought, waves and "particles / Of the mind" (*CP* 423), find a more ambitious compass in "An Ordinary Evening in New Haven," which ventures the question whether the quests for "God" and "reality"—or their synecdoches "heaven" and "New Haven"—are equivalent:

> The instinct for heaven had its counterpart:
> The instinct for earth, for New Haven, for his room,
> The gay tournamonde as of a single world
>
> In which he is and as and is are one
> For its counterpart a kind of counterpoint.
> (*CP* 476)

With the conflux of "heaven" and "earth," "as and is," solid object and reflective thought, "the enigmatical / Beauty of each beautiful enigma / Becomes amassed in a total double-thing" (*CP* 472). In this twinning, on "a windy night," "leaves in whirlings in the gutters, whirlings / Around and away, resembl[e] the presence of thought . . . of thoughts" (*CP* 473–74). Though the spiraling of leaves is first analogized to gyrations of thought, the actuality signified by those leaves disappears into the prowess of thought that transposes "imponderable" to "ponderable" and "lighten[s]" "heaviness . . . by light will" (*CP* 476). Thus

> The shadow of bare rock
> Becomes the rock of autumn, glittering
> Ponderable source of each imponderable,
> The weight we lift with the finger of a dream.
>
> The heaviness we lighten by light will,
> By the *hand of desire*, faint, sensitive, the soft
> Touch and trouble of *the touch of the actual hand.*
> (*CP* 476; italics mine)

Yet the poem's breadth does not reside in its distended theory in which the analogous categories "heaven" and "New Haven" orbit each other, or in the flipped reversals of metaphors ("the hand of desire" / "the actual hand"), but in "fidget[s] and "flickings" (*CP* 488), stirrings that turn up affinities whose ragged edges could never be jammed into the conceptual realms of counterpoint or counterpart. If what the poem calls "everything" (*CP* 471, 482) includes "the spirit's alchemicana" (*CP* 471), it grounds that "everything" in the visceral sense of the "high, night air" (*CP* 472), while also distilling the tensions that inhabit passages like the one above into the shock of this indelible image: "a visibility of thought, / In which hundreds of eyes, in one mind, see at once" (*CP* 488). In a mind resplendent with eyes, sensation trumps thought in the flush of phenomena that are catalyzed not crystallized, that don't fit each other as two into one, each ("half the world, half everything" [*CP* 481]) touching at angles or on surfaces, in a drift of experience that can't be tacked down or plumbed. At the poem's end "everything" includes

> The less legible meanings of sounds, the little reds
> Not often realized, the lighter words
> In the heavy drum of speech, the inner men
>
> Behind the outer shields, the sheets of music
> In the strokes of thunder, dead candles at the window
> When day comes, fire-foams in the motions of the sea,
>
> Flickings from finikin to fine finikin
> And the general fidget from busts of Constantine
> To photographs of the late president, Mr. Blank,
>
> These are the edgings and inchings of final form,
> The swarming activities of the formulae
> Of statement, directly and indirectly getting at,
>
> Like an evening evoking the spectrum of violet,
> A philosopher practicing scales on his piano,
> A woman writing a note and tearing it up.
>
> It is not in the premise that reality
> Is a solid. It may be a shade that traverses
> A dust, a force that traverses a shade.
>
> (*CP* 488–89)

"Finikin," a noun, alludes to the flashes of light ("flickings") "glistering"[20] in the froth turned up by the "motions of the sea," or to those motions themselves. Then the noun moves to gloss sculpture and photograph ("Flickings from finikin to fine finikin"). These shifts memorialize an emperor and a president, each mode superannuated in turn—as when an idealized bust of Constantine is superseded by the modern photographic image, and as in the poem's representation of the latter, where a public office is celebrated, but not the person, "Mr. Blank," its ephemeral tenant. "Flickings" / "fine finikin" / "fidget" are words pressed into relation not only alliteratively but also through the mobility of their grammatical objects that migrate from one reference to another, from "fire-foams" to forms of acclaim, each affected by the thrust of change, all "edgings and inchings of final form" in lieu of its evasive fact.

In kind, not one of the elusive phenomena that flit through the closing tercets holds—or ever has—a shape: not "the motions of the sea"; not "the little reds," which are "realized" *where*?; not "the less legible meanings of sounds," in which vibration and timbre echo as sense; not the "inner men"; and not Stevens's coinage of the word "finikin," whose usage is so idiosyncratic as to be minted anew. The shades of "violet" in "an evening" sky fluctuate; the practiced pianistic scales have an order, but not the structure of a musical composition—perhaps incidentally capturing the way this philosophical poet experiments with scales and their discrepancies. The "note" whose sense unfolds in writing, by a quirk, is rent rather than rendered. The stream of figures attest "reality / Is [not] a solid" (*CP* 489). In the near chiasm at the poem's conclusion—"It may be a shade that traverses / A dust, a force that traverses a shade"—the things that cross ("a shade," "a force") and the things that are crossed ("a dust," "a shade" [*CP* 489]), along with the verb "traverses" that implements the crossings, can't be extricated from, but also can't be identified with, each other.

These "swarming activities" (*CP* 488) are mere pulsings of experience, fragments that can't be claimed by the overwrought patterns of counterpart/counterpoint, even if they explicitly cross paths with, or depart from, such complements. Nor do they play a part in the wordplay of heaven/New Haven in which "heaven" seems to borrow its anagrammatic extra *e* from "New" in "New Haven," before turning into the heaviness of speech's "heavy drum" (*CP* 488). The "weight" of that "heaviness" (*CP* 476) pervades both "heaven" and "New Haven"—as well as the attempt to forge an equipoise between the two. In a different ontology, as in the poems to which I turn, the pulsings and "swarming[s]" (*CP* 488) float free of abstraction and design, evading the contrastive modes of expression that divide "An Ordinary Evening in New Haven."

iii

Part IV of "It Must Change" in "Notes Toward a Supreme Fiction" begins with a series of counterpoints:

> Two things of opposite natures seem to depend
> On one another, as a man depends
> On a woman, day on night, the imagined
>
> On the real. This is the origin of change.
> Winter and spring, cold copulars, embrace
> And forth the particulars of rapture come.
> (*CP* 392)

"Winter" and "spring," personify seasonal states drawn together by the cold that envelops each as the former shifts to the latter. When these "cold copulars . . . embrace," there is not only an identic merging (a *copular* verb joins an adjective or noun complement to the subject of a sentence, as in *to be*) but also a sexual merging (*copulate*) from which the issue is "rapture." Yet these lines abandon the symmetrical or slant personifications that precede and follow ("Morning and afternoon are clasped together / And North and South are an intrinsic couple / And sun and rain a plural, like two lovers" [*CP* 392]), for "cold copulars" do not emerge from contrary or proximate states. Rather the emphasis of the coupling is on the shared attribute of cold. While "the origin of change" (*CP* 392) "depend[s]" on "opposite natures," the lines expand the paradigm so that cold that is doubled morphs into ecstasy. The interest of the lines lies not only in a modification that annuls the pattern's banality, but also in a transport of emotion, "forth the particulars of rapture come," a word whose meaning—to "seize" and carry off[21]—relocates the coupling outside of any paradigm. This is a small example of how a single element can break through a template that initially confines it and assume a life of its own.

"Stars at Tallapoosa" undergoes a more intricate reorientation in its allusion to the pathetic fallacy of Walt Whitman's "Out of the Cradle Endlessly Rocking."[22] In Whitman's poem, a boy ventriloquizes the grief of a bird, a "lone singer" (58) perceived to have lost its mate. That heartbreak is mirrored in "that yellow half-moon . . . swollen as if with tears" (8); in "some old crone," the sea, "rocking the cradle" of waves (182); and in the boy's apostrophe to the bird whom he decrees his prototype: "O you singer, solitary . . . projecting me" (150). In distinction, Stevens's first two stanzas reject the pathetic fallacy of Whitman's poem:

> The lines are straight and swift between the stars.
> The night is not the cradle that they cry,
> The criers, undulating the deep-oceaned phrase.
> The lines are much too dark and much too sharp.
>
> The mind herein attains simplicity.
> There is no moon, on single, silvered leaf.
> The body is no body to be seen
> But is an eye that studies its black lid.
>
> Let these be your delight, secretive hunter,
> Wading the sea-lines, moist and ever-mingling
> Mounting the earth-lines, long and lax, lethargic.
> These lines are swift and fall without diverging.
>
> The melon-flower nor dew nor web of either
> Is like to these. But in yourself is like:
> A sheaf of brilliant arrows flying straight,
> Flying and falling straightway for their pleasure,
>
> Their pleasure that is all bright-edged and cold;
> Or, if not arrows, then the nimblest motions,

Making recoveries of young nakedness
And the lost vehemence the midnights hold.
(*CP* 71–72)

The mimesis of the earlier poem in which a bird's presumptive loss inspires a boy's song and his vocation as a poet are further declined in Stevens's own watery scenes on sea and soil (stanzas 3 and 4). For "sea-lines, moist and ever-mingling" and "earth-lines, long and lax, lethargic" are too flaccid to reflect the taut astronomical lines. When Stevens adds: "the melon-flower nor dew nor web of either / Is like to these," the cluster of entities that disable similitude suggests that "the lines . . . between the stars" rebuke any comparison: that nothing *could* be like them. But the inimitability of the "these" in the third stanza does not allude to lines in the constellations, but to Stevens's *poetic* lines, or at the least to the abstract lines in the mind. The simile then follows nonredundantly: the "eye that studies its black lid" sees that poetic lines, too, defy comparison to anything not innate, as expressed in a near tautology, "in yourself is like."

That the lines between the stars and poetic lines are each like nothing else becomes the tacit ground on which they are like each other, an accord secured by the description of both as unswerving. We see the contradiction in Stevens's first line, which distances itself from the confluences that engulf Whitman's poem and then restages affinity in the logic of shared incommensurability. This draws the interstellar lines, poetic lines, and abstract lines in the mind into the same orbit, though they do not merge into one (like counterparts), nor do they dispute each other (like counterpoints), nor are they superposable, nor do they infringe on each other. The poem keeps each at a remove from the other by almost negligible but distinct modes of allusion, as when the demonstrative pronoun "*these* lines" (italics mine) in stanza 3 names poetic or mental lines, while the first stanza evokes lines seen in galactic space. At the same time, though the two are not categorically comparable, the intercosmic lines are intimately recognizable to the "you" by a reference to something within whose correlate is overhead.

The twists and turns of the poem dispel likeness as Whitman establishes it. In reconstructing similitude on the basis of incommensurability, they create something like what Emerson called "an original relation to the universe"[23] established each time that prototypes—of the poem, of its relation to nature, of self, and perhaps also of universe—are not lenses through which perception is filtered. Prototypes mask the lone autonomy whereby a thing is first revealed in its singularity. Only then can a "relation" to it be "original." A vision purged of antecedents returns an innocence—"recoveries of young nakedness," a plural whose reclamation of ardor, agility, and "pleasure" does not cloy ("all bright-edged and cold")—that touches the sets of lines and, by inference, anything else in the universe also experienced as incomparable. The poem's expansion is reinforced by pronouns whose references are inclusive as in the triple reference to cosmic, poetic, and abstract lines of the mind in "*their* pleasure," *their* "recoveries," and "the lost vehemence the *midnights* hold" (italics mine). Of course poetic lines and the lines between the stars are both constellations patterned by the mind—there *are* no lines between the stars or on the page except by dint of the imagination—a source of similitude that is driven to the margins by the poem's fixation on the legitimacy of likeness under conditions of disparity that would seem to prohibit it.

In "Pieces," *not like* turns into a flurry of "is like . . . is like," everything in effect being game for inclusion:

> Tinsel in February, tinsel in August.
> There are things in a man besides his reason.
> Come home, wind, he kept crying and crying.
>
> Snow glistens in its instant air,
> Instant of millefiori bluely magnified—
> Come home, wind, he said as he climbed the stair—
>
> Crystal on crystal until crystal clouds
> Become an over-crystal out of ice,
> Exhaling these creations of itself.
>
> There is a sense in sounds beyond their meaning.
> The tinsel of August falling was like a flame
> That breathed on ground, more blue than red, more red

Than green, fidgets of all-related fire.
The wind is like a dog that runs away.
But it is like a horse. It is like motion

That lives in space. It is a person at night,
A member of the family, a tie,
An ethereal cousin, another milleman.
(*CP* 351)

The poem's title signals its relation to pianistic musical compositions, known by that term, whose contradictive moods conveyed by changes of key, dynamic, and speed are treated as one by the unification of an opus number.[24] Similarly, in Stevens's poem, elements without a formal structure are assembled collectively. The trope "fidgets of all-related fire" names agitations that flare into iridescence, but also the poem's brisk shifts that bind one condition with another (ice and fiery heat), one season with another (February and August); the assonance of those *i* notes in "gl*i*stens" / "*i*nstant" / "*cry*stal" / "*mill*efiori" / "*mill*eman" that swell into "a sense in sounds beyond their meaning"; as well as quirks of image and sensation ("things in a man besides his reason"). There is also a transferred epithet for water frozen on the "instant" that is almost anagrammatic—(g)listen/instan(t)—as if they share a subliminal materiality as crystallized syllables. In the last five lines, a more expansive reach across enmeshed objects syntactically bound by metaphor and simile pushes beyond any unifying alliance. The wind is wild but familiar, or familial, a member of the family but not the immediate family; it is generic ("a person at night"), yet elusive ("a motion . . . in space," an "ethereal cousin"). Though in the last stanza there are three similes, the third a personification that leads to straight metaphor (*is*, rather than *is like*), equating wind with embodied people, or personified relationships, in the final appositive "wind" is a "milleman," a neologism for the thousand-faceted man, too multitudinous to "come home," nothing whose parts could be domiciled, tethered, or even anatomized. Thus "wind" could not be assimilated to a single picture.

In this respect, the strange conceptual relations between "milleman" and the poem's other similes and tropes can be compared to the entangled particles of quantum theory. Particles are intertwined because measuring a particle in one place instantly affects the measurement of another particle and assigns it some intrinsic property even if the two are as far apart as New York and Honolulu, or are millions of miles apart.[25] Conceptual, rather than physical disparity, on a much-reduced scale, impacts relations in "Pieces," as when sequences link images that arise from spheres of discourse that share no frame of reference. They are drawn into "fidgets"; into an "over-crystal"; into the thousandth part of a whole that could not be numerically calculated—metaphoric designations for the poem's particulars that are sonically proximate, but at odds semantically ("milleman"/"millefiori"); extremes that are perceptually matched ("ice" and "fire") but structurally different, or syntactically hinged but asymmetrical, like the "motion that lives in space . . . a person at night," the former carried away by shifting velocities, the latter weighted down by a loose taxonomy ("a person") and an overspecification ("at night")—while the states "*beyond* . . . meaning" and "*besides* . . . reason" (italics mine) depart from common sense in the spatially distinct transgressions of proximity and exteriority. These uneven complements are more unmoored than the deviations that puncture the paradigms of counterparts and counterpoints, and more capricious than the stable contradiction in "Stars at Tallapoosa," a poem that rethinks the very idea of paradigm. Against the backdrop of Stevens's undermined referentiality and his coupling of heterogeneities (whether analogized to music or to physics), we can see that in "Pieces" Stevens's phenomenology of intertwined objects and perceptions defies all discrete ontologies of being or objecthood—in effect turning incommensurability into a metaphysics with no organizing matrix.

The problem of affinity that haunts all of Stevens's poems (what is "like," what defies likeness, and what usurps the structuring opposition that unifies the two) takes an unexpected turn in "The Motive for Metaphor," a poem so exhaustively discussed that I touch only on a striking disagreement—in two assessments I have arranged to oppose—about the relation of the poem's third and fourth stanzas regarding how to read likeness and unlikeness in states the poem contrasts:

You like it under the trees in autumn,
Because everything is half dead.
The wind moves like a cripple among the leaves
And repeats words without meaning.

In the same way, you were happy in spring,
With the half colors of quarter-things,
The slightly brighter sky, the melting clouds,
The single bird, the obscure moon—

The obscure moon lighting an obscure world
Of things that would never be quite expressed,
Where you yourself were not quite yourself,
And did not want nor have to be,

Desiring the exhilarations of changes:
The motive for metaphor, shrinking from
The weight of primary noon,
The A B C of being,

The ruddy temper, the hammer
Of red and blue, the hard sound—
Steel against intimation—the sharp flash,
The vital, arrogant, fatal, dominant X.
(*CP* 288)

The "motive for metaphor" is a response to "autumn" and "spring," incomplete seasons (that "would never be quite expressed"), that are compromised, as in the image of the uneven, halting pace of the breeze, which, in its limping rhythm, moves "like a cripple," in distinction to the consummate winter and summer. Through the third stanza, it seems that a world without fully revealed essence ("The single bird, the obscure moon") requires articulation—metaphoric expression being the compensation, if not the cure, for these half states. But though metaphor can approach the "A B C of being" only gleaned in "the half colors of quarter-things," in metaphor's compensation, the marrow of the "vital" can't be extracted from the "fatal" in the chain of metaphors that realize their inseparability. For the reader, there is also a grammatical crux in the break between the poem's first and second halves. In Beverly Maeder's words, the "grammatical ellipsis at the point of transition" means that "the syntax fails to establish a relation of coordination or subordination" between the first three and the last two stanzas. Therefore, "we must look to the juxtaposition established by the colon to detect another kind of grammatical parallel. And we find one in the morphological parallel between 'Desiring' and 'shrinking from.' They appear in chiasmus, prefiguring the final X, where they come together."[26] But "come together" how?

Maeder's conclusion is that in the indeterminacy of that "X," the "direction" of metaphor "is aleatory" (M 73) and is only "the beginning of an unstated, unfinished series XYZ" (M 72), and thus, I infer, is akin to the incomplete states of "autumn" and "spring," repeating the lack that metaphor was supposed to dispel: "the poem loosens metaphor from any essence" (M 72). Denis Donoghue likewise concludes that the "X" is disappointing—but decisively on another basis: "'The Motive for Metaphor' presents its experience as a blank failure" because "the things of the palpably external world are too dogged, too heavy, too sullen to be lifted" into a "spiritual consciousness" in which man "recognizes again his own self"[27]—a consciousness to which metaphor was to be the mode of access. In Donoghue's reading, metaphor is impotent against the "steel" that crushes "intimation" in the vast and complicated interplay of colors, sounds, and swagger—diverse manifestations of reality's heft and power. Though both agree about that undecidable "X," Maeder's is the more nuanced assessment, placing evasiveness in the ambivalence of the speaker ("Desiring" *and* "shrinking from") and not alone in the *X*'s indeterminacy. In both analyses, metaphor that was supposed to provide an escape from the "A B C of being" (in Donoghue's reading) and from the "half colors of quarter-things" (in Maeder's) fails to do so, an evaluation that unites the readings, notwithstanding the different glosses of that failure. The alliance of "Desiring" and "shrinking from" desire partly precipitates alternative exegeses as a response to the chiasmic force in which unlike morphs into like, in one of the intricate meanderings that structure the trajectory of Stevens's poems,[28] rather than from a canceled (x-ed out) equivalence or from the unfinished sequence of ABC . . . XYZ. Notwithstanding the distinctiveness of these poems—a diversity this essay has been at pains to elaborate—Stevens seems always to be writing a version of the same poem. Yet there is no paradigm for that poem, no way to typify it. In "Motive," for instance, the collapse of the distinction between the "vital" and the "fatal" presents a cohesion whose facets could never be disjoined—unlike the doublets that split down the middle, or are otherwise segregated—as in the "*motive* for metaphor" (italics mine) that is only one part of a dyad, the other part being the *success* of metaphor, which is named by antithesis only in Donoghue's analysis.

iv

"The Motive for Metaphor" raises questions about how things cohere, how far difference extends, what difference in any instant might be. In the preface to *The Order of Things*, Michel Foucault describes the transition from the classical to the modern age "at the end of the eighteenth and beginning of the nineteenth century" where, in what he calls the empiricity of "the middle region," perception is diverse and changeful. In "the middle region"—in relation to life sciences, economy, and language—heterogeneity is experiential.[29] If this is the release of the ordering principle into the world, it precedes formulation. Ad hoc heterogeneities are not under the yoke of fixed concept. Describing this emergence of "order in its primary state" (F xxi) in which "the system of positivities" is "transformed in a wholesale fashion" (F xxii), Foucault, the radical anti-metaphysical taxonomist of human culture, uncharacteristically sounds like Stevens's voicing of a transfigurative phenomenology in which resemblance and difference are matters of immediate, unscripted perception. In the preface, Foucault asks: What is "the threshold above which there is a difference and below which there is a similitude . . . indispensable for the establishment of even the simplest form of order"? "Order is . . . the hidden network that determines the way [things] confront one another, and also that which has no existence except in the grid created by a glance, an examination, a language; and it is only in the blank spaces of this grid that order manifests itself in depth as though already there, waiting in silence for the moment of its expression" (F xx). The passage continues, "Order" appears

> continuous and graduated or discontinuous and piecemeal, linked to space or constituted anew at each instant by the driving force of time, related to a series of variables or defined by separate systems of coherences, composed of resemblances which are either successive or corresponding, organized around increasing differences, etc. This middle region, then, insofar as it makes manifest the modes of being of order, can be posited as the most fundamental of all: anterior to words, perceptions, and gestures . . . more solid, more archaic, less dubious, always more 'true' than the theories that attempt to give those expressions explicit form, exhaustive application, or philosophical foundation. Thus, in every culture, between the use of what one might call the ordering codes and reflections upon order itself, there is the pure experience of order and its modes of being. (F xxi)

However contrastively sourced, Stevens's ensemble of relations that bring together things that are not isomorphic, that don't seem to go together (but that are also not a grab bag of oddities), with things that do evoke aspects of Foucault's characterization of "the pure experience of order and of its modes of being" (F xxi). Reaching further back for analogues: such relations depend on intuition that is each moment yet to be determined, like Kant's a prioris of time and space. In Stevens's poems, affinity can seep through walls of difference—as when no more could be figured from the babble of "hoobla-hoobla-hoobla-how" of the "Arabian in my room" than "Life's nonsense pierces us with strange relation" (*CP* 383). There are no tidy counterpoints or counterparts in "strange relation."

In "Domination of Black," entities estranged in space but conceptually proximate are swept together by the mind that turns from one to the other. The sequences that end "An Ordinary Evening in New Haven" brush against each other in a momentary contact revealing that "reality . . . may be a shade that traverses / A dust, a force that transverses a shade." "A dust" is *matter* without form; a force is a *vitalism*; a "shade" is a *diminution* of light or a *darkening* of hue (*CP* 489). The immaterial cast of light is syntactically but not semantically parallel to a coercive power ("a force") exerted upon it, interweaving what is static with what is dynamic. "Things of August" conjoins abstract—not material, objective—things: a "disused ambit of the soul / Or of a new aspect, bright in discovery" (*CP* 489); "[t]he speech of truth in its true solitude" (*CP* 490); "the endlessly emerging accords" (*CP* 493); "an expanse and the abstraction of an expanse" (*CP* 494). In "Ordinary Evening," even the elements of a simple declarative sentence pull against each other, as in the crossing of a negative employed to express a positive ("It is not in the premise that reality / Is a solid" [*CP* 489]), a proposition that defines itself in relation to forms of difference and possibility that can't be extracted from each other ("It is not. . . . It may be" [*CP* 489]). The conjunctions of such phenomena are incommensurable orderings of experience.

In his commonplace book, Stevens, reflecting on "the principle of order," cites a passage from Richard Storrs's *Divine Origin of Christianity* ("The philosopher could not love the indefinite and impersonal principle of order pervading the universe, any more than he could love atmospheres or oceans"[30]) and adds this rejoinder:

> For myself, the indefinite, the impersonal, atmospheres and oceans, and, above all, the principle of order are precisely what I love; and I dont see why, for a philosopher, they should not be the ultimate inamorata. The premise to Storrs is that the universe is explicable only in terms of humanity.[31]

Such revisionary principles of order are at the core of the "ultimate inamorata"—that is, of the entanglements that become enlargements across Stevens's poems. At the threshold of the audible, the sound of the word "inamorata" for the love object perhaps contains a flicker of the enormousness Stevens spells out elsewhere. Order can be discerned in the combination of things separated by time, space, and concept that give onto each other in the same way they might if they were physically proximate. The logic of such arrangements is parsed by Alfred North Whitehead in a passage Stevens copied in "A Collect of Philosophy": "My theory involves the entire abandonment of the notion that simple location is the primary way in which things are involved in space-time. In a certain sense, everything is everywhere at all times, for every location involves an aspect of itself in every other location. Thus every spatio-temporal standpoint mirrors the world" (*CPP* 858).

Whitehead's proposition is not the same as Blake's "To See a World in a Grain of Sand"[32] because what is seen is not that each thing is representative of the whole, but rather that if each thing "involves an aspect of itself in every other location" (*CPP* 858), then all things stand on common ground and are commensurable. In Edgar Allan Poe's *Eureka*, which Stevens is presumed to have read,[33] Poe expressed his grasp of common ground: "If I venture to displace, by even the billionth part of an inch, the microscopical speck of dust which lies now on the point of my finger . . . I have done a deed which shakes the Moon in her path, which causes the Sun to be no longer the Sun, and which alters forever the destiny of the multitudinous myriads of stars that roll and glow in the majestic presence of their Creator."[34] Though Stevens disparages Leibniz as a "poet without flash," he insists that *Monadology* "transforms reality. Moreover, in a system of monads, we come, in the end, to a man who is not only a man but sea and mountain, too, and to a God who is not only all these: man and sea and mountain but a God as well" (*CPP* 853). These ideas—everything everywhere (Whitehead); ubiquitous consanguinity (Poe); monadic creation in which immaterial, indivisible substances are synchronized with each other about which, Stevens wrote, Leibniz "held that reality consists of a mass of monads, like bees clinging to a branch, although for him the branch was merely a different set of monads" (*CPP* 852)—may have played a modest part in the immersive impression of experience registered in "Things of August" in which "differences lost / Difference and were *one*" (*CP* 494; italics mine). In the pun, a *won*/lost dichotomy hovers over this line—the victory of category over instant, union over multiplicity, won from dispersion into similitude and nameable form:

When was it that the particles became
The whole man, that tempers and beliefs became
Temper and belief and that differences lost
Difference and were one? It had to be
In the presence of a solitude of the self,

An expanse and the abstraction of an expanse,
A zone of time without the ticking of clocks,
A color that moved us with forgetfulness.
When was it we heard the voice of union?

Was it when we sat in the park and the archaic form
Of a woman with a cloud on her shoulder rose
Against the trees and then against the sky
And the sense of the archaic touched us at once
In a movement of the outlines of similarity?
We resembled one another at the sight.
The forgetful color of the autumn day
Was full of the archaic forms, giants
Of sense, evoking one thing in many men,
Evoking an archaic space, vanishing
In the space, leaving an outline of the size
Of the impersonal person, the wanderer,
The father, the ancestor, the bearded peer,
The total of human shadows bright as glass.
(*CP* 494)

Stevens's "archaic forms" in "archaic space" antedate the time before perception shattered the "outlines of similarity" into jagged parts. In that totality, these forms are "giants / Of sense," the epitome of abstraction itself, first personified and then disseminated: "evoking one thing in many men" (*CP* 494). Such forms evince "a new text of the world" (*CP* 494) in which the "archaic" and the latent cannot be riven. In "Lebensweisheitspielerei" (*CP* 504), a neologism that is virtually untranslatable because of the asymmetrical senses of "life"/"wisdom"/"play"—life wisdom *as* play? the tomfoolery, gimmick, or pastime of life wisdom?—one cannot deduce how such concepts comport with each other, even as the title that condenses them into one disallows their fracture, maintaining its ground on the other side of paraphrase. The poem titled by this portmanteau also blends discrete senses. The world is "a dwindled sphere" of "indigence / That is an indigence of the light" (*CP* 505) from which "the proud and strong / Have departed. / . . . / those that are left are the unaccomplished" (*CP* 504). Though one privation follows another, these oxymorons—"a *stellar pallor* . . . hangs on the threads. . . . / in the *stale grandeur* of annihilation" (*CP* 505; italics mine)—are porous to each other, not sequentially or appositionally, but compressed at close range in the attributive adjective. We see a similar contiguity in the hermetic "One of the Inhabitants of the West," where "At evening's one star / And its pastoral text . . . A reader of the text, / A reader without a body, / . . . reads quietly: . . . 'I am the archangel of evening and praise / This one star's blaze.'" The "reader" adds: "'Suppose it was a drop of blood . . . / So much guilt lies buried / Beneath the innocence / Of autumn days'" (*CP* 503–4).

"Blaze" and "blood" are entangled marks that reach across lines that would segregate each. So, too, that anonymous "he" of the poems whose moods are appraised and plumbed, both expels and marks the presence of a lingering "I." The improbable tag "mannerism"—"The mannerism of nature caught in a glass / And there become a spirit's mannerism" (*CP* 519)—evokes "nature" and spirit," joining the two by a word that applies to neither. Stevens's clusters and couplings recall the thread of incommensurables, the likenings at play and at risk, in this book's previous essays, each author probing in a unique way the motive for metaphor and for plainer forms of transposition—as in Stevens's "Time in its weather . . . weather in words and words in sounds of sound" (*CP* 332). Emerson's "beauty" and "chaos" mesh in figures that seal their common plight; Whitman's scalar "translations" bond and blur past and future, "you" and "I"; Dickinson's tropes map wayward ties that interweave abstraction and sensation; Cather's visionary figures repel the underplots that hold them up, but return to find their only life grounded in that sure foundation. Across these metaphoric and ontological junctures, we feel, in "the sharp flash" of "[s]teel against intimation," the sparks let fly from "the hammer" blows (*CP* 288), which efface disparity across heterogeneities that come to constitute each other in the relaxed paradox of their shared difference.

In "Connoisseur of Chaos," Stevens waves away the logic of uniform sense for "the immense disorder of truths" (*CP* 216): "We cannot go back" to the time "when bishops' books / Resolved the world" (*CP* 215). Plural, teeming, anarchic rather than archival, "truths," like entangled objects, do not agree in kind, form, locale, or import. They are "not like statuary, posed / For a vista in the Louvre. They are things chalked / On the sidewalk so that the pensive man may see" (*CP* 216) the ambit of their changes: "suppose the disorder of truths should ever come / To an order, most Plantagenet, most fixed." Then: "A great disorder is an order" (*CP* 216). Viewed on that "sidewalk" is not a swap. Rather, "The pensive man . . . sees that eagle float / For which the intricate Alps are a single nest"—sees the welter of "chaos" and the "nest" of repose that inheres within it distilled as one (*CP* 216). The grammar of that nexus is not just that "everything is everywhere at all times" (Whitehead [*CPP* 858]), but that such entanglements occur in a single event in which things are in a fluid relationship that Stevens described as "a universal iridescence, a dithering of presences and . . . a complex of differences" (*CPP* 858) so that "even in the case of [an] object, the boundaries are not clear."[35] In the glut of that simultaneity, Stevens finds a refuge, a fate, and a poetic method.

Acknowledgments

My first debt of thanks is to my students and colleagues in the Department of English at Princeton University, where I presented an early version of "Whitman's Translations," and to students and colleagues in one-time seminars on Dickinson's off-the-map scenes in English departments at the University of Chicago, Columbia University, New York University, the University of Utah, and the University of North Carolina at Chapel Hill, in which the attendees raised questions that deepened my understanding of both poets. Thanks are due to the English department at New York University, which generously granted me Visiting Scholar appointments and indispensable access to Bobst Library. T. J. Clark, Theo Davis, Judith Grossman, Richard Halpern, Susan Howe, the late Janet Malcolm, Michael Jonik, George Kateb, Ross Posnock, Eric Sundquist, Jane Tompkins, and Marta Werner all read some of the essays; their insights improved the final versions. Colin Dayan, Elizabeth Falsey, the late Jonathan Goldberg, and Michael Moon read all of them; their comments sharpened my thinking and writing in fundamental ways. Interlocutors prized for their skepticism at decisive moments, Branka Arsić, Neil Hertz, and Garrett Stewart read these essays more than once. I appreciate the support of Alan Thomas, my unparalleled editor at the Press since 1989. Ann Goldstein's willingness to copyedit pages of text, often at the last moment, has been an act of pure friendship. I am grateful to Barry Weller, whose acute suggestions and laborious proofing of my manuscripts over four decades have helped bring them up to standard substantively as well as technically. One decade earlier, I met Garrett Stewart, when we were assistant professors at Boston University, and have since counted on the gift of his rare collaborative thinking about intellectual problems distant from those in which he is engaged. As the reader will see throughout, Stewart's theory of the subvocal production in the sounding of phonetic language has awakened my ear to the aurality of silent reading.

My book is dedicated to the memory of Janet Malcolm and Jonathan Goldberg, drawn into an affinity—its own zone in the expansive territory occupied by the likeness of things unlike—through the loss of these incomparable friends.

Notes

Introduction

1. Wallace Stevens, "Conversation with Three Women of New England," in *Opus Posthumous*, ed. Samuel French Morse (New York: Knopf, 1957), 108–9; hereafter abbreviated *OP* and cited parenthetically.
2. Lawrence M. Krauss, *A Universe from Nothing: Why There Is Something Rather Than Nothing* (New York: Free Press, 2012), 17; cited in Leo Bersani, *Thoughts and Things* (Chicago: University of Chicago Press, 2015), 77.
3. Alfred North Whitehead, *Process and Reality: An Essay in Cosmology*, Gifford Lectures delivered at the University of Edinburgh, 1927–28, ed. David Ray Griffin and Donald W. Sherburne (New York: Free Press, 1985), 35, 36; hereafter abbreviated *PR* and cited parenthetically.
4. Cited in Benson Mates, *The Philosophy of Leibniz: Metaphysics and Language* (New York: Oxford University Press, 1986), 219.
5. William James, *The Works of William James: Essays in Radical Empiricism* (Cambridge, MA: Harvard University Press, 1977), 9, 8.
6. I am indebted to Kenneth Reinhard for this example.
7. Leo Bersani, *Thoughts and Things* (Chicago: University of Chicago Press, 2015), 78, 79.
8. Bersani, 82.
9. For the clarity of this explanation and some of the language, I am indebted to an email from Richard Halpern. For a novel analysis of Leibniz's writing that considers its "stylistic, rhetorical, and even poetic dimensions, not just the logical and conceptual ones," see Richard Halpern, *Leibnizing: A Philosopher in Motion* (New York: Columbia University Press, 2023), xii. Halpern argues that Leibniz's "philosophical originality results in part" from the way in which "disparate intellectual realms are allowed to seep into one another" (xiv).
10. William James, cited by John J. McDermott in the introduction to James's *Essays in Radical Empiricism* (Cambridge, MA: Harvard University Press, 1976), xxvi.

11. Christopher Ricks, "William Wordsworth: 'A Pure Organic Pleasure from the Lines,'" in *The Force of Poetry* (Oxford: Clarendon Press, 1984), 91. Ricks's point is "no fragmentation into separateness; but also no dissolution within a greedily engrossing unity" (91).
12. Emily Dickinson's poems are identified by their first line and/or by the numbers assigned them by R. W. Franklin, ed., *The Poems of Emily Dickinson*, Variorum Edition, 3 vols. (Cambridge, MA: Harvard University Press, 1998); hereafter abbreviated F and cited parenthetically. When a first line is used in lieu of a title, I follow the practice of omitting punctuation and, except in the first word, capitals. Quotations are from "My period had come for prayer" (F 525); "Because I could not stop for death" (F 479); "Of all the sounds despatched abroad" (F 334).
13. Whitehead wrote: "I have adopted the term 'prehension' to express the activity whereby an actual entity effects its own concretion of other things" (52). See also *PR* 51, 56–57. Elsewhere: "The 'production of novel togetherness' is the ultimate notion embodied in the term 'concrescence.'" Its "sole appeal is to intuition" (21–22).
14. Gottfried Leibniz, *Leibniz's Monadology: A New Translation and Guide*, ed. Lloyd Strickland (Edinburgh: Edinburgh University Press, 2014), 119. For Leibniz, another kind of comprehensiveness—here in the form of supernatural clairvoyance—pertains to a substance's "thoughts and perceptions": "Nothing can in fact happen to us except thoughts and perceptions, and all our future thoughts and perceptions are only the consequences . . . of our preceding ones, so that if I were capable of considering distinctly everything that is happening to me or appearing to me at this hour, I could see in it everything that will ever happen or appear to me" (cited in Mates, *The Philosophy of Leibniz*, 196).
15. These distinctions are introduced in "Of the Nature and Origin of the Mind," in the *Ethics*. *A Spinoza Reader: The Ethics and Other Works*, ed. and trans. Edwin Curley (Princeton, NJ: Princeton University Press, 1994), 141 (II P40S2); hereafter abbreviated *Et*. For the reader's convenience, the first number refers to the page of the Curley translation. Following Curley (xxxv), in the parenthetical citation that follows, Roman numerals denote parts of the *Ethics*. Arabic numerals are used for axioms, definitions, propositions, and the like. A = Axiom; P = Proposition; D (following a Roman numeral) = Definition; D (following P + an Arabic numeral) = Demonstration of the Proposition; C = Corollary; S = Scholium. So, above, "II P40S2" indicates book II, proposition 40, scholium 2 of the *Ethics*.
16. Wallace Stevens, "A Collect of Philosophy," in *Collected Poetry and Prose*, ed. Frank Kermode and Joan Richardson (New York: Library of America 1997), 853; hereafter abbreviated *CPP* and cited parenthetically.
17. See Richard Halpern, "Metaphorical Clumping," which argues the inverse of Stevens's argument: namely, that "analogical thinking is foundational for Leibniz." Halpern, *Leibnizing*, 37.

18. Willa Cather, "The Novel Démeublé," in *Not Under Forty* (Lincoln: University of Nebraska Press, 1968), 50.
19. Ralph Waldo Emerson, "Experience," in *Essays and Lectures*, ed. Joel Porte (New York: Library of America, 1983), 485; hereafter abbreviated E and cited parenthetically. All references to Emerson's essays are to this edition.
20. Wallace Stevens, "The Man with the Blue Guitar," in *The Collected Poems* (New York: Vintage, 1990), 165; hereafter abbreviated *CP* and cited parenthetically.
21. Walt Whitman, "Crossing Brooklyn Ferry," in *Leaves of Grass and Other Writings*, ed. Michael Moon (New York: Norton Critical, 2002), 6:71; hereafter abbreviated CBF and cited parenthetically. All citations to Whitman's works are to this edition. Where any of Whitman's poems are divided into parts, the first numeral indicates section; the second, line number.
22. Willa Cather, *The Professor's House* (New York: Vintage, 1973), 252–53; hereafter abbreviated *PH* and cited parenthetically.
23. Whitman, "Song of Myself," in *Leaves of Grass and Other Writings*, ed. Moon (3:47); hereafter abbreviated SM and cited parenthetically. The first numeral indicates section; the second, line number.
24. Henri Bergson, *Creative Evolution*, trans. Arthur Mitchell (Mineola, NY: Dover, 1998), 47; hereafter abbreviated *CE* and cited parenthetically. Stevens also read Bergson's *L'Intuition philosophique*, as well as Bergson on comedy.
25. Such passages might also be considered as *generically* philosophical in terms suggested belatedly to me by Paul North, who introduced "homeotics," a field defined by relations structured by likeness, as a "challenge to ontology." North, *Bizarre-Privileged Items in the Universe: The Logic of Likeness* (New York: Zone Books, 2021), 61. I say *belatedly* since I read this book only after the completion of my manuscript. Retrospectively for me, it provides a way of understanding the wider sphere of phenomena in which the literary texts I discuss might find a place as a subset. In addition to North's range of captivating examples of likeness, he charts the ways in which philosophers and scientists such as Aristotle, Plato, Plotinus, Kant, Darwin, Wittgenstein, and others formulated discordant notions of likeness. North's characterizations of likeness from diverse vantages amplify: "A thing is a plenum of likenesses" (61). "A thing is likenesses through and through, with no remainder" (103). "What we call a 'thing' is surrounded by a halo of partial things, traits, pieces, manners, affects . . . that are in some ways kin to it. . . . Penumbral elements make travesties of individuals" (62). "Likenesses . . . are first and foremost fungible and unstructured" (134). "Another aspect of homeosis that distances it from signification, . . . phenomenological intention, . . . aesthetic mimesis, or metaphysical causality, is bidirectionality" (135).

    In my essays *un*likeness is the pivotal term, though it is linked to likeness, while in North's book *likeness* is the operative term, though linked to *un*likeness. The anomaly is the same from a different direction, with a different scope, different coordinates, a different emphasis and in relation to divergent objects (or *things* in North's vocabulary). My objects are literary texts, but they similarly default on interpretive meanings, shying away from discursive language, while still giving rise to something meaningful and felt.

26. Walter Benjamin, *The Arcades Project*, trans. Howard Eiland and Kevin McLaughlin (Cambridge, MA: Harvard University Press, 1999), 460; hereafter abbreviated *AP* and cited parenthetically.
27. A transcription from Whitman's "Talbot Wilson" notebook (leaf 19 recto, leaf 19 verso) in the Walt Whitman Archive, https://whitmanarchive.org/manuscripts/notebooks/transcriptions/loc.00141.html.
28. Willa Cather, *My Ántonia* (New York: Barnes & Noble Classics, 1994), 45; hereafter abbreviated *Á* and cited parenthetically.
29. Writing of Cather to Leonard C. van Geyzel on December 9, 1940 (Letter 417), Stevens declared: "You may think she is more or less formless. Nevertheless, we have nothing better than she is." *Letters of Wallace Stevens*, ed. Holly Stevens (Berkeley: University of California Press, 1996), 381.
30. Edgar Allan Poe, *The Science Fiction of Edgar Allan Poe*, ed. Harold Beaver (New York: Penguin, 1978), 292; hereafter abbreviated EAP and cited parenthetically.
31. Jorge Luis Borges, "The Aleph," in *The Aleph and Other Stories*, trans. Andrew Hurley (New York: Penguin, 2004), 127; hereafter abbreviated A and cited parenthetically.
32. Michel de Montaigne, "Of Experience," in *The Complete Essays of Montaigne*, trans. Donald M. Frame (Stanford, CA: Stanford University Press, 1965), 821.
33. Emerson, "The Poet," in *Essays and Lectures*, ed. Porte, 460.
34. Herman Melville, *Moby-Dick*, An Authoritative Text, 2nd ed., ed. Hershel Parker and Harrison Hayford (New York: Norton Critical Edition, 2002), 140.
35. I have addressed the relation of these incommensurables in *Choosing Not Choosing: Dickinson's Fascicles* (Chicago: University of Chicago Press, 1992); *Writing Nature: Henry Thoreau's Journal* (Chicago: University of Chicago Press, 1985); and *The Corporeal Self: Allegories of the Body in Melville and Hawthorne* (Baltimore: Johns Hopkins University Press, 1981; pbk., New York: Columbia University Press, 1991). *Lyric Time: Dickinson and the Limits of Genre* (Baltimore: Johns Hopkins University Press, 1979) considers the relation between temporal continuity and temporal stasis, at odds but conjoined, in the ruptured wholes of Dickinson's lyrics.
36. F. Scott Fitzgerald, *The Great Gatsby* (New York: Union Square and Co., 2022), 146.

Beginning to Be

1. Ralph Waldo Emerson, *Nature*, in *Essays and Lectures*, ed. Joel Porte (New York: Library of America, 1983), 31; hereafter abbreviated *N* and cited parenthetically. All references to Emerson's essays are to this edition.
2. Emerson, "The American Scholar," 67.

3. Emerson, "Nominalist and Realist," 580; hereafter abbreviated NR and cited parenthetically.
4. Emerson, "Uses of Great Men," in *Representative Men*, 625; hereafter abbreviated U and cited parenthetically.
5. Emerson, "Fate," 955; hereafter abbreviated F and cited parenthetically.
6. Emerson, "The Over-soul," 385; hereafter abbreviated OS and cited parenthetically.
7. Emerson, "Worship," 1076.
8. Emerson, "The Divinity School Address," 89; hereafter abbreviated DSA and cited parenthetically.
9. Emerson, "Montaigne or the Skeptic," 709; hereafter abbreviated M and cited parenthetically.
10. Emerson, "Experience," 473; hereafter abbreviated E and cited parenthetically.
11. The depreciation of the person in Emerson's writing is examined in "The Way of Life by Abandonment: Emerson's Impersonal"; Emerson's dissociation from his own person is explored in "Representing Grief: Emerson's 'Experience,'" both in Sharon Cameron, *Impersonality: Seven Essays* (Chicago: University of Chicago Press, 2007), 53–78, 79–107.
12. Emerson, "The Poet," 467; hereafter abbreviated P and cited parenthetically.
13. Emerson, "Circles," 404; hereafter abbreviated C and cited parenthetically.
14. "Intuitive" is Spinoza's word for "knowledge of the third kind," which Spinoza calls "the intellectual love of God" (*Et* 261, 260; V P36S). For abbreviations in reference to the *Ethics*, see note 15 in the Introduction.

    For Spinoza there are three distinguishable kinds of knowledge: "Knowledge of the first kind" is "represented to us through the senses in a way which is mutilated, confused, and without order." "The second kind of knowledge" arises "from the fact that we have common notions and adequate ideas of the properties of things." This Spinoza calls "reason." In the "third kind," called "intuitive knowledge," "knowing proceeds from an adequate idea . . . of the essence of things" (*Et* 141; II P40S2). I will return to these distinctions and their pertinence for Emerson.
15. "Lived transition" is Deleuze's characterization of a person's continuous movement between the kinds of knowledge—that is, between "adequate" and inadequate ideas, and therefore between sadness and joy. Gilles Deleuze, *Spinoza: The Velocities of Thought*, lecture 2, December 2, 1980, The Deleuze Seminars, https://deleuze.cla.purdue.edu/lecture/lecture-02/. Deleuze describes the third kind of knowledge as "thinking at absolute speed," thinking "that goes simultaneously to the deepest level . . . , that possesses a maximum amplitude proceeding like a bolt of lightning." In the third kind of knowledge, "everything is contracted" as distinct from "the relative slowness of the first four books."
16. Emerson learned of Spinoza's philosophy through Goethe (Gustaaf Van Cromphout, *Emerson's Modernity and the Example of Goethe* [Columbia:

University of Missouri Press, 1990], 26–40), and also through the seventeenth-century Pierre Bayle's five-volume *Historical and Critical Dictionary*, which he checked out from Harvard College Library in 1824. See Adam Adler's honors thesis, "Emerson's Hidden Influence: What Can Spinoza Tell the Boy?" Georgia State University, 2007, https://doi.org/10.57709/1061169. "The Divinity School Address," *Nature*, and "Power" especially reveal Spinoza's influence on Emerson.

In addition, Emerson imparted Spinoza to Charles Sanders Peirce: "through his re-definition of the notion of 'power' and 'endeavor,'" Emerson transmitted the "Spinozian-Emersonian tradition" that "acted like a virus . . . hidden in the folds of Peirce's reflections." Rossella Fabbrichesi, "Spinoza, Emerson, and Peirce: Re-thinking the Genealogy of Pragmatism, 2019 Presidential Address," *Transactions of the Charles S. Peirce Society* 55, no. 2 (Spring 2019): 103, https://www.jstor.org/stable/10.2979/trancharpeirsoc.55.2.01. In other words, the origins of pragmatism, according to Fabbrichesi, are not a modern phenomenon, but can be traced back through Emerson to Spinoza.

17. In Spinoza's multiple characterizations, individuals are human "bodies . . . distinguished from one another by reason of motion and rest, speed and slowness, and not by reason of substance" (*Et* 125; II P13L); but the same word also describes "the parts of an individual" that compose his "composite body" (*Et* 126; II P13A3); and in addition, there is a "third kind of individual . . . composed of a number of individuals of a different nature." From this sequence, Spinoza invites us to conclude that "if we proceed in this way to infinity, we shall easily conceive that the whole of nature is one individual" (*Et* 127; II P13L7S).
18. "Display" is Charles Altieri's characterization of what might "clarify" Wittgenstein's assertion that ethical concerns "could not be said but had to be shown": "The role of display in late Wittgenstein extends to the claim that agents cannot be expected to be argued into changing values, but have to be led to 'look at the world in a different way.'" Such displays not only have an aesthetic effect, but they also have an "ethical" effect. Altieri, "The Poverty of Moral Theory in Literary Discourse: A Plea for Recognizing the Multiplicity of Value Frameworks," *Soundings: An Interdisciplinary Journal* (Spring/Summer 2011): 45, 52. The argument is amplified in Altieri's *Reckoning with the Imagination: Wittgenstein and the Aesthetics of Literary Experience* (Ithaca, NY: Cornell University Press), 2015.

    For Emerson, too, change, and the compunction of an ethical imperative do not come about by argument, but by radical shifts of perspective.
19. Emerson, "Compensation," 302.
20. Emerson, "Spiritual Laws," 305.
21. Emerson, "Illusions," 1121; hereafter abbreviated I and cited parenthetically. The slippage (between "trifles" that never had value and challenges that wound

Thor's pride in the Norse myth that Emerson appropriates) is Emerson's. It's an odd slippage, since the competitions Thor fails initially seem merely humiliating, not at all like things of consequence. As the above discussion suggests, there is a similar slippage between "us who are contending" and "he" who contends (I 1121).

22. Emerson, not Thor, is omitting the portrayal of realization as an experienced phenomenon, but its preclusion might be understood in relation to a distinction in "Intellect" between "intellect receptive," which involves spontaneous intuitions, and "intellect constructive," which molds these so that "thoughts, sentences, poems, plans, designs, systems" can be produced from a structuring of such insights ("Intellect," 422). The passage in "Illusions" is not concerned with this distinction, but it clarifies what is missing from the representation of Thor's discovery: revelation of this magnitude might precipitate wonder rather than a cool acknowledgment of an inscrutable truth.
23. *Dictionary of Untranslatables: A Philosophical Lexicon*, ed. Barbara Cassin; trans. Steven Rendall, Christian Hubert, Jeffrey Mehlman, Nathan Stein, and Michael Syrotinski; translation ed. by Emily Apter, Jacques Lezra, and Michael Wood (Princeton, NJ: Princeton University Press, 2014), 772.
24. Theodor W. Adorno, "The Essay as Form," in *Notes to Literature*, vol. 1, ed. Rolf Tiedemann, trans. Shierry Weber Nicholsen (New York: Columbia University Press, 1991), 22, 23. In relation to the essayist's "accentuation of the partial against the total, in its fragmentary character," Adorno quotes Georg Lukács on "the essayist" who "adapts himself to this smallness—the eternal smallness of the most profound work of the intellect in the face of life" (9–10). This discrepancy also applies to Emerson's paratactic images.
25. I am modifying a phrase of Simon Jarvis's: a "rhythm intervoluted with thinking." Jarvis, "Superversive Poetics: Browning's *Fifine at the Fair*," *MLQ* 77, no. 1 (March 2016): 137. Jarvis's phrase is situated within an argument about how an "individual line" in Browning's poem *Fifine at the Fair* has "value in itself" and exploits aesthetic intensities in a way that actively "refuses the usual schemata of literary mereology" (130). Jarvis calls such a line "superversive" because it elevates "composition and technique"—specifically, "the play between syntactic and metrical segmentation"—above "theme and representation" (139). Thus "for each metrically virtuosic poem, there might be some single line which constitutes something like the poem's zenith, its noncompare of a rhythm intervoluted with thinking" (137).

    I adopt Jarvis's phrase to signify the disproportionate importance of image to exposition at certain moments of Emerson's essays discussed above, and to emphasize the work these images do to heal the conceptual divisions that have preceded them—whether between "Fate" and "freedom" (F 953); or between the necessity of our "ruin" and the "universal benefit" which that ruin procures

(F 967); or even between the economic calculations that measure cost in relation to return with respect to the "pain" that constitutes "ruin" ("whatever lames or paralyzes you, draws in with it the divinity, in some form, to repay" [F 967])—in Emerson's prose.

26. The *OED* links the two words in its first example of "the world or universe as an ordered and harmonious system." 1650: "As the greater World is called Cosmus from the beauty thereof" (J. Bulwer *Anthropometamorphosis* xv. 149).
27. Such an exclusion is examined in Geoffrey Hartman's analysis of the phrase "the voice of the shuttle" from "Sophocles . . . on the theme of Tereus and Philomela," which gains its "power" from the "elision of middle terms and overspecification of end terms." Hartman, "The Voice of the Shuttle: Language from the Point of View of Literature," in *Beyond Formalism: Literary Essays, 1958–70* (New Haven, CT: Yale University Press, 1970), 338. Hartman adds that such phrases might "have little meaning without a story. . . . [Y]et once a story is found, their suggestiveness is not absorbed but rather potentiated" (337). Similarly, the power of Emerson's images is intensified by restoring them to their place in the essay's tangle of casuistic arguments for and against fate, and in the propositions that declare beauty can compensate for fate, as discussed above.
28. For instance: "I do not wonder at a snow-flake, a shell, a summer landscape, or the glory of the stars; but at the necessity of beauty" (F 967).
29. I am recalling Agamben's citation and gloss of Aristotle's *De anima* in which a potential also implies a lack: "the principle of sight 'in some way possesses color,' and its colors are light and darkness, actuality and potentiality, presence and privation. . . . The greatness—and also the abyss—of human potentiality is that it is first of all potential not to act, *potential for darkness*." Giorgio Agamben, "On Potentiality," in *Potentialities: Collected Essays in Philosophy*, ed. and trans. Daniel Heller-Roazen (Stanford, CA: Stanford University Press, 1999), 181.
30. In "An Approach to Unapproachable America," Richard Poirier takes up the dualism of the figures "Culture" and Power," associating "culture" with conventions of pastoral at the beginning of the paragraph discussed above and "power" with Emerson's sensational description of "the ecstasy in the desert." Poirier, "An Approach to Unapproachable America," *Raritan* 26, no. 9 (2007): 1, 3. The association of the desert with power is nowhere in the passage, but, Poirier reports, it is given in the journal phrase from which the passage comes: "the sunbright Mecca of the Desart of Infinite Power" (6), a figure whose genitive Emerson drops when he transfers the passage from journal to essay. As Poirier acknowledges, "any relations between power and culture are left only to inference" (6). Still, as intimated above, I would agree that this omission is irrelevant to the fact that some crucial tension is, in Altieri's term, "displayed" (see note 18, above) in the contrast between the calculable stages enumerated in

Emerson's paragraph and what could never be calculated or anticipated, because its power is primordial.

In distinction, Stanley Cavell's analysis of the same passage argues that Emerson's finding himself in loss (of Waldo, at the child's death) is compensated by the idea of founding America and the concomitant discovery that "if I have found a new America, then I have to declare myself the first philosopher of this new region, the founder of the nation's thought." Cavell, *This New Yet Unapproachable America: Lectures After Emerson After Wittgenstein*, The 1987 Frederick Ives Carpenter Lectures (Chicago: University of Chicago Press, 1989), 106. Cavell calls these associations "fantasizing" (107).

In diverse ways, Emerson's passage throws critics off-balance—as it did me when in my 1986 "Representing Grief: Emerson's Experience," I did not consider the Mecca-America passage because I could not see how its range could be assimilated to the expression of so much channeled grief in the essay as a whole.

31. There would be a darker, historical reading of the passage in which America's manifest destiny involves the metaphorical overcoming of Muslims, as it did in the attempted removal and obliteration of Native Americans. The context of Emerson's passage seems to drive such a gloss into the margins, but not out of acknowledgment.
32. Thus unlike Emerson's "The Poet," where the "ravishment of the intellect" enables "passage out into free space" only through the "escape" of "the custody of that body in which [man] is pent up" (P 460), in the Mecca-America passage, freedom is an incarnated experience.
33. Walter Benjamin, *The Arcades Project*, trans. Howard Eiland and Kevin McLaughlin (Cambridge, MA: Harvard University Press, 1999), 460, 461, 462, 463, 464; hereafter abbreviated *AP* and cited parenthetically.
34. Although Benjamin's "dialectical images" (*AP* 462, 463) are usually understood to be the means by which a materialist history of the nineteenth century will be revealed, demonstrating "knowledge [that] comes only in lightning flashes" (*AP* 456) inseparable from the "primal history of the present" (*AP* 462), this is not always the context of the term, as in Benjamin's example of Proust's lost and found time whose juncture equally prompts an "awakening" (*AP* 464). "Dialectical image" also sheds its historical frame in Adorno's description of the interactive relation of myth and enlightenment in Max Horkheimer and Theodor W. Adorno, *Dialectic of Enlightenment*, trans. John Cumming (New York: Continuum, 2002). And when it is concluded by Giorgio Agamben in "Aby Warburg and the Nameless Science" that for Warburg a specific image "is neither an external object nor an intrapsychical entity" but reveals the "the play of mental alienation" and "pure historical matter" (Agamben, "Aby Warburg and the Nameless Science," in *Potentialities*, 102–3), Agamben's use of the term "dialectical image" (103)—as in my description of the juncture of Emerson's

paratactic images—comes to include diversely contrasted images and ideas that are inseparable.

35. Needless to say, Spinoza's philosophy ought ideally to be examined in its own right. I touch perfunctorily on certain aspects of it here only as a reference point for my consideration of Emerson, but direct my reader to Pierre Macherey, *Hegel and Spinoza*, trans. Susan M. Ruddick (Minneapolis: University of Minnesota Press, 2011); Étienne Balibar, "Spinoza's Three Gods and the Modes of Communication," *European Journal of Philosophy* 20, no. 1 (2012); Étienne Balibar, "A Note on 'Consciousness/Conscience' in the *Ethics*," reprinted as "Postscript," in *Identity and Difference: John Locke and the Invention of Consciousness*, trans. Warren Montag (New York: Verso, 2013); Gilles Deleuze, *Spinoza: Practical Philosophy*, trans. Robert Hurley (San Francisco: City Lights Books, 1988); Gilles Deleuze, *Expressionism in Philosophy*, trans. Martin Joughin (Princeton, NJ: Princeton University Press, 1968); and Warren Montag, *Bodies, Masses, Power: Spinoza and His Contemporaries* (New York: Verso, 1999).
36. This is Pierre Macherey's gloss in his *Hegel and Spinoza*, trans. Ruddick, 68.
37. Cited in Deleuze, *Spinoza: Velocities of Thought*, lecture 14, March 24, 1981, The Deleuze Seminars, https://deleuze.cla.purdue.edu/lecture/lecture-14-0/. On April 3, 1663, in a letter to Lodewijk Meyer, Spinoza wrote: "we can arbitrarily delimit the existence and duration of Modes . . . ; and we can conceive this duration as greater or less, and divisible into parts. But Eternity and Substance, being conceivable only as infinite, cannot be thus treated without annulling our conception of them." Spinoza, *Complete Works*, trans. Samuel Shirley, ed. Michael L. Morgan (Indianapolis: Hackett, 2002), 788.
38. Étienne Balibar, "A Note on 'Consciousness/Conscience' in the *Ethics*," in *Studia Spinozana* 8 (Königshausen & Neuman, 1992), 49–50; hereafter abbreviated NCC and cited parenthetically. The essay is reprinted as "Postscript" in *Identity and Difference: John Locke and the Invention of Consciousness*, trans. Warren Montag (New York: Verso, 2013). Page numbers are to the essay publication in *Studia Spinozana*.

    Balibar's understanding of "consciousness" in the *Ethics* is unique. In the etymological and philosophical history of the words "*conscientia*" and "*conscius esse*" that he establishes, the Latin word "'*conscientia*'" becomes "link[ed]" with "'epistemology,' 'psychology,' and 'ethics' in Spinoza's philosophy" (NCC 38) in such a way that in the *Ethics* for Spinoza "consciousness" and "conscience" come to "refer exactly to the same phenomena" (NCC 46). This "phenomenology of consciousness-conscience . . . is tantamount to defining the Essence of Man" (NCC 47). However, in Balibar's analysis, "consciousness" and "knowledge" are *not* the same thing.

    "*Each kind* of knowledge can be accompanied by some sort or degree of consciousness" that pertains to "the way *a relationship* can be built within knowledge between these different 'objects,'" namely, the "Mind, 'its' Body, God, the 'things' in general" (NCC 47, 48). In the third kind of knowledge "the Mind . . . [is] conscious of *its own Body* from the point of view of eternity" with "its singular essence and powers deriving causally from God (or Nature) as a proximate cause" (NCC 48). Balibar emphasizes: "It is not *a Body* . . . that is conceived from the point of view of eternity, it is 'my Body'" that is "conceived from the point of view of eternity" (NCC 48), not as an idea, but as "an immanent consequence of 'intuitive science'" (NCC 49)—something spontaneously and immediately experienced.

39. Deleuze coins the word "mystic" to describe Spinoza's characterization of the third kind of knowledge (Deleuze, *Spinoza: Velocities of Thought*, lecture 14, https://deleuze.cla.purdue.edu/lecture/lecture-14-0/) and "suggests there is no such thing as a 'God of the second kind,' but only a *transition towards the understanding of God*, whose idea always belongs to the third kind, through the development of increasingly adequate representations of nature, and the joy it provokes." Balibar, "Spinoza's Three Gods and the Modes of Communication," 39; hereafter abbreviated STG. For Balibar, in distinction, there are "*three ideas of God*" which are related to, but not identical with, "the *three kinds of knowledge*. . . . [K]inds of knowledge are kinds of the knowledge of God, not in the mystical sense, but in the practical sense" (STG 40). Balibar elaborates "the impossibility of reducing the essence of God to a single idea, or a single name for its idea" by proposing "a *triplicity*: *three Gods* whose ideas are incompatible, but nevertheless form parts of a single process of communication" (STG 29). In this uniform process, "every idea which refers to God is true (or has 'truth content')" (STG 32). The "truth content" of the second idea of God crucially concerns the neighbor. Moreover, "the practical rule of loving one's neighbour . . . is not a means towards an *external* goal, but it performs its own result" (STG 39).
40. "The more each thing is perfect, the more reality it has" (*Et* 263; V P40).

Whitman's Translations

1. A transcription from Whitman's "Talbot Wilson" notebook (leaf 19 recto, leaf 19 verso) in the Walt Whitman Archive, which also includes scans of Whitman's pages. The text cited omits the cross-outs included in the archive's transcriptions: https://whitmanarchive.org/manuscripts/notebooks/transcriptions/loc.00141.html. My thanks to Ed Folsom for helping me locate this passage.
2. Walt Whitman, "Out of the Cradle Endlessly Rocking," in *Leaves of Grass and Other Writings*, ed. Michael Moon (New York: Norton Critical Edition, 2002), 22. All citations to Whitman's works are to this edition. Further passages of "Cradle" are cited parenthetically and abbreviated OC. Where any of Whitman's poems are divided into parts, the first numeral indicates section; the second, line number.
3. In biology there is a process called "translation" that denotes a step in protein biosynthesis in which the genetic code is transformed to produce a particular sequence of amino acids.

For a comprehensive discussion of the importance of translation to Whitman's poetry, see Colleen Glenney Boggs's "Specimens of Translation in Walt Whitman's Poetry" (*Arizona Quarterly* 58, no. 3 [2002]), which demonstrates that Whitman's "comments in *Specimen Days* and his linguistic practices in *Leaves of Grass* reconfigured the discourse of a specific kind of literary anthology, the specimen collection" (34). "As a literary conceit, translation is the consummate specimen; since no two translations will be exactly the same" (39). This conceit is then examined in relation to "the antebellum press which published the reciprocal and often collaborative translations of such men of letters as Longfellow and the German poet Ferdinand Freiligrath" (40). The latter part of Boggs's essay turns to Whitman's use of the word "translation" in his own poetry and includes an especially fine reading of linguistic nativism in sections 1 and 6 of "Song of Myself" (44–46).

4. Whitman, "Song of Myself," 21:423–24; hereafter abbreviated SM and cited parenthetically.
5. Walter Benjamin, "On Language as Such and on the Language of Man," in *Selected Writings*, vol. 1, *1913–1926*, ed. Marcus Bullock and Michael W. Jennings (Cambridge, MA: Harvard University Press, 1996), 69; hereafter abbreviated LS and cited parenthetically.

"The linguistic being of things is their language" (LS 64). The language of a "mental entity," or what the translator of Benjamin's *Selected Writings* alternately calls a "mental being" (LS 63)—even though the noun phrase translated is in each instance "*geistige Wesen*" (the essence or nature of something)—is "that which is . . . communicable" in it (LS 63). The phrase "mental entity" suggests that what is communicated by a thing is a cognitive datum as distinct from a thinking thing, whereas "mental being" implies a personification in which human existence is attributed to a thing. The confusion introduced by the translator is immediately clarified in Benjamin's claim that the "conception" (LS 69) or "knowledge of things" (LS 71) enables man to discern what *in* them is communicable, and thereby to express his own "mental being" (*das geistige Wesen des Menschen*), hence to translate "the mute into the sonic . . . the nameless into name" (LS 70).

On the diverse connotations of Benjamin's use of the word "translation" in general, and on the relation of God's "creative Word" to "Adamic naming," Carol Jacobs writes: "Benjamin's language has its own word to mark the difference of human cognition in Adamic naming. It is 'conception.'" Jacobs, "The Monstrosity of Translation: 'The Task of the Translator,'" in *In the Language of Walter Benjamin* (Baltimore: Johns Hopkins University Press, 1999), 107.

In Giorgio Agamben's related, but distinct, theory of the Stoic "sayable" and the Platonic "idea," "the linguistic element that belongs to the idea—the sayable—is not simply the name, but the translation, or what is translatable in the name." Agamben, "On the Sayable and the Idea," in *What Is Philosophy?*, trans. Lorenzo Chiesa (Stanford, CA: Stanford University Press, 2018), 69.

6. Whitman, "Preface 1855," *Leaves of Grass*, 1st ed. (*Leaves of Grass and Other Writings*, 631); hereafter abbreviated P and cited parenthetically. Numerals refer to page numbers.
7. In relation to such consolidations, see Werner Hamacher, "The Word *Wolke*—If It Is One," in *Benjamin's Ground: New Readings of Walter Benjamin*, ed. Rainer Nägele (Detroit: Wayne State University Press, 1988). In Hamacher's analysis, the "changing, unstable, ungraspable way" in which words (especially the word for "cloud") in Benjamin's *Berlin Childhood Around Nineteen Hundred* "enter into a relationship of likeness with others *always in a completely new, original, and nondeducible way*" (164–65) recalls the semantic inequalities in Whitman's conjunctions that also "resist translation" (166), although in Benjamin single words correspond to alternatives, whereas in Whitman's poetry incomparable phenomena are explicitly joined in ostensible similitude.
8. The Preface concludes its exposition of a "prudence suitable for immortality" (P 631) by identifying a governing principle that also rules the disjunctive couplings discussed above—a sublime indifference to difference that "divides not the living from the dead" (P 633): "only that person has no great prudence to learn . . . who in his spirit in any emergency whatever neither hurries or avoids death" (P 633). This serene disinterest issues from "spirit" rather than disposition; is neutral with regard to outcome; does not consider fate, embraced or avoided, as calamitous; and is absolute; it can sustain composure in any extremity.
9. The term is Deleuze's in "Whitman," in *Essays Critical and Clinical*, trans. Daniel W. Smith and Michael A. Greco (Minneapolis: University of Minnesota Press, 1997), 58.
10. Georges Poulet, "Phenomenology of Reading," *New Literary History* 1, no. 1 (October 1969): 54, 55. For such "intersubjective transaction[s]" in Whitman's writing, see Vincent J. Bertolini, "'Hinting and Reminding': The Rhetoric of Performative Embodiment in *Leaves of Grass*," *ELH* 69, no. 4 (Winter 2002): 1064; and Kerry C. Larsen's analysis of the tensions in such exchanges between the "I" and "you" in *Whitman's Drama of Consensus* (Chicago: University of Chicago Press, 1988), xxiii, 3–29.
11. Poulet, "Phenomenology of Reading," 58.
12. Émile Benveniste, "The Nature of Pronouns," in *Problems of General Linguistics*, trans. Mary Elizabeth Meek (Coral Gables: University of Miami Press, 1971), 218.
13. Benveniste, "Subjectivity in Language," in *Problems of General Linguistics*, 225.
14. For analyses of the characterizations in quotations, as well as for a consideration of the problems raised by such approximations, see "Identity" and "Mereology," *Stanford Encyclopedia of Philosophy*, https://plato.stanford.edu/entries/identity/ and https://plato.stanford.edu/entries/mereology.
15. Barbara Johnson, "Abortion, Animation, and Apostrophe," *Diacritics* 16, no. 1 (Spring 1986): 30.

16. The phrases, and the calculation, are from Marion K. McInnes, "Following You: Second Person in Walt Whitman's 'As I Ebb'd with the Ocean of Life,'" *Walt Whitman Quarterly Review* 35, no. 2 (2017): 156, 160.
17. In "As I Ebb'd with the Ocean of Life," the section and lines to which McInnes refers are 2:27–29.
18. Benveniste, "The Nature of Pronouns," 218.
19. Barbara Johnson writes: "addressing something reveals the nature of the subject, not of the object." In Whitman's case, to adapt Johnson's words, "being-with" is how the subject that is Whitman constitutes himself and his "democratic ideal." Johnson, *Persons and Things* (Cambridge, MA: Harvard University Press, 2008), 9.
20. "Identity," *Stanford Encyclopedia of Philosophy*, https://plato.stanford.edu/entries/identity/.
21. Whitman, "Song of Prudence," 33; hereafter abbreviated SP and cited parenthetically by line number. Michael Moon notes: "except for the two opening lines, this 1856 poem is taken, practically in its entirety, from the 1855 Preface" (*Leaves of Grass and Other Writings*, 314).
22. Wai Chee Dimock, "Whitman, Syntax, and Political Theory," in *Whitman and Cultural Studies*, ed. Betsy Erkkila and Jay Grossman (New York: Oxford University Press, 1996), 67, 70; Allen Grossman, "The Poetics of Union in Whitman and Lincoln: An Inquiry Toward the Relationship of Art and Policy," in *The American Renaissance Reconsidered: Selected Papers from the English Institute, 1982–83*, ed. Walter Benn Michaels and Donald Pease (Baltimore: Johns Hopkins University Press), 193, 194; Charles Altieri, "Spectacular Antispectacle: Ecstasy and Nationality in Whitman and His Heirs," *American Literary History* 11, no. 1 (Spring 1999): 59, 53; Ryan Cull, "'We Fathom You Not, We Love You': Walt Whitman's Social Ontology and Radical Democracy," *Criticism* 56, no. 4 (2014): 763, 762; Gilles Deleuze, "Whitman," in *Essays Critical and Clinical*, trans. Daniel W. Smith and Michael A. Greco (Minneapolis: University of Minnesota Press, 1997), 57; Jane Bennett, "Whitman's Sympathies," *Political Research Quarterly* 69, no. 3 (2016): 608; Michael Moon, "Solitude, Singularity, Whitman vis-à-vis Fourier," *ELH* 73, no. 2 (2006): 310, 313, 304.

    Among other powerful theorizations of Whitman's I/you pairings, see D. H. Lawrence's celebrated analysis of Whitman's inclusiveness as "mentalized." True sympathy, Lawrence insisted, would include "the bitterest hate" as well as "passionate love." Lawrence, "Whitman," in *Studies in Classic American Literature* (New York: Viking, 1971), 165, 177. See also Mitchell Breitweiser's "Who Speaks in Whitman's Poems?," which posits a bifurcation in Whitman's poetry between an "I" that is "a particular man" and an "I" for whom "dependence on specific individuality is cancelled." In *The American Renaissance: New Dimensions*, ed. Harry R. Garvin (Lewisburg, PA: Bucknell University Press, 1983], 126, 130); Angus Fletcher's analysis of Whitman's invention of the "environment-poem" dominated by an "iconography of the wave" and "the present participial phrase-unit" that, more than any "I" or "self," surrounds the reader by incorporating him in "wave-like forms, rhythms and structures." Fletcher, *A New Theory for American Poetry:*

Democracy, the Environment and the Future of Imagination (Cambridge, MA: Harvard University Press, 2004), 103, 9, 156; George Kateb's characterization of Whitman's self as "collage-like" and "actualized in all directions" with "unexpressed potentiality." Kateb, *The Inner Ocean: Individualism and Democratic Culture* (Ithaca, NY: Cornell University Press, 1992), 249, 258; and Philip Fisher's analysis of "democratic space" achieved by an "aesthetics" of "social space," where shared "unhistoricized moments of experience" displace political entities, since all experience is the same. For Fisher, this equality is epitomized by "The Sleepers," in which "sleep cancels all differences, all identities," and consciousness itself. Fisher, "Democratic Social Space: Melville, Whitman, and the Promise of American Transparency," *Representations* 24 (Fall 1988): 68, 69, 71–72. Finally, see Mark Noble's "Whitman," which argues that Whitman "borrows from Lucretius a materialist mechanics of subjectivity, in which the sentient body is composed and sustained by the flow of objects toward it," an "atomism" that constitutes not only "the body of a singular subject" but also the "body politic." Noble, "Whitman's Atom: Sex and Death in the 'Wide Flat Space' of *Leaves of Grass*," in *American Poetic Materialism from Whitman to Stevens* (Cambridge: Cambridge University Press, 2015), 49, 51; and Cristin Ellis's analysis of "Whitman's inheritance from Spiritualism's bioelectrical theology," in which "a bioelectric subject" is "granted identity not despite but because of the body's nervous entanglement with the world." Ellis, *Antebellum Posthuman: Race and Materiality in the Mid-Nineteenth Century* (New York: Fordham University Press, 2018), 98.

23. Whitman, "Native Moments," 12.
24. Whitman, "Are You the New Person Drawn Toward Me?," 8.
25. Roman Jakobson, "On Linguistic Aspects of Translation," in *The Translation Studies Reader*, ed. Lawrence Venuti (London: Routledge, 2000), 114.
26. José Ortega y Gasset, "The Misery and the Splendor of Translation," trans. Elizabeth Gamble Miller, in *The Translation Studies Reader*, 4th ed., ed. Lawrence Venuti (New York: Routledge, 2021), 57.
27. Whitman, "Song of the Answerer," 1:33.
28. I am thinking of the conclusion to "Crossing Brooklyn Ferry": "We fathom you not—we love you" (9:129), where all "appearances" (9:120) are conceived as "dumb, beautiful ministers" (9:126). In "Crossing Brooklyn Ferry," everything is embraced without being "fathom[ed]."
29. Such a split is theorized by Giorgio Agamben's claim via Benveniste that there is a crisis point (he calls it a "fracture") in which a wedge is driven between the semiotic and the semantic: "The semiotic (the sign) must be *recognized*; the semantic (discourse) must be *understood*." Agamben adds: "Benveniste identified in translation the point at which one grasps the difference between [the] semiotic and semantic." In "the idea . . . the sign reaches a threshold, where it crosses into the semantic." Only the "signified thing" can be "enunciated" and thus translated. Agamben, "On the Sayable and the Idea," in *What Is Philosophy?*, 63, 62, 69, 63.
30. Walter Benjamin, "The Task of the Translator," in *Selected Writings*, vol. 1, 260–63; abbreviated TT and cited parenthetically.

31. A good translation "gives voice to the *intention* of the original not as reproduction but as harmony, as a supplement to the language in which it expresses itself" (TT 260). But "supplement" also points to a more comprehensive movement away not only from the sense of the original, but from "all sense" (TT 261). For Benjamin, "pure language" is empty of significance—even of the hint of sense that precedes enunciated discourse (TT 257, 261).

    In Samuel Weber's formulation: "language that is pure of everything that is outside it is a language that would consist of pure signifying" without a signified. Weber, *Benjamin's -abilities* (Cambridge, MA: Harvard University Press, 2008), 74–75. Translation is closer to "pure language" than an original because of the "differential character of every translation," which reveals "the concentration of gaps" that "takes shape [in translation's] mismatch of content and language." Peter Fenves, *Arresting Language: From Leibniz to Benjamin* (Stanford, CA: Stanford University Press, 2001), 332–33. In other words, the gaps and "silences" lamented by José Ortega y Gasset as constituting the "difficulty" of translating from one language to another are a boon that gives new, unidiomatic meaning to the expression *lost in translation*, if the goal is "pure language." "By reproducing the syntactic arrangement of words from one language to another according to the precept of 'syntactic literalness,' the movement of translation disrupts the grammatical rules that create meaning and institutes in their stead a sequence that does not add up to a whole" (Weber, 93). For Benjamin "the only whole is 'every language as a whole'" (Fenves, 333).
32. Werner Hamacher, "'Disgregation of the Will': Nietzsche on the Individual and Individuality," in *Premises: Essays on Philosophy and Literature from Kant to Celan*, trans. Peter Fenves (Stanford, CA: Stanford University Press, 1999), 148, 159.
33. Ralph Waldo Emerson, "The Over-soul," in *Essays and Lectures*, ed. Joel Porte (New York: Library of America, 1983), 398.
34. Whitman, "So Long," 24; hereafter abbreviated SL and cited parenthetically.
35. Whitman, "When Lilacs Last in the Dooryard Bloom'd" (4:24); hereafter abbreviated WL and cited parenthetically.
36. Whitman, "Passage to India" (9:230, 231); further citations are parenthetical and abbreviated PI.
37. Giorgio Agamben, "On the Concept of Demand," in *What Is Philosophy?*, 30; abbreviated D and cited parenthetically.

Done with the Compass, Done with the Chart

1. Texts for Dickinson's poems are from *The Poems of Emily Dickinson*, Variorum Edition, 3 vols., ed. R. W. Franklin (Cambridge, MA: Harvard University Press, Belknap Press, 1998); hereafter abbreviated F and cited parenthetically. Where Dickinson provides variants to a word or to phrases, a superscript plus sign precedes the word or words to which there are alternatives, given at the poem's end. Dickinson never titled her poems; I follow the practice of identifying

them by the poem's first line, minus punctuation and, with the exception of the first word, without capitalization, and/or by the number Franklin assigned them in his Variorum Edition. In accordance with Franklin, I retain Dickinson's eccentric spellings of words like "opon" for "upon," "ought" for "aught," "snapt" for "snapped," and "it's" for the possessive pronoun as well as for the contraction of "it is." Also following Franklin, I use a spaced hyphen, rather than an en or em dash for the varying length and position of the dashes in Dickinson's manuscripts. The title of my essay includes a quotation from F 269.

2. Sharon Cameron, *Lyric Time: Dickinson and the Limits of Genre* (Baltimore: Johns Hopkins University Press, 1979) and *Choosing Not Choosing: Dickinson's Fascicles* (Chicago: University of Chicago Press, 1992).
3. Yvor Winters distinguished between poems that represent "the daily realization of the immanence of death" and poems in which a speaker *experiences* death or "eternity"; he called the latter "fraudulent" because they "trespass beyond knowable boundaries." Winters, "Emily Dickinson and the Limits of Judgment," in *The Recognition of Emily Dickinson: Selected Criticism Since 1890*, ed. Caesar R. Blake and Carlton F. Wells (Ann Arbor: University of Michigan Press, 1968), 192. Geoffrey Hartman argued that the poems could not be fraudulent because they inhabit a liminal space where they "stay profane . . . on the threshold of vision." Hartman, "The Voice of the Shuttle: Language from the Point of View of Literature," in *Beyond Formalism: Literary Essays, 1958–1970* (New Haven, CT: Yale University Press, 1970), 350. For Robert Weisbuch, the poems evade fraudulence because they sever analogies from experience: "The poems do not lack a situational matrix . . . but mimetic situations are . . . transported to a world of analogical language which exists in parallel to a world of experience." Weisbuch, *Emily Dickinson's Poetry* (Chicago: University of Chicago Press, 1972), 19. Thomas Foster submitted that Dickinson substitutes space for place, specifically by producing an "alternative textual space" for the "construction of a feminine poetic voice." Foster, "Homelessness at Home: Placing Emily Dickinson in [Women's] History," in *Transformations of Domesticity in Modern Women's Writing* (London: Palgrave, 2002), 26.

   Such accounts segregate poems that violate epistemological limits from those that don't (Winters, Hartman, and—in regard to bifurcating the poem so that the situational is not compromised by the analogic—Weisbuch), or by translating place to space, specifically one cordoned off by gender (Foster).
4. Geoffrey Hartman, "The Voice of the Shuttle: Language from the Point of View of Literature," in *Beyond Formalism*, 350.
5. The temporal disparity Dickinson italicizes anticipates a cognate moment when, glossing "Mr. Waley's" translation of a Chinese poem ("Swiftly the years, beyond recall / Solemn the stillness of this spring morning"), William Empson writes: "The human mind has two main scales on which to measure time. The large one takes the length of a human life as its unit. . . . The small one takes as its unit the conscious moment. . . . The scales are so far apart as almost to give the effect

of defining two dimensions; they do not come into contact because what is too large to be conceived by the one is still too small to be conceived by the other." Empson, *Seven Types of Ambiguity* (New York: New Directions, 1966), 23–24.

6. Elaine Scarry connects the fluid transit between the literal and the figural in *Wuthering Heights* to an observation of John Searle's about "the astonishing and mystifying capacity of our brains to distinguish (and move effortlessly back and forth) between fiction and the real world, a feat that is not attributable to language since, as Searle notices, nouns, verbs, prepositions, adjectives, and adverbs all act in identical ways in the two realms." Scarry, "Windburn on Planet Brontë," in *On Style in Victorian Fiction*, ed. Daniel Tyler (New York: University of Cambridge Press, 2021), 165. Scarry argues that Brontë's "handling of the figurative and the literal . . . in their own modest and miniature way parallel[s] the distinction between the fictive and the real" (165). She elaborates the terms in which Brontë thwarts the distinction between these oppositions by the boundary crossings in which, for example, "the figurative" is literal(ized) (166) in action, or in which the two change places (167).

   In eliminating the difference between figure and act, fiction has a resource unavailable to poetry. Above I discuss the versatile ways in which Dickinson's poems slide from abstraction to sensation, a pairing that is loosely linked with, but not equivalent to, the figural and the literal.
7. Charles R. Anderson, *Emily Dickinson's Poetry: Stairway of Surprise* (New York: Doubleday Anchor, 1966), 320.
8. In "I read my sentence steadily" (F 432), the "I" of the poem's first line also surrenders individuality, a loss precipitated in both poems by an "extremity -" (F 432).
9. Freud quotes the philosopher Alexander Bain, who wrote that each of our conceptions is acquired in relation to its opposite: "If everything that we can know is viewed as a transition from something else, every experience must have two sides; and either every name must have a double meaning, or else for every meaning there must be two names." Bain, "The Antithetical Sense of Primal Words," quoted in Sigmund Freud, *On Creativity and the Unconscious* (New York: Harper and Row, 1958), 60. Hegel expressed the fundamental importance of antithesis in the notion that thinking itself lies in the ability to negate that which is immediately before us.
10. *The Emily Dickinson Lexicon* is a comprehensive dictionary of words and variants found in Dickinson's collected poems and is partly based on her dictionary, Webster's 1844 *American Dictionary of the English Language*, vols. I and II, and *The Oxford English Dictionary*. See Emily Dickinson Archive, https://www.edickinson.org/words.
11. John Donne, "Holy Sonnet 1," https://www.poetryfoundation.org/poems/44113/holy-sonnets-thou-hast-made-me-and-shall-thy-work-decay.
12. In John Fletcher's analysis, "a rising tide of erotic encroachment" is construed to a different end: the dissolution of "gentlewomanly composure and self-containment" by which the speaker fears she will be "devoured" within an

"opposition of . . . masculine and feminine" "positioning." Fletcher, "Poetry, Gender, and Primal Fantasy," in *Formations of Fantasy*, ed. Victor Burgin, James Donald, and Cora Kaplan (London: Methuen, 1986), 135, 136, 135. Thus she "disengag[es herself]" from the threat (137). Above, I argue that the poem's end merely suggests a mutuality ("we met the Solid Town -") following the conclusion of the physical act.

13. Dickinson's "Ought" is a variant of the archaic "aught" (meaning "all, everything"), part of the English language since the twelfth century. Dickinson would have seen it used in Shakespeare, as in *The Winter's Tale*: "if you know aught which does behoove my knowledge . . . imprison [it] not" (https://www.merriam-webster.com/dictionary/aught).
14. John Ashbery, "Self-Portrait in a Convex Mirror," in *Self-Portrait in a Convex Mirror* (New York: Viking, 1975).
15. Paul de Man, "Hypogram and Inscription: Michael Riffaterre's Poetics of Reading," *Semiotics* 11 (Winter 1981): 33. The central point of de Man's deconstructive argument, published in a review of Riffaterre's 1978 *Semiotics of Poetry*, is to contest Riffaterre's claim that the "materiality" of a poem by Victor Hugo, "as distinct from the phenomenality . . . take[s] place" not in "the materiality of the mind, or of time, or of the carillon—none of which exist, except in the figure of prosopopoeia"—but, de Man insists, in "the materiality of an inscription" (35). In an analysis of the same poem that revises the claims of both Riffaterre and de Man, Garrett Stewart argues that Hugo's poem "'actuates'" not by "inscription alone," nor merely by description, as Riffaterre asserts, but by the "sounded sense of an echo" in the "phonetic hinge-work of" the poem's "internal rhyme." Stewart, *Book, Text, Medium: Cross-Sectional Reading for a Digital Age* (New York: Cambridge University Press, 2020), 222–24.
16. De Man, "Hypogram and Inscription," 33. Descartes and Hegel are the two philosophers de Man names to exemplify the dependability of sense certainty. Yet both philosophers are committed to arguing the delusory nature of the senses. In "First Meditation," Descartes identifies the numerous ways in which "the senses deceive" (René Descartes, *Meditations on First Philosophy*, trans. and ed. John Cottingham [Cambridge: Cambridge University Press, 2020], 16), while in *Phenomenology of Spirit* on "Sense-Certainty," Hegel writes: "he who is initiated into these Mysteries [of the bread and the wine] not only comes to doubt the being of sensuous things, but to despair of it; in part he brings about the nothingness of such things himself in his dealings with them, and in part he sees them reduce themselves to nothingness. Even the animals are not shut out from this wisdom but, on the contrary, show themselves to be most profoundly initiated into it; for they do not just stand idly in front of sensuous things as if these possessed intrinsic being, but assured of their nothingness, they fall to without ceremony and eat them up" (G. W. F. Hegel, *Phenomenology of Spirit*, trans. A. V. Miller [Oxford: Oxford University Press 1977], 65).

Although most of de Man's concluding examples are corrective glosses of the Hugo poem, he equivocates when he writes that perception itself is "hallucinatory" and "uncanny": "one never 'has' a hallucination the way one has a sore foot from kicking the proverbial stone. Just as the hypothesis of dreaming undoes the certainty of sleep, the hypothesis, or the figure, of [perception which may be a] hallucination, undoes sense certainty" (34). Such sentences link "hallucination" and the "uncanny" (34) to a context outside of writing. For de Man, the bottom line with regard to writing is that "[p]rosopopoeia undoes the distinction between reference and signification on which all semiotic systems depend" (34). In his expansion of the point, the figurative *giving face* in poetry becomes only an exaggeration of all of language, and of consciousness too.

17. For J. V. Cunningham, the poem depicts "a nature experience yet [is] theological in form." Cunningham, "Sorting Out: The Case of Dickinson," *Southern Review* 5, no. 2 (April 1969): 436.
18. De Man, "Hypogram and Inscription," 34.
19. Leela Gandhi, "Invisible, Inc.," *ELH* 88, no. 2 (Summer 2021): 424. Gandhi is arguing against the idea that "abstraction is associated with the violence of capital . . . that cuts us off from life itself" (421). Although "chiasmatic abstraction becomes" identified with "modernity" (424), she asserts "there are no intrinsic historical or geographical limits" on the chiasmatic relation she describes (424). Her examples of "abstraction" are offered across disciplinary contexts—among others, abstract art; "ecumenical epistemology, willing to name Confucius, Socrates, Buddha, Jesus, and Zarathustra in the same breath" (426); political theory; and philosophy (especially that of Karl Jaspers in regard to his notion of "axiality" [426])—but her declared "focus" is "abstraction as a form of knowledge" (425). "Jaspers's concept of an Axial Age" identifies a "period between about 800 to 200 BCE in which there was . . . a largely serendipitous advance . . . of a universal tendency toward abstract thinking across . . . Palestine, China, India, Persia, and Greece" (426). "Axial consciousness" seeks to "overcome . . . epistemologies of the hidden" (428).
20. Gandhi, 425.
21. Gandhi, 432.
22. No enumeration of other paradigms, of which there are many—most recently, *Essays from the English Institute 2019: Abstraction* (*ELH* 88, no. 2 [Summer 2021]), entirely addressed to the topic of abstraction—would lead to a different conclusion. As argued above, Dickinson's poems exhibit a versatility that defies paradigm. I sketch the two theories above because they exemplify extremes of scope: one limited, the other comprehensive.

Something like Nebraska and Something like Virginia

1. Willa Cather, *The Professor's House* (New York: Vintage, 1973), 273–74; hereafter abbreviated *PH* and cited parenthetically.

2. Willa Cather, *My Ántonia* (New York: Barnes & Noble Classics, 1994), 64; hereafter abbreviated *Á* and cited parenthetically.
3. Willa Cather, "The Novel Démeublé," in *Not Under Forty* (Lincoln: University of Nebraska Press, 1988), 50; hereafter abbreviated *NUF* and cited parenthetically.
4. Jonathan Goldberg provides a far-reaching analysis of the ways in which "the thing not named" resonates across almost every aspect of Cather's writing, including gender and race, breath and voice, music and Cather's dynamic relation to the singer Olive Fremstad. Goldberg, *Willa Cather and Others* (Durham, NC: Duke University Press, 2001). With comparable scope, Christopher Nealon examines the genealogies that haunt Cather's fiction when, in Cather's phrase, "children of the moon" flee their families to form "an affiliation" with "something larger—with a community," even a "race of dreamers," of "slaves," "captives," and "prisoners." Nealon, *Foundlings: Lesbian and Gay Historical Emotion Before Stonewall* (Durham, NC: Duke University Press, 2001), 79, 78. See also Judith Butler, "Dangerous Crossing: Willa Cather's Masculine Names," in *Bodies That Matter: On the Discursive Limits of Sex* (New York: Routledge 1993); Eve Sedgwick, "Willa Cather and Others," in *Tendencies* (Durham, NC: Duke University Press, 1993); and Marilee Lindemann, *Willa Cather: Queering America* (New York: Columbia University Press, 1999).

   One way or another, for Goldberg, Nealon, Butler, Sedgwick, and Lindemann, "the thing not named" is at least a question of sexuality and gender, and, in the best of these analyses, casts a more pervasive, equally queer shadow.
5. With some exceptions, Cather's critics have attended to narrative's onward movement—this includes attention to portraits of ethnically diverse Nebraska settlers; farm life on the prairie; lyrical snapshots of the pictorial splendor of the landscapes that, far from a backdrop, assume their own visual continuity—rather than examining passages whose mutations have a limited evolution outside of the novels' ongoing storylines.

   Among the best exceptions are Richard H. Millington, who wrote of Cather's "'anti-novelistic' behavior" ("Willa Cather's American Modernism," in *The Cambridge Companion to Willa Cather*, ed. Marilee Lindemann [Cambridge: Cambridge University Press, 2005], 62) in relation to a modernism Cather practices in her fiction's "resistance to the related ideas of 'depth' and 'development'" (61)—in effect, "withdrawing its interest from psychological conceptions of character and the moralizing trajectories of action that underwrite Victorian narrative." Instead, Cather invests in "forms of feeling cut free from the depth-seeking, ending-hungry, explanation-driven trajectories of Victorian culture" (63).

   In a related vein, John Plotz defines Cather's modernism against representational norms of American realism and naturalism—through what he calls "semidetached aesthetic experience" ("Overtones and Empty Rooms: Willa Cather's Semidetached Modernism," *Novel* 50, no. 1 [2017]: 60), whereby a given situation is shown to possess a surplus that is often an inverse of what is supplemented (as when, for instance, the "incantatory" and the "humdrum" [57], "opera music" and "ordinary Pittsburg grime" [64], are overlaid on each other, demonstrating fiction's "capacity to inhabit" "aesthetic dreaming and the world of hard facts . . . simultaneously" [57]).

David Hill cites "the brain neurologist Antonio Damasio" to explain how "the ongoing creation of momentary 'core' consciousness," which might appear unified, is actually composed of a series of "quantum-like pulses of consciousness-building" that defies "plotted progression" in the construction of experience and identity in Cather's *My Ántonia*. Hill, "The Quotidian Sublime: Cognitive Perspectives on Identity-Formation in Willa Cather's *My Ántonia*," *Arizona Quarterly* 61, no. 2 (2005): 110, 120. That explanation is Bergsonian in its emphasis on upsurges that disrupt sequence, though Hill's explanatory framework is cognitive, not philosophical.

Such arguments about how Cather's writing breaks free of progression and development (Millington, Hill) and of unitary representations of experience (Plotz) are cognate to my understanding that in Cather's writing, transposition loosens the boundaries around the fixtures that situate identity and category. In distinction to these arguments, the tenor of the transpositions I consider do not focus on Cather's modifications of literary tradition, whether the Victorian narrative or the American movements of realism and naturalism, but are essentially metaphysical.

6. Willa Cather, *Willa Cather: Stories, Poems, and Other Writings*, ed. Sharon O'Brien (New York: Library of America, 1992), 960; hereafter abbreviated *W* and cited parenthetically. In her review of *Death Comes to the Archbishop*, Cather describes "prose" that is "without accent, with none of the artificial elements of composition," in which writing is not "force[d] . . . up" and in which "the mood is the thing" (*W* 960).
7. Henri Bergson, *Creative Evolution*, trans. Arthur Mitchell (Mineola, NY: Dover, 1998), 47; hereafter abbreviated *CE* and cited parenthetically. When Cather read Bergson's *Creative Evolution* (translated into English a year earlier), she wrote to Elizabeth Shepley Sergeant: "I think the first two chapters . . . of 'Creative Evolution' glorious." *The Selected Letters of Willa Cather*, ed. Andrew Jewel and Janis Stout (New York: Vintage, 2014), 168; hereafter abbreviated *L* and cited parenthetically. In 1913, a year after Cather read Bergson, she wrote *O Pioneers!* and named its central character Alexandra Bergson.

In *Bergson and American Culture: The Worlds of Willa Cather and Wallace Stevens* (Chapel Hill: University of North Carolina Press, 1990), Tom Quirk matches language and concept in Cather's novels to passages in *Creative Evolution* of which they are reminiscent. Such point-by-point correlations are forced. A more compelling understanding of Cather's relation to *Creative Evolution* is found in Loretta Wasserman's earlier "The Music of Time: Henri Bergson and Willa Cather," *American Literature* 57, no. 2 (May 1985), specifically in relation to Bergson's "two forms of time: clock time, or chronological time" revealed in "measured separate units," which is "the time of science and practical affairs," and, in distinction, "Bergson's 'duration'" that "is experienced or lived time" within "the ceaseless flow of qualitative change" composed of "layered simultaneous moments" (229). Wasserman offers a particularly brilliant reading of St. Peter's ossified time and "another way of apprehending the past" that is "spontaneous and intuitive" (236), as exemplified by Louis Marsellus.

8. Bergson wrote: "Intuition and intellect represent two opposite directions of the work of consciousness" (*CE* 267). "Intuition . . . pierces the darkness of the night in which the intellect leaves us. . . . Intuition is mind itself, and in a certain sense, life itself" (*CE* 267–68). He also described "life" as an "immense wave" that "spreads outwards" and is "converted into oscillation" (*CE* 266), perhaps akin to the fluctuation that sometimes defines the properties of Cather's characters whose traits waver between the personal and impersonal.
9. "Radical mechanism implies a metaphysic in which the totality of the real is postulated complete in eternity, and in which the apparent duration of things expresses merely the infirmity of a mind that cannot know everything at once. . . . Finalism" is "only inverted mechanism. . . . It substitutes the attraction of the future for the impulsion of the past" (*CE* 39). Both mechanism and finalism suggest the whole is given in the past and the future and that therefore there is no possibility of change. See pages 39–59 of *Creative Evolution* for Bergson's extended descriptions of this aspect of his metaphysic.
10. Willa Cather, *O Pioneers!* (New York: Vintage Classics, 1992), 43; hereafter abbreviated *OP* and cited parenthetically.
11. *Webster's*: from Middle French or Latin; Middle French *metaphore*, from Latin *metaphora*, from Greek *metapherein* to transfer, from *meta-* + *pherein* to bear.
12. Willa Cather, *The Song of the Lark* (Boston: Houghton Mifflin, 1988), 395, 409; hereafter abbreviated *SL* and cited parenthetically.
13. In "the grass was the country, as the water is the sea," the analogy segregates "grass" and "sea" on either side of the comparison. In the second trope ("the red of the grass" is "the color of . . . certain seaweeds when they are first washed up") grass and some aspect of sea—"seaweeds"—are made congruent by virtue of seaweed's "red" grass-like color despite its customary habitation in water. So while the first analogy drives a line between the parts of the comparison of "grass" and "sea," the second analogy (the shared color, the similitude of plant and "washed up" plant-like algae) draws the two together, almost amalgamating them in a metonymic transposition into "the whole country," whose segments cannot be breached (*Á* 9).
14. The inscription that Cather, or Edith Lewis, or both, chose for Cather's tombstone is from *My Ántonia* (*Á* 12).
15. Willa Cather, *Lucy Gayheart* (New York: Vintage Classics, 1995), 190; hereafter abbreviated *LG* and cited parenthetically.
16. Willa Cather, *One of Ours* (Cleveland: First Belt, 2019), 65; hereafter abbreviated *OO* and cited parenthetically.

17. Cather based the Tom Outland story on Richard Wetherill's exploration of Mesa Verde in 1888.
18. Though not disembodied in the way that D. A. Miller describes Jane Austen's style as what displaces Austen's person for "an out-of-body voice" and "a free indirect style, in which the narrator's way of *saying* is constantly both mimicking, and distancing itself from, the character's way of *seeing*." Miller, *Jane Austen; or, The Secret of Style* (Princeton, NJ: Princeton University Press, 2003), 1, 27. Cather never vacates the page. Her narrator is a sympathetic presence, not an ironic absence, sympathetic less to character than to the transpositions that overshadow characters while directly passing through them. Cather described *O Pioneers!* as "a slow-moving story, without 'action,' without 'humor,' without a 'hero'" (*W* 964).
19. In "My First Novels (There Were Two)," Cather distinguishes *Alexander's Bridge*, which is "very like what painters call a studio picture," "very shallow" and "conventional," from *O Pioneers!*—"'the novel of the soil,'" in which "everything was spontaneous" (*W* 963). In *Death Comes to the Archbishop*, the prose is subdued and the events depicted, episodic. Cather wrote, "I had all my life wanted to do something in the style of legend, which is absolutely the reverse of dramatic treatment," "with none of the artificial elements of composition" (*W* 960). Cather identified her style in *Shadows on the Rock* as "not too conclusive, not too definite: a series of pictures remembered rather than experienced" (*W* 966) to characterize a style that is atmospheric.
20. Cather described this economy in "The Novel Démeublé": "How wonderful it would be if we could throw all the furniture out of the window; and along with it, all the meaningless reiterations concerning physical sensations . . . and leave the room as bare as the stage of a Greek theatre, or as that house into which the glory of the Pentecost descended; leave the scene bare for the play of emotions, great and little—for the nursery tale, no less than the tragedy, is killed by tasteless amplitude" (*NUF* 51).
21. Willa Cather, "Old Mrs. Harris," in *Collected Stories* (New York: Vintage Classics, 1992), 306; hereafter abbreviated OMH and cited parenthetically.
22. As Ian F. A. Bell writes, "Not only does [Professor St. Peter] seem unaware of the Magnificat as the first writing of the nativity, but he misapplies his passage from another text, the 'Litany of the Blessed Virgin,' better known as the 'Litany of Loreto,' and he seems to misremember its main catalogue of symbols (the Litany has the 'Tower of David,' not the 'Lily of Zion')." Bell, "Re-Writing America: Origin and Gender in Willa Cather's 'The Professor's House,'" *Yearbook of English Studies* 24 (1994): 12.
23. Edith Lewis, *Willa Cather Living: A Personal Record* (Lincoln: University of Nebraska Press, 2000).
24. "My Antonomasia" are Susan Howe's words in the prose poem "Since." Susan Howe, *Concordance* (New York: New Directions, 2020), 26.

    Onomastics, the study of names, is of corollary interest to antonomasia in Cather's writing, since the drift described above also bears on the name of the central character in *One of Ours*, Claude Wheeler, who is "annoyed" to hear his name pronounced "Clod" by Reverend Arthur Weldon (OO 121). Enid, his wife, "amiable, but inflexible" (OO 124) and, above all, unloving, also pronounces his name as if it were spelled "Clod" (OO 190). "Clawd" is mistreated as "Clod" until he comes into his own in France as "Clode" in a pronunciation never given but tacit in the Cather voice to arc, via transposition, across the whole waste of his stateside life to his transfiguration in the "hazy enchantment" (OO 369) of France. When in 1914 he thinks of joining American troops to fight German bullets, "Paris suddenly seemed to have become the capital, not of France, but of the world!" (OO 159). As his ship arrives in France, "the coast that rose before him . . . was like a pillar of eternity" (OO 288). When Claude meets Madame Joubert, who calls his "a very good French name" (OO 316), the possessive in the novel's title might refer not to the Midwesterners Claude abhors, but to the French whose values reflect his own. In the end, however, Claude remains an alien, one of the "children of the moon" (OO 189) who belong to no one.

25. Theodor Adorno, "On the Contemporary Relationship of Philosophy and Music," in *Essays on Music* (Berkeley: University of California Press, 2002), 140. Adorno writes: "As language, music tends toward pure naming, the absolute unity of object and sign, which in its immediacy is lost to all human knowledge." In another formulation: "[I]n music, what is at stake is not meaning, but gestures. To the extent that music is language, it is, like notation in music history, a language sedimented from gestures" (139). For this reason, "music provides the prototype of untranslatability" (142).
26. Theodor Adorno, "Punctuation Marks," in *Notes to Literature*, vol. 1, ed. Rolf Tiedemann, trans. Shierry Weber Nicholsen (New York: Columbia University Press, 1991), 92; hereafter abbreviated TA and cited parenthetically.
27. Willa Cather, "Two Friends," in *Collected Stories*, 330, 323; hereafter abbreviated TF and cited parenthetically.
28. Willa Cather, "Before Breakfast," in *Collected Stories*, 399.
29. Philippe Lacoue-Labarthe, "The Echo of the Subject," in *Typography: Mimesis, Philosophy, Politics* (Stanford, CA: Stanford University Press, 1989), 200–201.
30. In "The Novel Démeublé," "as if unconsciously" describes how "the material investiture" of Hawthorne's *The Scarlet Letter* is "presented" (49)—"one can scarcely ever see the actual surroundings of the people; one feels them, rather, in the dusk" (50)—and leads directly to Cather's description of her own compositional aspiration and method: "to present [the] scene by suggestion rather than by enumeration" (48).

Wallace Stevens's Entangled Objects

1. Quotations from my first three sentences are, respectively, from Wallace Stevens, *The Collected Poems* (New York: Vintage, 1982): "The Latest Freed Man," 205; "A Primitive Like an Orb," 442, 441; and "Chocorua to Its Neighbor," 296. Poems from this edition are hereafter abbreviated *CP* and cited parenthetically.

2. Fredric Jameson: "we have to do . . . with a play between whole 'systems' of connotation . . . in which the reference withdraws in order the more surely to foreground style or representation as its new object." Jameson, "Wallace Stevens," in *Critical Essays on Wallace Stevens*, ed. Steven Gould Axelrod and Helen Deese (Boston: G. K. Hall, 1988), 186–87.

Steven Shaviro: "opposites . . . coexist without coinciding and without interacting dialectically" so that "similitude" is produced "without correspondence"; it is "indefinitely repeatable" and "takes the place of any epistemological conclusions." Thus, "the logic of Stevens's poetry is repetitive and accretive, not dialectical and progressive." Shaviro, "That Which Is Always Beginning: Stevens's Poetry of Affirmation," in *Critical Essays on Wallace Stevens*, ed. Axelrod and Deese, 197–98, 193, 208.

Joseph Riddell: Even though the poems are "hung upon what is at bottom rhetorical statement," they "are very near to what Henry James provocatively called 'felt thought'" that "progresses in rhythm not in substance." Riddell, "Wallace Stevens' 'Visibility of Thought,'" *PMLA* 77, no. 4 (September 1962): 483, 486.

Helen Vendler, writing of a passage in "Like Decorations in a Nigger Cemetery": Stevens presents "the journey back and forth between antithetical states." These may "interpenetrat[e]" but cannot be identified with each other. Vendler, *On Extended Wings: Wallace Stevens' Longer Poems* (Cambridge, MA: Harvard University Press, 1969), 74.

R. P. Blackmur: Stevens "turn[ed] an idea or a conviction 'into a feeling which did not exist, even in his own mind, until he had put it down in words.'" Paul Mariani, quoting Blackmur in Mariani, *The Whole of the Harmonium: The Life of Wallace Stevens* (New York: Simon and Schuster, 2016), 177.

Of Stevens's juxtapositions like those considered in this essay, Charles Altieri writes in relation to *Harmonium*: "Perhaps there can be structures that fully engage the mind precisely because they yield to modes of linkage for which the mind has no categories." Altieri, *Wallace Stevens and the Demands of Modernity: Toward a Phenomenology of Value* (Ithaca, NY: Cornell University Press, 2013), 66. While Altieri privileges the "aspectual thinking" (sometimes "aspectual seeing") introduced in Stevens's poems by "the grammar of 'as'" (217), that is, of simile, to indicate the dominance of a non-epistemic phenomenology of value, Edward Alexander complements Altieri's analysis by demonstrating the grammatical "counterpoint" of "as"—namely, the importance of "the partitive 'of'" that "invokes the relationship between a particular local instance of value and a scale or measure of value." Alexander, "'Not a Choice Between but Of': Revisiting Stevens' Other Major Grammatical Operator," *Wallace Stevens Journal* 39, no. 1 (Spring 2015). Alexander's argument tacks down the phenomenologically infused "aspectual seeing" in which "of" is the grammatical "woof to [the] warp of" "as" (68).

The evacuation of what Stevens called "content" and what the critics cited above variously identify as "reference," "substance," "statement," "conclusion," and "category" as these are subsumed by mood, style, and novel feeling points to the effect of ungrounded similes that displace cognitive anchors.

3. Ralph Waldo Emerson, "Fate," in *Essays and Lectures*, ed. Joel Porte (New York: Library of America, 1983), 967.
4. Emily Dickinson, "The tint I cannot take is best" (F 696). Dickinson's poems are identified by their first line and the number Franklin assigned them in *The Poems of Emily Dickinson*, Variorum Edition, 3 vols., ed. R. W. Franklin (Cambridge, MA: Harvard University Press, 1998). When a first line is given as a title, I omit punctuation and, except in the first word, capitals.
5. Willa Cather, O *Pioneers!* (New York: Vintage Classics, 1992), 146.
6. The word "fidgets" comes from "Pieces" (*CP* 352), a poem I discuss later.
7. John Cage, *A Year from Monday: New Lectures and Writings* (Middletown, CT: Wesleyan University Press, 1967), 122. The sentences are from a chapter titled "Rhythm Etc." initially composed in 1961 in response to a request from a professor of Visual Design at MIT asking Cage if he could write something on "form," along with "rhythm, proportion, symmetry, beauty, balance, etc." (120). Cage wrote: "Symmetry. Pure symmetry. Doesn't exist" (123).
8. Cage, 122.
9. Roger Gilbert, "Whitman and Stevens: Certain Phenomena of Sound," *Wallace Stevens Journal* 40, no. 1 (Spring 2016): 67.
10. Wallace Stevens, "Conversation with Three Women of New England," in *Opus Posthumous*, ed. Samuel French Morse (New York: Knopf, 1972), 109.
11. Altieri's major claim in *Wallace Stevens and the Demands of Modernity* is that in Stevens's compositions, the "distrust [of] description, proposition, and system" (6) helps "establish the place of value in a world of fact" (8). For Stevens, as understood by Altieri, categories are containers of knowledge that enforce divisions between aspects of experience. In the dissolution of those structures, an intensely experienced world emerges in which things are not matters of empirical fact, ethical proclamation, or conceptual knowledge, but rather have an affective—a phenomenological—value. This shift, Altieri argues, is represented in the grammar of "as" and in the "*aspectual thinking*" (43) in which resemblance, comparison, and, above all, simile displace the rigid copula that determines which things are this or that.
12. Wallace Stevens, *Collected Poetry and Prose*, ed. Frank Kermode and Joan Richardson (New York: Library of America, 1997), 712; hereafter abbreviated *CPP* and cited parenthetically.
13. The passage is from Gilles Deleuze, *Difference and Repetition*, trans. Paul Patton (New York: Columbia University Press, 1994), 37. Though his subject is theoretical and Stevens's name never appears within it, Deleuze's distinction between the univocity of being that everything possesses, within which there are inequalities, inadvertently glosses the difficulty of assessing the objects in Stevens's appositions. It is because all things possess "univocal being," notwithstanding the individuated differences of particular phenomena within it, that

objects can be drawn together. By the same token, it is because those differences, often contrarieties, cry out as such within the parallel structure and grammar of Stevens's sequences, appositions, and similes—that is, precisely because specific entities are not the same and not equal—that it is difficult to discern when these figures reflect each other from when they refute each other. In a poem like "The Motive for Metaphor," that obstructive difficulty hampers a decisive resolution to the cryptic relation of the two halves of the poem, as discussed within.

14. Letter to L. W. Payne Jr., March 31, 1928, *Letters of Wallace Stevens*, ed. Holly Stevens (Berkeley: University of California Press, 1996), 251 (*L* 279). This and subsequent citations of Stevens's letters, abbreviated *L* and cited parenthetically, refer to the letter (not the page) number.
15. Arden Reed, *Romantic Weather: The Climates of Coleridge and Baudelaire* (Hanover, NH: University Press of New England, 1983), 11–12.
16. Mark J. Bruhn exemplifies the nonsense words, neologisms, and word combinations that drive sound and sense apart in Stevens's poems, along with the "chiasms" and the "kinesthetic rhythms" that "'capture the manner in which experience is actually *sensed*, in the blaze of all of its affect and meaning-laden intensity,' prior to its translation into language-mediated sense." Bruhn, "A Mirror on the Mind: Stevens, Chiasmus, and Autism Spectrum Disorder," *Wallace Stevens Journal* 39, no. 2 (Fall 2015): 182. Bruhn quotes Michael Burke, a cognitive literary theorist, on "rhetorical schemes," like that of the chiasmus, "which may momentarily but not entirely overwhelm the . . . semantic content" (193). Bruhn adds: "Chiasmus is not a mere linguistic figure learned through exposure to literary discourse but rather a pre-linguistic cognitive pattern, or even neural disposition, grounded in the bilateral, mirror-symmetrical organization of the visual cortex" (193). The bibliography of scientific works on which Bruhn's argument is constructed is fascinating.

    Among the many fine essays on Stevens's depictions of sound, see "Wallace Stevens and the 'The Less Legible Meanings of Sounds,'" ed. Natalie Gerber, special issue, *Wallace Stevens Journal* 33, no. 1 (Spring 2009), especially Alan Filreis, "Sound at an Impasse" (15–23); Beverly Maeder, "Sound and Sensuous Awakening in *Harmonium*" (24–43); and Peter Middleton, "The 'Final Finding of the Ear': Wallace Stevens' Modernist Soundscapes" (61–82).

    Middleton argues that Stevens exploits the "interdependence of two different modes of generating meaningfulness, discursive reasoning and the complex encoding of phonemes" (67). For Stevens, "sound" is "a mode of thought" for "utopian aspirations expressed in words at the borders of sense" (78). In a stunning analysis of "Notes Toward a Supreme Fiction," Middleton clarifies: "Beneath the surface of what reads as if it were philosophical instruction in a form of phenomenological reduction . . . is an accompanying narrative of phonic transformations, 'less legible meanings of sounds' . . . based initially on reflexive use of the two vowels of the word 'begin'" with which that poem opens (63–64).

In *The Deed of Reading* and *Reading Voices*, Garrett Stewart compels attention to "the silent sounding of phonetic language" in what he calls "'secondary vocality' to indicate the suppressed but potent aurality of silent reading" in Stevens's poems, among others. Stewart, *The Deed of Reading: Literature, Language, Writing, Philosophy* (Ithaca, NY: Cornell University Press, 2015), 42; and *Reading Voices: Literature and the Phonotext* (Berkeley: University of California Press, 1990). See, for instance, Stewart's analysis of the ontological core of "are" in the way "Things as they are / Are changed upon the blue guitar" in *Deed* (32–33) and a cross-word case of sound in a more blatant homophonic pun (for collective "aims") in another Stevens title, "United Dames of America," in *Reading Voices* (46).

17. Samuel Taylor Coleridge, "The Eolian Harp," https://www.poetryfoundation.org/poems/52301/the-eolian-harp.
18. In a letter to Hi Simons, January 12, 1943, Stevens confirms: "The Arabian is the moon; the undecipherable vagueness of the moonlight is the unscrawled fores: the unformed handwriting" (*L* 469). "Fores" is what the "future casts" shapelessly in front of us, but the word also retains the whiff of *force*.
19. Anglo-Norman *percer, percier, perser, perzer* and Old French, Middle French *percer, perser* (also in Old French as *percier, persier*; . . . French *percer*) to pierce through, to penetrate; c. 1100; also in figurative contexts (*Oxford English Dictionary*).

    This kind of penetration has a different ingress than sense. In "Le Monocle de Mon Oncle," it is registered for the reader in a phonetic rhyme that distills a shared fate: "Remember how the crickets came / Out of their mother grass, like little kin, / In the pale nights, when your first imagery / Found inklings of your bond to all that dust" (*CP* 15). Little *kin* conduces to "*ink*lings" almost as objective cause to subjective effect (italics mine). As in "Things of August," where such "sounds are long in the living of the ear" (*CP* 489), resonance binds creatures that have no common tongue.
20. The *OED* defines the adjective "finikin," of Dutch origin, from the seventeenth century, as "dainty, fastidious, mincing; excessively precise in trifles. Also of things: Over-delicately wrought or finished; also, insignificant, paltry, trifling." And, in a eulogistic sense: "Dainty, pretty. *Obsolete*." Example from 1749: "A finikin lass, Did shine like glistering gold." The "obsolete" example has been removed from the 2023 online version of the *OED*, presumably because of its racism.
21. "Rapture": "transport of mind." But also "from *raptura*, seizing, influenced by 'rapt' rapt *v.* + -ure *suffix*. Formed within English by derivation. Compare capture *n.* . . . earlier rapt *n.* and raption *n.* . . . ancient Greek ἁρπάζειν to snatch away, to seize." For origin in Greek and Latin, see *Oxford English Dictionary* https://www.oed.com/dictionary/rapture_n?tab=etymology#26674341.
22. The parenthetical numbers after the quotations that follow refer to the lines of Whitman's poem.

23. Ralph Waldo Emerson, *Nature*, in *Essays and Lectures*, ed. Porte, 7.
24. Stevens owned a recording of Schoenberg's "Klavierstücke," Op. 11, No. 2 and, according to Michael O. Stegman, had a wide and varied record collection. Stegman, "Wallace Stevens and Music: A Discography of Stevens' Phonograph Record Collection," *Wallace Stevens Journal* 3, nos. 3/4, Commemorative Issue (Fall 1979): 93. It would have been surprising if he had not been familiar with the generic term "pieces" that was sometimes more variation than theme, as in Webern's "Drei Kleine Stücke," Op. 1.

    Writing to Ronald Lane Latimer on November 26, 1935, Stevens averred that "an appropriate experiment would be to write poetry without music and without color" (*L* 331). This would give you Schoenberg. "Without music" is Stevens's judgment that twelve-tone music is without the functional tonality of major and minor scales and the proclivity within those melodies and chords to create tension and resolution. "Pieces," like atonal music, avoids resolution conceptually while managing to sound resolved.
25. Stevens was interested in the developments of modern physics as they emerged around him. In "A Collect of Philosophy," he alludes to Max Planck's relation to quantum theory, calling him "the patriarch of all modern physicists," and he concludes: "It is unexpected to have to recognize even in Planck the presence of the poet" (*CPP* 866–67). Joan Richardson documents the context for Stevens's knowledge of quantum physics in *Wallace Stevens: A Biography: The Later Years, 1923–1955* (New York: William Morrow, 1988), 73, 156. Dana Wilde argues that the interrelations posited by quantum theory—in which the measurement of one particle affects that of another, and in which the mind observing the subatomic particle affects the phenomenon it observes—have a parallel in Stevens's poetry, where "the imagination" can't be separated from the "physical world" to which it gives "form and order." Wilde, "Wallace Stevens, Modern Physics, and Wholeness," *Wallace Stevens Journal* 20, no. 1 (Spring 1996): 5. Mark Noble particularizes Stevens's relation to the "concepts of epistemological 'uncertainty' and 'complementarity'" in the 1920s writing of Niels Bohr and Werner Heisenberg as these "sugges[t] to Stevens any number of experiments in the multiplication and compilation of poetic vantages." Noble, *American Poetic Materialism from Whitman to Stevens* (Cambridge: Cambridge University Press, 2015), 142–82; quotes on 169, 165.

    Quantum entanglement was discovered experimentally only after Stevens's death with the publication of Bell's theorem in 1964. Stevens was a layman and probably would not have engaged such technical issues. But he could have imbibed certain philosophical premonitions of quantum entanglement from both Whitehead and Leibniz, as well as from the genealogy of ideas that permeated the intellectual atmosphere around Harvard, as in the papers ultimately published in William James's *Essays in Radical Empiricism*.
26. Beverly Maeder, "World and Word *Au Pays de la Métaphore*," in *Wallace Stevens' Experimental Language: The Lion in the Lute* (New York: St. Martin's Press, 1999), 70; abbreviated M and hereafter cited parenthetically.

Maeder's is one of the most lucid analyses of the poem—until its end where she glosses the chain of metaphors that lead to the "X" by calling them allusions to other texts, a specificity the poem resists.

27. Denis Donoghue, "The Motive for Metaphor," *Hudson Review* (Winter 2013): 560, 561, https://hudsonreview.com/2013/03/the-motive-for-metaphor-2. In Donoghue's reading, Hegel's logic and some of his language are implemented to describe the source of that failure.
28. In another manifestation of this meandering, Garrett Stewart, in an email, hears "Stevens's proclivity for sound play in the internal echo of 'mo *tiv for*' and 'me *ti for*'"—a cross-drift of sound consonant with the motive force in which *like* and *unlike* cannot be driven apart.
29. Michel Foucault, *The Order of Things: An Archaeology of the Human Sciences* (New York: Vintage, 1994) xxii, xxi; further references are abbreviated F and are noted parenthetically.

    In an early review, George Steiner quotes this passage: "Philology, biology, and political economy were established, not in the places formerly occupied by general grammar, natural history, and the analysis of wealth, but in an area where those forms of knowledge did not exist, in the space they left blank, in the deep gaps that separated their broad theoretical segments and that were filled with the murmur of the ontological continuum. The object of knowledge in the nineteenth century is formed in the very place where the Classical plenitude of being has fallen silent. Inversely, a new philosophical space was to emerge in the place where the objects of Classical knowledge dissolved" (*New York Times*, February 28, 1971).

    See Foucault's "Labour, Life, Language," in *The Order of Things* (250–302), where the "order in its pure primary state" (xxi), touched on above, is described in detail. See also "On the Ways of Writing History," where Foucault discusses with Raymond Bellour this epistemological break, in Michel Foucault, *Aesthetics, Method, and Epistemology*, vol. 2, ed. James D. Faubion, trans. Robert Hurley et al. (New York: New Press), 279–95; quote on 282.
30. Richard S. Storrs, *The Divine Origin of Christianity Indicated by Its Historical Effects* (New York: Anson D. F. Randolph, 1884), 89.
31. *Sur Plusieurs Beaux Sujets*: *Wallace Stevens' Commonplace Book: A Facsimile and Transcription*, ed. Milton J. Bates (Stanford, CA: Stanford University Press, 1989), 33. The next entry Stevens added is by Mario Rossi: "the great interests of man: air and light, the joy of having a body, the voluptuousness of looking" (33–35) (Mario Rossi and J. M. Hone, *Swift; or, The Egotist* [London: Gollancz, 1934]).
32. William Blake, *Auguries of Innocence*, https://www.poetryfoundation.org/poems/43650/auguries-of-innocence.
33. Describing Stevens's composition of "The Noble Rider and the Sound of Words," Joan Richardson writes: "In calling attention to 'the sound of words,' he approached the mystical realistically, calling on his reading in modern physics. A

text that he did not name but . . . seemed to recall was Edgar Allan Poe's *Eureka*, in which Pascal's thought experiment of conjuring the movement of one stone on the sea floor that affects the universe with the waves it generates was translated into the effect that every word uttered has the power of transforming the shape of all things." Richardson, *Wallace Stevens: A Biography: The Later Years, 1923–1955*, 181.

34. Edgar Allan Poe, *Eureka*, in *The Science Fiction of Edgar Allan Poe*, ed. Harold Beaver (New York: Penguin, 1978), 236.
35. Cage, *A Year from Monday*, 122.

Index